Helping Struggling Learners Succeed in School

Harriet D. Porton

Boston   Columbus   Indianapolis   New York   San Francisco   Upper Saddle River
Amsterdam   Cape Town   Dubai   London   Madrid   Milan   Munich   Paris   Montréal   Toronto
Delhi   Mexico City   São Paulo   Sydney   Hong Kong   Seoul   Singapore   Taipei   Tokyo

Vice President and Editorial Director: Jeffery W. Johnston
Executive Editor: Ann Castel Davis
Editorial Assistant: Penny Burleson
Vice President, Director of Marketing: Margaret Waples
Marketing Manager: Joanna Sabella
Senior Managing Editor: Pamela D. Bennett
Production Manager: Susan EW Hannahs
Senior Art Director: Jayne Conte

Cover Designer: Suzanne Behnke
Cover Art: Corbis
Full-Service Project Management: Vivek Khandelwal, Element LLC
Composition: Element LLC
Printer/Bindery: Edwards Brothers Malloy
Cover Printer: Lehigh-Phoenix
Text Font: Palatino LT Std Roman

Credits and acknowledgments for materials borrowed from other sources and reproduced, with permission, in this textbook appear on the appropriate page within the text.

Every effort has been made to provide accurate and current Internet information in this book. However, the Internet and information posted on it are constantly changing, so it is inevitable that some of the Internet addresses listed in this textbook will change.

Library of Congress Cataloging-in-Publication Data
Porton, Harriet D.
  Helping struggling learners succeed in school / Harriet D. Porton. — 1st ed.
    p. cm.
  ISBN 978-0-13-290247-2
  1. Remedial teaching—Planning. 2. Effective teaching. I. Title.
  LB1029.R4P67 2012
  371.9--dc23   2012004648

10 9 8 7 6 5 4 3 2 1

ISBN 10: 0-13-290247-8
ISBN 13: 978-0-13-290247-2

*This book is dedicated to the memory of my mom,
Rosalie Blumenthal Dorfman.*

*And it is dedicated to the people who are with me now: my wonderful
husband, Steve, my loving children, my fabulous grandchildren, my
incredible Aunt Lucille, and all of the students I have taught since 1966
who have shared with me their caring, curiosity, and wisdom.*

Thank you!

PREFACE

In 1990, my principal, Doris Williams, who was also one of my closest friends, scheduled me to teach a tenth-grade English inclusion class (general education students and special education students taught by the content general educator and a special educator) with a brand new special educator. In addition, one of the students we were assigned to teach was a youngster I will refer to as "Lemoyne." According to his former special educator, during the previous school year Lemoyne had stolen a car and chose to drive it up and down the street in front of the home where he had "borrowed" it. When the car owner, who is Caucasian, saw a young African American male driving the family car up and down the street in front of his home, he called the police. The officers arrested  Lemoyne, but first they took him home to notify his mother that he was being taken to a juvenile facility to be charged with grand theft auto. Lemoyne's mother was tired of seeing her son being brought home by the police. As soon as she could get close enough to Lemoyne, she hit him so hard that the police handcuffed her for child abuse; Lemoyne was already in cuffs for stealing the car, and the family rode off to the police station.

I told Doris I was beginning to think I was too old to teach. My life stories no longer matched those of my students, and I could not imagine surviving the ordeal of seeing my mother in handcuffs. Every day my students lived with traumas far more devastating than those I had ever known. I knew I had to get help so that I could continue to reach the children I would be teaching for the next 10 to 20 years. I knew after more than 20 years in the classroom, I could still be and still wanted to be an effective teacher. However, I was beginning to doubt my ability to relate to my students the way I always had. I wasn't sure if the traditional techniques and methods that had worked for my generation and for the generations of students I had taught from the mid-1960s could still work with the students who were beginning to show up in my current classes in ever greater numbers. Not only were these students less prepared for the academic rigors of high school life, but also they were suffering from psychosocial issues I knew I did not have the background to handle. Fortunately, Goucher College and Sheppard Pratt Hospital had recently been awarded a grant to train an elite group of teachers in the art and science of working with at-risk students. I applied immediately! Happily, I was accepted, and I started my course work that September. And thus Doris, Joppatowne High School, and I started on our new journey of discovery. I would like to take the time now to acknowledge my Goucher College–Sheppard Pratt experience—the faculty, my fellow students, and the free flow of ideas.

Twenty years later I still remember Lemoyne and the anxiety I felt knowing the depth of his need and the dearth of my knowledge. I know that when I started my student teaching experience in 1965 at a middle school that had grants from Johns Hopkins University and the Ford Foundation, I never expected to be writing this book. During my student teaching experience, we took our seventh graders to the opera, the ballet, and other cultural events many Friday afternoons, and we had an experienced professor from Johns Hopkins who came to our school and graded our students' papers for us. I was completely unprepared for the world of teaching that I was about to enter. Fortunately for me, at my first teaching job in the Bronx, JHS #113, I was mentored by a caring and dedicated principal who took an interest in a 5'0" teacher who weighed about 100 pounds; it was he who taught me how to establish routines and rapport. I had always wanted to teach, and Mr. Liebson made sure I knew how.

Mr. Liebson was my first mentor, but he certainly was not my last. Over the years, many other professionals and students have been instrumental in helping me to develop, refine, and reinforce my skills. When my own children were very young,

I accepted a job teaching first grade in the Bronx. The school was overcrowded, and the first graders and their teachers came to school from 7:30 until 12. The first year I was told that phonics was the only way to teach reading. The following year there was a change in administration; all the phonics books and materials were put away, and we were told to teach using a whole language approach. The year after that a new approach was introduced. At that point, one of the veteran teachers told me to close my door and blend phonics and whole language instruction together so that all of my students could learn to read.

After many more challenges, I learned from both experience and course work that in order to make a difference in my students' lives, I had to make reading not only accessible, but also meaningful for my students. I taught English at Joppatowne High School in Joppatowne, Maryland, for 26 years; for the last 10 years, by choice I taught English 9. A highlight of that curriculum for me was teaching *The Odyssey*. My students always enjoyed the adventures, the humor, and the cunning of Odysseus. One year I had a particularly lovely group of students who were very attached to me. The students started referring to Odysseus as O because they liked him so much. One day in the middle of a lesson, one of my very favorite students looked up at me and said: "O be the man, Mrs. Porton." He could think of no higher compliment; I knew I had reached a child who had never found meaning in literature before.

I told myself that day, if I ever wrote a book, that would be its title. Unfortunately, no one would ever know what a book by that title could possibly mean! In order to compromise, I created a less noble, but more understandable title and included the story here and other stories about O and my students inside the text as well.

In this book, we will be using the terms *at risk learners* and *struggling learners* interchangeably. Both names describe the challenging, but uniquely rewarding population of students that can be found in every school in the United States. More importantly, although at-risk students may not be cognitively impaired, throughout this book I will continue to make the point that this population does not succeed without appropriate interventions and differentiated instruction. I will be using the following categories to capture the essence of these struggling learners: (1) children who live in unstable families and communities, (2) children who are unsuccessful in meeting school-based standards, (3) children who have an external locus of control, and (4) children who have a limited and/or grim notion of the future.

The book is divided into four parts. Part One deals with planning, which must be approached with an eye to transparency when working with struggling learners. Perhaps the greatest departure from standard procedures comes from the management techniques that are discussed in Part Two. The third part deals with instruction. The chapters in this section provide many innovative ideas for linking real-world experiences with academic pursuits for those teachers who believe in themselves and maintain high expectations for the struggling learners they teach. Finally, Part Four covers issues surrounding assessment. Unless all of these pieces are in place and are congruent, many struggling learners are unlikely to have access to the success they are capable of achieving.

So, from Mr. Liebson, Mrs. Williams, Lemoyne, and everyone in between and after, please join us on this journey of discovery. You will meet some wonderful folks along the way; you will uncover new ways of teaching and learning; you will read some terribly sad stories and some wonderfully joyous ones. Most importantly, I hope that you will walk away with effective ways to teach and reach those who matter most—*all* your students.

Harriet D. Porton

ACKNOWLEDGMENTS

I wish to start by thanking my editor, Ann Davis, for her support and guidance throughout my work on this book. She was incredibly generous with her time and talent and was a constant source of wisdom and friendship. Her assistant, Penny Burleson, has been an invaluable aid to me, and I appreciate all that they have done to move this text from proposal to production. At the end of the writing process lurk the final details that most authors who love writing but don't love tedious details really resist. The reference section was my nightmare. I wish to acknowledge the help that Mary Stoddard gave me. She had been a student of mine at the College of Notre Dame, and she was very skillful, thorough, and knowledgeable.

Knowing that "the grown-up ship" pulled away from the dock and left me behind, I recruited a group of friends, colleagues, and relatives who sent me funny emails and encouraging notes throughout this process. I wish to publicly thank my "Cheerleaders" now for their tremendous support: Betsy Cooper, Bob Alper, Steve Blumenthal, Mike and Karen Friedman, Normajean Boyd, Russ Holmes, Joe Noone, Maryann Brown, Mindy Hayes, Greta Cephas, Paula Robertson, Dolores Winston, Karen Cifranick, Linda Kaniecki, Mary Ann Crimi, Robbie Keen, Adele Wilson, Michelle Muscello, Trisha Swam, Cyndi and Joe Tirone, Claudia Duffy, Alison Weaver, Susie Neuberger, Lisa Booth, Rachel Cassidy, Susan Levin, Debby Watson, David and Jen Schwartz, and Lilly.

In addition, after I wrote each chapter, I asked current practitioners to read it over to be sure that my content was relevant and accurate. I also asked experts in their fields to read for accuracy. I wish to thank the following for their expertise: Eva Skolnick-Acker, Shaudon Pinkney-Matthews, Debby Watson, Doris Williams, Gary Thrift, Eli Velder, Hanoch Flum, Barbara Leonard, Jill Bateman, Anthony Dallman-Jones, and J. Robert Dorfman.

Also, I would like to thank the following reviewers: Amy Baer, Minnesota State University, Mankato; Gloria Dye, Washburn University; Jan Heinitz, Concordia University; Marty Horning, University of Wisconsin, Milwaukee; Beverly Johns, MacMurray College; and Jackie Powell, University of West Georgia.

Finally, I wish to thank my brother and sister, J. Robert Dorfman and Susan Levin, who allowed me to share stories from our childhood, and my two children, Debby Watson and David Schwartz, who allowed me to share stories from their childhood! And I wish to thank all of the students at all the schools where I have had the honor and privilege to teach—thank you for all that you have helped me to learn.

BRIEF CONTENTS

PART ONE   Planning   1

    Chapter 1   How to Plan for Instruction   3

    Chapter 2   Identifying Struggling Learners   19

    Chapter 3   Effective Grouping Strategies   35

    Chapter 4   Practices of Reflective Planners   47

PART TWO   Management   59

    Chapter 5   Successful Management Skills: Rules, Routines, and Boundaries   61

    Chapter 6   Guidelines for Effective Classroom Management   75

    Chapter 7   Mistakes in Management   89

    Chapter 8   Practices of Reflective Managers   101

PART THREE   Instruction   111

    Chapter 9   Guidelines for Effective Instruction   113

    Chapter 10   Discovery Learning   131

    Chapter 11   Practices of Reflective Teachers   145

PART FOUR   Assessment   157

    Chapter 12   How to Create Effective Assessments   159

    Chapter 13   Formative Versus Summative Assessments   173

    Chapter 14   Practices of Reflective Assessors   185

Appendix 1   Figures, Tables, and Templates   197

Appendix 2   Interstate New Teacher Assessment and Support
Consortium Standards   219

References   223

Index   229

CONTENTS

Preface   v

Acknowledgments   vii

PART ONE   Planning   1

Chapter 1   How to Plan for Instruction   3

The Instructional Triangle   4

Goal   4

Strategies   5

Assessment   6

Lesson Plans   7

Formatting the Lesson Plan   7

A Student Teacher's Story   8

Differentiated Instruction   12

Guidelines   12

Differentiation in Practice   12

Summary   16

Chapter 2   Identifying Struggling Learners   19

Children Who Live in Unstable Families
and Communities   22

Divorce   22

Substance Abuse   23

Poverty   23

What Does This Mean for You?   24

How Do You Plan with These Students in Mind?   25

Children Who Are Unsuccessful in Meeting
School-Based Standards   25

Attendance   25

Retention in Grade   26

Expectations of Those in Authority   26

What Does This Mean for You?   27

Children Who Have an External Locus of Control   28

Attribution   28

Connections Between Effort and Success   28

No Ownership of Failure or Success   29

Classroom Applications   29

Children Who Have a Limited and/or Grim
Notion of the Future   30

Generational Incarceration   30

Generational Poverty   31

Long-Term Effects of Gender Bias   32

How Do You Plan with These Students in Mind?   33

Summary   34

Chapter 3 Effective Grouping Strategies   35

Grouping Students   36

History of Tracking and Grouping   36

Current Schoolwide Practices in Grouping   37

Cooperative Learning   38

Definition of Cooperative Learning   38

Creating a Successful Group   38

Are Ability Groups Always Harmful?   40

Grouping by Effort   41

Grouping by Talents, Interests, or Values   41

Talents   42

Interests   42

Values   42

Grouping by Gender   43

Single-Gender Teams   44

Valuing Contributions Made by All   44

Summary   45

Chapter 4 Practices of Reflective Planners   47

Why Should Teachers Be Reflective?   48

Let's Reflect on What We Have Learned So Far   49

Let's Practice Reflecting Together   50

Summary   53

Your Turn   53

Reflections About Planning   56

Summary   57

PART TWO   Management   59

Chapter 5 Successful Management Skills: Rules, Routines, and Boundaries   61

Defining Rules, Routines, and Boundaries   62

Rules   62

Routines   63

Boundaries   63

Why Successful Classroom Management Is So Critical   64

Routines: Your Best Friend   64

Establishing Routines   64

Establishing Clear Boundaries   65

Some Benefits of Boundaries   66

Student–Teacher Relationships and Management   66

Develop a Positive Rapport with Your Students   67

A Sense of Humor Is a Valuable Asset   67

Benefits, but No Burdens, Come with Positive Relationships   67

Creating a Productive Room Arrangement   68

You Must Be Able to Reach Any Child Quickly   68

Every Child Must Be Able to See and Hear You When You Are Teaching   68

You Must Be Able to See All Your Students All the Time   68

Decorate Your Classroom So That It Is Welcoming   69

Provide Easy Access to the Technology in Your Room   69

Your Energy Is the Key to Students' Well-Being   69

A Quick Intervention Is Worth a Lot   70

Clear the Field   71

Handle Defiance Without Confrontation   71

Summary   72

Chapter 6 Guidelines for Effective Classroom Management   75

The New Reality in Our Classrooms   76

Why Are Today's Children So Angry?   76

How Can You Help?   76

"If It Is to Be, It Is Up to Me"   77

The Importance of Dressing Like a Professional   78

How Do You Stop the Noise?   78

Guidelines for Effective Praise   78

Current Brain Research   80

Elementary School   80

Middle School   81

High School   81

Harriet's Helpful Hints   82

Summary   86

Chapter 7 Mistakes in Management   89

Every Mistake Is Not a Felony   90

Why Is It Important to Have a Neat Classroom?   90

What Went Wrong with My Lesson?   91

Where Is the Routine?   91

What Should I Do About Mean Girls?   93

Mistakes That Cannot Be Forgiven   93

Wall of Shame   93

Targeting a Child   94

I Had to Move My Car   95

Teachers Who Ignore Their Students   96

Fixable Versus Unforgivable Errors   97

Should You Become a Teacher?   98

Guidelines for Ineffective Praise   98

General Education Students   99

Struggling Learners   99

Gender Issues   99

Summary   99

Chapter 8 Practices of Reflective Managers   101

Let's Reflect on What We Have Learned   102

Rules, Routines, and Boundaries   103

Room Arrangement   104

Positive Student–Teacher Relationships   104

Be a Professional   104

Ginott and Brophy   105

Brain Research   105

Harriet's Helpful Hints   105

Fixable Versus Egregious Errors   106

Struggling Learners and the Effects of Teacher Quality   106

Guidelines for Ineffective Praise   107

When You Reflect   107

Your Turn   107

Summary   110

PART THREE   Instruction   111

Chapter 9   Guidelines for Effective Instruction   113

A Veteran's Plan   114

Does This Meet Our Standards for a Successful Lesson?   116

Why Did It Work?   116

What Can Teachers Do?   117

To Kill a Mockingbird and Self-Efficacy   117

What Did the Students Say?   118

A Novice's Lesson Plan   118

Instructional Triangle   118

Evaluating the Plan   119

The Plan in Action   120

Let's Review   121

Effective Classroom Discussions   121

Results Depend on Preparation and Effort   121

Staying on Track   122

Assessing the Discussion   122

Lesson Plan on Classroom Discussions   122

Primary-Level Reading Lesson Plan   124

A Few Reflections on the Lesson   129

Summary   129

Chapter 10   Discovery Learning   131

Constructivism   132

Reviewing the Instructional Triangle
and Lesson Plan Template   133

Instructional Triangle and Constructivist Learning Theory   133

Lesson Plan Template and Discovery Learning   134

It's Nice, But How Do You Do It?   134

"My Name"   135

The All Stars Problem-Solving Game   136

Technology, Science and Discovery Learning   139

High School Science and Discovery Learning   140

Climatology   141

Summary   144

Chapter 11 Practices of Reflective Teachers   145

    Looking Back   146

      Your Turn   146

    Back to Bandura   146

      Your Turn   147

    Meet Marzano   147

      Your Turn   148

    Have You Had Any Good Class Discussions Lately?   148

      Your Turn   148

    Primary Reading Lesson   150

      Your Turn   151

    Discovery Learning   151

      Your Turn   152

    Alignment and Alliances   152

      Your Turn   152

    Getting to Know You   153

      Your Turn   154

    Creating and Implementing an Effective Lesson   154

      Your Turn   155

      Summary   155

PART FOUR   Assessment   157

Chapter 12 How to Create Effective Assessments   159

    Teacher-Made Assessments   160

      The Connections Among Goals, Strategies, and Assessments   161

      The Uses of the Assessment Results   161

      The Integrity of the Process   162

    Rubrics   163

      Creating a Rubric   164

      Grading with a Rubric   165

      Rubrics from a Learner's Point of View   165

    Data Analysis   166

      From Goal to Assessment and Beyond   166

    Alternative Types of Assessments   168

      Concerns Related to Sharing Group Grades   168

      Decision-Making Matrix   169

      Summary   171

Chapter 13 Formative Versus Summative Assessments   173

    Formative Assessment   174

      Vocabulary   174

      When and How Do We Use Formative Assessments?   175

      An Example of a Formative Assessment   175

      Reluctant Workers   176

    Summative Assessments   177

      An Example of a Summative Assessment   177

High-Stakes Tests and Struggling Learners   178

    Historical Context of the Accountability Movement   178

    Unintended Negative Consequences of the Policy   179

    What Research Tells Us   180

    Matching Theory to Practice   181

        Summary   183

Chapter 14   Practices of Reflective Assessors   185

Assessment   186

    Effective Daily Assessments   186

    How Do We Reflect on Our Success on Daily Assessments?   186

    Formative and Summative Assessments   187

    High-Stakes Testing and Struggling Learners   188

What Have We Learned About Struggling Learners?   189

    Successful Strategies   191

    Your Turn   192

    How Do We Know We Are Being Effective?   192

    Effective Planning   192

    Effective Management   193

    Rules, Routines, and Boundaries   193

    Your Turn   193

    Room Arrangement   193

    Angry Children   193

    Effective Praise   194

    Effective Instruction   194

        Summary   195

Appendix 1   Figures, Tables, and Templates   197

*Appendix 2   Interstate New Teacher Assessment and Support
Consortium Standards   219*

References   223

Index   229

Part One

Planning

Chapter 1   How to Plan for Instruction

Chapter 2   Identifying Struggling Learners

Chapter 3   Effective Grouping Strategies

Chapter 4   Practices of Reflective Planners

How to Plan for Instruction

Tell me, and I will forget
Show me, and I may not remember
Involve me, and I will understand.

NATIVE AMERICAN PROVERB

From the first time you walk into your classroom until the day you retire, the only thing under your complete control will take place before a single child walks into your room. It's called *planning*. Planning requires careful thought and deliberation. Without it, any learning that takes place is accidental and incidental. With it, you determine what you want your students to learn or be able to do for each part of the day. Your children will be involved in activities that will motivate and involve them in their pursuit of knowledge in a way that is respectful to them as individual learners. Your assessments will help you to evaluate how well the children mastered the day's skills and to determine how to plan the next step in the teaching–learning process. It is very challenging to write a good plan, because an effective plan requires a great deal of time, thought, and effort.

In this chapter, we will first discuss a new paradigm for examining instruction: the instructional triangle. Next, we will review a lesson plan format that has utility in many content areas, and finally, we will discuss the importance of differentiated instruction.

Effective teachers know what they are teaching and why. They use a format for planning that resonates with their own organizational strategies, and that helps them to stay focused on the essentials of good teaching. Since learning takes place one student at a time, some form of differentiated instruction is a requirement for reaching every child each day.

THE INSTRUCTIONAL TRIANGLE

Goal

At the top of the instructional triangle (Figure 1.1), you will find the statement of the day's goal: What do you want your students to know or be able to do? In the past, teachers were free to create their own goals. However, in an attempt to address the effects of dissatisfaction with public schools across the United States, many school systems have institutionalized assessments designed to test their students' academic performance. According to Jacob (2001), proponents of high-stakes testing believe that these exams "help raise achievement levels by focusing school goals" (p. 99). Therefore, in order to help students reach mastery on the exams, most states have created curriculum guides that all public school teachers are required to follow.

Consequently, before you begin to plan any lesson, you must find out if what you will be teaching is assessed on the statewide test. If it is, you must be sure your plan addresses the statewide curriculum for the lesson's topic. Specifically, your goal for the lesson must come from the state's curriculum guidelines or the upcoming Common Core State Standards for the grade and content you are teaching.

SPECIFIC OBJECTIVES FOR DAILY LESSONS   If you are a public school teacher, you are probably using a statewide curriculum guide that clearly articulates the goals for your lessons. However, it is up to you to write the specific objective for each

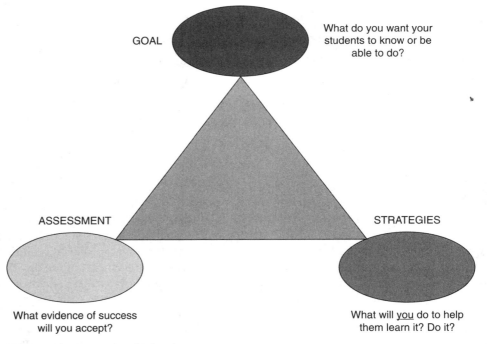

GOAL — What do you want your students to know or be able to do?

ASSESSMENT — What evidence of success will you accept?

STRATEGIES — What will <u>you</u> do to help them learn it? Do it?

FIGURE 1.1   The Instructional Triangle

daily lesson. Behaviorists (e.g., Mager, 1972), normally require an objective to answer three questions:

1. What behavior? Refer to Bloom's (1956) Taxonomy for a very useful list of terms and related questions that will give you clarity and direction: for example,
   a. Knowledge—Do you want the children to be able to define or distinguish?
   b. Comprehension—Do you want the children to be able to translate or restate?
   c. Application—Do you want the children to be able to generalize or organize?
   d. Evaluate—Do you want the children to be able to justify or assess?
2. Under what conditions? Where will the children demonstrate their learning?
3. How well? What are your criteria for the children's success?

Objectives must be phrased in measurable outcomes, not activities. You cannot use objectives that require students to demonstrate how they feel, such as "Students will enjoy/appreciate/value...," since feelings cannot be objectively measured or observed (Clark, 2010).

The objective for each day's lesson is further determined by whether you want your students to learn or store information (declarative knowledge) or to be able to perform a task (procedural knowledge) during instruction. According to Marzano (1992), "Many theorists believe there are different types of knowledge, each involving somewhat different learning processes" (p. 32); Marzano uses the binary system of declarative and procedural knowledge for classifying learning.

DECLARATIVE KNOWLEDGE   Planning instruction that is declarative in nature is very difficult because teachers have to sift through all the information and data and determine how to help their students find meaning in the information; Marzano (1992) refers to that process as *constructing meaning*. If your students have completed that task, the next step is to help them *organize* the data in a system that will help them to see its utility in its broader context. Finally, if the students are close to being tested or are at the end of the unit of study, they are ready to *store* the information in a manner that will provide them with easy access to the material. Ask yourself, Will the goal of my declarative lesson plan help my students construct meaning?

PROCEDURAL KNOWLEDGE   If you are teaching your children a step-by-step process, you will need to create a procedural lesson plan. Some theorists in the field believe that planning for a procedural lesson is as challenging as it is for a declarative lesson because teachers can make the mistake of thinking that students need to know more procedures than they really do (Marzano, 1992). Thoughtful planning helps to eliminate that problem. Ask yourself, What do my students need to be able to do by the end of this lesson? Only include those procedures the students really need to master during the lesson in order to reach the day's goal.

When you have answered those questions, you can formulate your objectives. After you write the objectives in your own language, write them again in the students' language because the students will have to be able to understand and meet the goals/objectives for the day's lesson.

Strategies

After you have selected your goal and daily objective, you will need to create a specific set of strategies and activities that are designed to help students master the material you want them to learn for the day's lesson. The first step is to measure the students' prior knowledge of today's topic. It is relatively easy to measure the students' prior knowledge on any topic. Using the drill/warm-up, ask them simple questions that assess their basic prior knowledge of the topic.

MOTIVATION   Following that, students will need to be motivated in order to become actively involved in the lesson. During motivation, you help your students understand what they are learning and *why*. During this part of the lesson, you give students some information about the highlights of the lesson and, most importantly, help them to understand the importance of this lesson in the context of what they have been learning and in terms of their own lives.

For example, when I taught first grade, I found that even the most reluctant learners were easily engaged if I used a variety of interesting devices to help the children get ready for the fun we were going to have and if I explained what we were going to learn and why. When I first introduced subtraction, I took one very bright little boy aside and told him what I planned to do. Next, I took my coat and walked just outside my classroom door. Now the children were intrigued. I came back in with the coat over my head, put the subtraction sign on the blackboard, and said, "I am Lady Take Away. I am here to take away one little boy." Then I went over to the designated child and walked him outside our door. My children loved the setup for subtraction, and none of them ever forgot either the symbol for subtraction or what it means to take away.

However, as many children grow older, they become more recalcitrant, and if they are not given the purpose for what they will be learning, they will not participate. Teachers who are skillful at motivational activities understand the value of exposing children of all ages to both the joy that is part of learning and the rationale for every lesson.

ACTIVITIES   Students who are provided with a variety of techniques and modalities of instruction have more opportunities to understand and interact with their world (Gardner, 1983). Some children learn by touching, others by hearing, and others by seeing. Therefore, all modalities of learning have to be available for all learners to be successful. For instance, if you talk all the time, visual learners will not have equal access to success. Many successful teachers use technology, which keeps visual learners very stimulated, while they are addressing auditory learners, and manipulatives have become a required part of many curricula to help kinesthetic learners find success.

When I taught students how to pass the Functional Citizenship Test, I had to do some "drill and kill" exercises because of some of the incredibly trivial information that was always on the test. However, there were also some important concepts that the students needed to know to be informed citizens. When I created the strategies for teaching the court systems, we held mock trials. Unfortunately, some of my students had spent more time in court than their youth might lead one to expect; therefore, they were savvy about courtroom procedures, and our courtroom "dramas" were fairly accurate. We always found the defendant guilty so the person could be moved through either the state or the federal court hierarchy. This simple role-playing strategy helped my students store and retrieve knowledge of the court system when they took the test. We also played lots of quick recall games to reinforce bits of isolated information, such as "How long does a state district court judge sit?"

Once you know what you want your children to learn and be able to do and you have created the strategies you believe will help every child attain mastery of that goal, you are ready to create the assessment for the day's lesson. The assessment will provide you with evidence of the extent to which each child has achieved mastery of the day's goal.

Assessment

The assessment should measure each student's mastery of the content covered during the class (middle and high school) or during the segment of the day (elementary school) you have devoted to this topic. Chapter 12 is devoted to explaining how to match instruction to assessment, but for now, it is important to remember that the assessment must measure the skills and knowledge the students are supposed to be learning. For any assessment to be effective, every part of the goal for the day must be assessed, and the assessment must match the way the students practiced learning the material.

STRUGGLING LEARNERS AND ASSESSMENT   Since this book is specifically geared to help you succeed with struggling learners, you need to remember their worldview of adults. According to Sagor (1993), struggling learners are very mistrustful of adults; their schema for teachers is negative, and their expectation is that you will be unfair, unresponsive, and unlikely to meet their needs. Struggling learners' prior experiences in school have taught them to doubt that strategies and types of assessment will provide them with the opportunities they need to be successful.

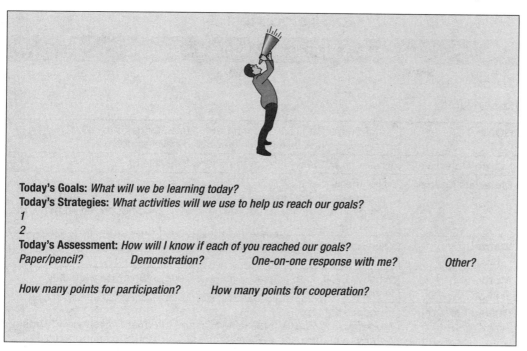

Today's Goals: *What will we be learning today?*
Today's Strategies: *What activities will we use to help us reach our goals?*
1
2
Today's Assessment: *How will I know if each of you reached our goals?*
Paper/pencil?   Demonstration?   One-on-one response with me?   Other?

How many points for participation?   How many points for cooperation?

FIGURE 1.2   Message Board

Even if an assessment has very little point value or is only a small fraction of the total grade for their report card, struggling learners have to be convinced that they can be successful. They need to see the intrinsic link between how and what they were taught and how they are being assessed. For this reason, your daily goal, instruction, and assessment must match closely in every feature, or you can betray your children's trust in you.

As part of the schedule for the day, create a simple, but valuable message board (Figure 1.2). This should be laminated so you just fill in the details every day. Then, when your students enter your classroom, they will know where to look to see what they will be doing that day. They will know their activities and their assessments. For children whose lives are filled with chaos, this order provides some of the security that is essential for their success in school.

LESSON PLANS

Formatting the Lesson Plan

Once you understand the essentials of the instructional triangle, you are ready to use any lesson plan format. Some content areas require a specific style of plan because it has greater utility than others. The 5 E plan was widely used for math and science, and many school systems required its use. For other content areas, you can use Template 1.1, a fairly simplistic, generic form that seems to work well with cooperative learning, across the cognitive spectrum, across grades, and across disciplines.

In order to help you match this lesson plan to the instructional triangle, look at the first column in Template 1.1. You will find the INSTRUCTION section where you see GOAL and Lesson Objective in the top two rows of the template. STRATEGIES begin with Drill/Warm-Up and continue through Independent Practice. ASSESSMENT is the last formal step in the lesson plan. Although Closure is a required part of every lesson, it is much more informal; it does not require a response from every student, and your purpose is to hear from the children regarding their feelings and attitudes toward the day's learning and activities. Take notes on anything that the children tell you that will help to inform your future instructional decisions. Always collect and evaluate the children's homework. However, if you make homework meaningless and trivial, you will get little of it turned in, and any homework that is done will reflect the quality of your assignment.

Template 1.1

Lesson Planning Template—Generic	

Lesson Title:

Lesson Unit:

GOAL	(State Curriculum) (SC) Common Core State Standards (CCSS) Statewide or local systemwide goal /Grade level standard
Lesson Objective	As a result of today's lesson, students will be able to
Materials Needed	Make the list. Check to see that all items are present. During the lesson, if you find you need something not on the list, write the item in the margin.
Warm-Up Time:	Use this to *activate prior knowledge.*
Motivation Time:	What will you do to engage students in today's topic? *Why* are they learning the new information?
Guided Practice Time:	Introduce the topic. *Model* how to construct meaning/organize information/store new learning *or* how to perform the task/create the product/share the performance.
Independent Practice Time:	Working with their teams, *students practice* the new learning. During this phase, errors are eliminated, strengths are praised, and students learn from each other. Using differentiated group assignments will help students with the wide variety of skills, interests, and abilities they need to succeed. Discovery learning is the essence of this phase.
Assessment Time:	*Each student must supply evidence of the extent to which he mastered content or skill development as described in today's goal.* Use data from this assessment for tomorrow's instruction.
Closure Time:	Ask students a question about key attitudes and learning in today's lesson: What did you learn today? What was the best part of today's lesson? What did you learn from each other today? How are you going to use today's lesson?
Homework	Make homework relevant and practice oriented. Do not assign drill and kill exercises!

A Student Teacher's Story

Ms. Flippy wants to teach English. She is having a difficult time with her fifth-period 9th graders. She thinks they are rude and indifferent to the literature she asks them to read. I was anxious to see how well she had integrated what we had been talking about regarding her management problems and her previous issues with planning.

This was my first formal observation. I had visited her once before because I always plan an informal visit with my student teachers so I can learn how much they know and can do before we begin our formal observations together. At her informal, Ms. Flippy handed me a list of what she wanted to accomplish, the book she was going to use during the lesson, and the names of the students who were "bad." During the debriefing of that visit, I showed her the instructional triangle and the lesson plan format in Template 1.1. Her plan for my first formal visit is shown in Table 1.1. My notes to her are in *italics*.

Although Ms. Flippy had indeed mastered the concept of what goes into each section of a plan, she had missed the basic premise of the instructional triangle. There is a mismatch among her instructional objectives, her strategies, and her assessments. It was not a surprise to me that when she started to teach, she quickly lost control of her students.

Ms. Flippy did not know how to match her plans to the children she was teaching. She was so worried about controlling her students that she lost her focus on how to teach

TABLE 1.1	Lesson Plan—9th Grade 5th Period	
GOAL	Lesson Goal (SC) I.Ib Students will read fiction in order to understand an author's use of various literary devices.	
This is your day's objective!	Lesson Objective As a result of today's lesson, students will be able to <u>understand point of view as a literary device by identifying the point of view used in the story we will read in class</u>. *Good!*	
Materials Needed	<u>Adventures in Reading</u> Quiz	
Warm up Time: 5 minutes	What is point of view? (5 points) *How can you grade students on a topic you have not taught them? In order to access their prior knowledge, this is fine. However, it cannot be graded drill!*	
Motivation Time: 10 minutes	Have you ever known anyone who has died? Brief discussion of the students' experiences with death. *I like this as a discussion topic. You needed to plan how to tie this into today's goals, etc.*	
Guided Practice Time: 15 minutes	I will teach them the points of view they need to know for this lesson—Omniscient/Limited Omniscient/First Person Involved/First Person Uninvolved. The students are expected to take notes on the 4 types of points of view and put their notes in the Classwork section of their English notebooks. *This is **telling**, not teaching. Your students were struggling to learn the material this way. Can you think of more engaging ways of involving your students? Make this a focus lesson so that by the end of class they all practice telling a story in each point of view.*	
Independent Practice Time: 15 minutes	Students will read "Before the End of Summer," pp. 65–76. When they have finished reading, they will write down the point of view they believe this story is written in and cite 3 examples from the story that support their choice. *All the children are not really ready to do this. If you look at p. 77, the text tells them the point of view this is written in. Save the story for the next day's lesson, & do something different w. it.*	
Assessment Time: 10 minutes	Students will be given a graded quiz that requires them to match definitions to the appropriate points of view. Students may not use their notes for this quiz. (20 points) *This **does not match** instructional goals or strategies.*	
Closure Time: 5 minutes	Did you like today's story? Explain *Good!*	
Homework	Write 5 starting sentences for short stories from each type of point of view. A total of 20 sentences will be due tomorrow (20 points). ***Why?***	

them. When we debriefed, she told me she was sure that, if she could get the students to read the story, they would see how easy it is to determine point of view. She thought she could just tell the children about point of view, and like herself as a young enthusiastic reader, they would internalize the concept and be ready for the next step. However, if careful planning does not precede instruction, not many of the outcomes anyone hopes for are likely to occur.

Ms. Flippy and her cooperating teacher agreed that Ms. Flippy needed to work on planning how to motivate her students. She recognized the need to capture their interest, and that's why she had the idea of discussing their prior knowledge about knowing someone who had died. However, that topic did not tie into the goals, strategies, or assessments of the day, and the students did not want to stop talking about it when Ms. Flippy wanted to move on. She had a lot of trouble recognizing those students in the class who are intrinsically motivated and those who are not. This is a critical issue in identifying students who may be at risk. Therefore, we agreed that Ms. Flippy needed to have a better method of observing her students while her cooperating teacher was teaching. Many

TABLE 1.2	Observation Topic: Motivation					
Student's Name	Time	Activities	Student's Involvement			Observations
			A	S	W	
1		Warm-Up				
		Motivation				
		Guided Practice				
		Independent Practice				
		Assessment				
		Closure				
2		Warm-Up				
		Motivation				
		Guided Practice				
		Independent Practice				
		Assessment				
		Closure				
3		Warm-Up				
		Motivation				
		Guided Practice				
		Independent Practice				
		Assessment				
		Closure				

A stands for Actively involved; **S** stands for Somewhat involved; **W** stands for Withdrawn from the activity.

student teachers need an observation checklist so that they know what to look for before they take over many teaching responsibilities. A sample of one is shown in Table 1.2.

The cooperating teacher and Ms. Flippy selected a highly motivated student, a student with average motivation, and a poorly motivated student so that at regular intervals Ms. Flippy could keep a record of how all three types of students perform. In this way, she can better plan how frequently she needs to change activities (timing), how much more motivation some students need than others, and how each student reacts to different types of activities.

RELATIONSHIP BETWEEN MOTIVATION AND ACADEMIC ABILITY   Since motivation is such a critical issue, we spent a lot of time on this issue. It is important to remember that motivation and academic ability are not necessarily positively correlated; however, intrinsic motivation is positively correlated to future academic success. In a study of ability and student motivation, researchers found that development of intrinsic motivation in younger students, as early as the primary grades, is important, since it normally influences later academic achievement. Thus, intrinsic motivation may be *the* key factor in determining achievement behavior (Goldberg, 1994; Gottfried, 1990).

Anecdotally, over 45 years of teaching experience have made it clear to me that students who struggle with very simple academic tasks can be very highly motivated and their cognitively skilled counterparts can be very difficult to encourage. The critical difference appears to be whether or not the motivation is extrinsic or intrinsic. "Students who become intrinsically motivated during the elementary school years have a higher chance of success in the future" (Messali, 2010). Finally, research and experience indicate that no matter how skilled or unskilled your students may be, it is your job to be sure that your motivational techniques provide a reason for every student to believe that what he will be learning is both personally meaningful and intellectually purposeful.

STRATEGIES   Next, we talked about what Ms. Flippy needed to include in her strategies that would provide opportunities for all her students to master the content she wanted them to learn. Her objective—"As a result of today's lesson, students will be able to understand point of view as a literary device by identifying the point of view used in the story we will read in class"—was fine. Next, she had to decide if she was teaching declarative or procedural knowledge. We agreed that it was declarative. She had not given the students any prior instruction on this topic, so she was in the first phase of instruction: constructing meaning (Marzano, 1992).

As we talked our way through the planning process, Ms. Flippy realized that she needed to be wary of assuming that her students shared her likes and dislikes. She was an English major because she liked reading. Many of her students did not read well, although some did. She taught her lesson for auditory learners, but she had not provided strategies that would allow her visual or kinesthetic learners to master the material. We were not in the business of fixing blame; we wanted to fix the problem. That became our mantra.

SUCCESS   During her second formal observation, Ms. Flippy showed marked improvement. As shown in Table 1.3, her goals, strategies, and assessment are now aligned. Her

TABLE 1.3   9th-GRADE LESSON PLAN

GOAL	(SC) I.Ib Students will read fiction in order to understand an author's use of various literary devices.
Lesson Objective	As a result of today's lesson, students will be able to understand the use of the First Person Uninvolved point of view in Harper Lee's (1960) *To Kill a Mockingbird*.
Materials Needed	Each team needs a placemat and every student needs a copy of the novel.
Warm-Up	1. Define First Person Uninvolved. 2. Define First Person Involved. 3. Who is Scout? 4. Who is telling the story? How do you know?
Motivation	Harper Lee has a large number of interesting characters who could tell her story. What would have happened if Boo told the story? Since the students have read only the introduction, they know only that Boo is a scary man who lives next door, comes out at night, and eats squirrels. From his point of view, the story should sound very different.
Guided Practice	I am going to hide something in front of the class. The teams will have to write their version of what they saw me do. After #-3 from each team reports, we will discuss the importance of perspective in understanding what we see and how we interpret it. The students will read Chapter 1 in the novel. Guided question: How does Scout's telling the story affect what we know and how we understand what is happening in the character's life?
Independent Practice	Each team will be given its own set of questions related to the guided practice in Chapter 1. Using a Gallery Walk, each team will display its answers so that by the end of this practice each team will have a better understanding of Harper Lee's use of First Person Uninvolved. These notes will be kept and added to as we continue to read the novel.
Assessment	1. Write a sentence from Dill's point of view. 2. Write a sentence from Atticus's point of view. 3. Write a sentence from the teacher's point of view. 4. Write a sentence from Jem's point of view. Each sentence must reveal your understanding of the major problem Scout faced her first day of school.
Closure	Who is your favorite character in the novel? Why?
Homework	Write a paragraph about our class today using the First Person Involved point of view. Be prepared to share it with your team tomorrow.

homework is more appropriate. Her motivation led her into the discussion she needed, and her lesson was a success.

DIFFERENTIATED INSTRUCTION

Historically, elementary teachers brought small groups of children to work with them for reading instruction long before anyone named it "differentiated instruction." It just made good sense to teach children to read by placing them in small groups based on their skills and abilities and having them work with their teacher one group at a time. Today many teachers self-report that they are advocates of differentiated instruction, but in practice, that is not often the case. Their reluctance to implement differentiated instruction may be a reflection not of their discontent with its theory, but rather of their view that it is too time consuming to put into practice. However, using what you already know about planning for instruction, you can easily plan for differentiated instruction.

Guidelines

The basic premises of differentiated instruction are that no group is static and groups can change during each topic, each group should change fundamentally from topic to topic, and assessments must guide future instructional decisions.

Based on your prior assessments, divide your class into the following groups:

1. *Enrichment*—Students in this group have shown proficiency _on this topic_. Their assessments consistently reveal their ability to grasp the concepts and complete enrichment work with little to no teacher support. Students who show that they cannot sustain the rigors of this group's work should be moved down to the next group.
2. *At grade level*—Students in this group can do the work _on this topic_ with teacher support. Their assessments consistently reveal that with some simple reteaching, they are able to understand and grasp the concepts at their expected grade level. If a student appears bored, he may need to try the enrichment group to see if more-challenging work might be more appropriate.
3. *Struggling learners*—Students in this group struggle to understand the work _on this topic_. Typically, they have trouble reading, maintaining their attention, and believing that they are capable of mastering this subject. Motivation is critical: Students must be given multiple opportunities to approach the task using all of their learning modalities, especially a hands-on approach. They must be reminded that they can do the work with the teacher's help. A teacher's negative approach can help to destroy any hope in a struggling child.

Routines are the basic building blocks of differentiation. First, you must "think your way through" the lesson to determine what routines you need to have in each section of the plan. You will need to determine if you have to teach the routine ahead of time or review it before you teach the plan as written so that the routine has been internalized by your students. Finally, your daily routines must be in place:

- routine for changing groups
- routine for serving as student helpers
- routine for distributing materials
- routine for coming to work with the teacher
- routine for returning to desks quietly and starting seat work

In order to make these guidelines more accessible to you, I have included Template 1.2, designed specifically for a differentiated lesson plan.

Differentiation in Practice

One of my very favorite student teachers, Ms. Dimples, was working with a group of fifth graders in a school that serves a broad demographic area. Although the cooperating teacher had established excellent routines for the children, neither the cooperating teacher nor Ms. Dimples had found much success in motivating a "low ability" group that they had been assigned to teach.

Template 1.2

Lesson Planning Template II—Differentiation	

Lesson Title:

Lesson Unit:

GOAL	State Curriculum (SC) Common Core State Standards (CCSS) Statewide or local systemwide goal Grade level standard
Lesson Objective	As a result of today's lesson, students will be able to
Materials Needed	Make the list. Check to see that all items are present. During the lesson, if you find you need something not on the list, write the item in the margin.
Warm-Up Time:	Use this to activate prior knowledge. Each of the three groups should have a warm-up that addresses the assessment from the previous day.
Motivation Time:	*(Whole group)* What will you do to engage students in today's topic? Why are they learning the new information?
Guided Practice Time:	While groups 2 and 3 are working on their warm-up, call group 1 for guided practice. From now on, the process is the same, but the expectations reflect the nature of each of the groups. Introduce the topic. Model the task/product/performance.
Independent Practice Time:	Working with their groups, students practice the new learning. During this phase, errors are eliminated, strengths are praised, and students learn from each other. When group 1 is sent back to do independent practice, group 2 is brought up for guided practice. When group 2 is sent back, group 3 comes up. In the meantime, if group 1 is finished, targeted students can help group 2 students with their independent practice. When group 3 returns for independent practice, groups 1 and 2 can come up and demonstrate their products or skills together.
Assessment Time:	Each student must supply evidence of the extent to which he mastered content or skill development as described in today's goal. *This does not have to be a paper/pencil assessment; demonstration of processes should be performed, not assessed, using a paper/pencil format.* Use data from this assessment for tomorrow's instruction.
Closure Time:	*(Whole group)* Ask students a question about key attitudes and learning in today's lesson: What did you learn today? What was the best part of today's lesson? What did you learn from each other today? How are you going to use today's lesson?
Homework	Homework Make homework relevant and practice oriented. Each group should get its own homework assignment. Avoid drill and kill exercises, especially for the below-grade-level group!

The fifth-grade team had decided to divide their responsibilities according to teachers' strengths and aptitudes. Unfortunately for me (a lifelong math phobic), Ms. Dimples was working with the one person on the team who loved teaching math.

I volunteered to do a demonstration lesson in math in order to show how careful planning and effective instruction can help engage disengaged learners even in a subject area that has been a real torment for them. The cooperating teacher, seeing the terror in my eyes and knowing the limitations of the students, assigned me a topic that even I could understand: units of time. As I planned for the lesson, I went over my notes from my prior observations of Ms. Dimples' work with this class. My notes included the following:

1. Ms. Dimples did not plan for differentiated instruction, even though the children were clearly not a homogeneous group.
2. Ms. Dimples' plan did not utilize a variety of teaching and learning styles and preferences.
3. By the time the children got to the part of the lesson where they could work together, they were frustrated and exhausted.
4. All of the students were assigned a "reteach" workbook assignment whether they needed it or not.

I then wrote my plan with the children's needs in mind (see Table 1.4). I also created the worksheets shown in Figure 1.3 for each of the groups.

TABLE 1.4 Mrs. Porton's Math Lesson Plan

GOAL	(SC) There is no statewide or local systemwide curriculum goal for this lesson.
Lesson Objective	As a result of today's lesson, students will be able to determine equivalent units of time by converting minutes, seconds, and hours.
Materials Needed	Stuffed animals/Worksheets*/Using data from prior assessments, class work, and behavior, the teachers put their students in three groups. (*Did not use too much)
Drill/Warm-Up **Time: 5 minutes**	On the overhead: 1. How many pennies in a dime? 2. How many nickels in a quarter? 3. How many fingers on one hand? 4. How many branches of government in the federal government? (A topic recently covered in class)
Motivation **Time: 8 minutes** (Kids loved this)	Stuffed animal show. Using the stuffed animals, demonstrate that in math we can use sets to count up and down, multiply and divide, and make distribution even and more accessible. The seconds will be the smallest animals, the minutes will be the next in size, and the hours will be the largest. (Students respond to concrete objects first before they can respond to numbers.)
Guided Practice **Time: 10 minutes** (I connected this to splitting the atom.) (Teachers formed the groups; I chose the leaders.)	In Dr. Porton's graduate advanced calculus class, the students have decided that they are going to test the hypothesis that the hour can be divided into smaller units. Therefore, groups will try the following experiment. Watch out for dangerous flying objects! (To keep all alert, I thought I would throw stuffed animals in air—never necessary.) 1. Students in group 1 will be given the smallest animals (these represent the seconds). They are to speak in high squeaky voices. Based on the motivation, group 1 has to determine how many seconds are in a minute. 2. Students in group 2 will be given the middle-size animals (these represents the minutes). They are to speak in regular voices. Based on the motivation, group 2 has to determine how many minutes are in an hour. 3. The two students in group 3 will be given Moose the Hour. I have a large stuffed moose, which I brought in with the other stuffed animals. The size ratios of the toys helps the visual learners, the discussions help the auditory learners, and the manipulation of the toys helps the kinesthetic learners.
Independent Practice Time: 10 minutes	Working with their groups, each student will be given worksheets to practice equivalent parts by determining how to convert seconds into minutes, minutes into hours, and hours into minutes.
Assessment **Time: 5 minutes** (100% mastery!)	Exit ticket: For Seconds and Minutes Groups—You have to go from your home to my home so you can give me a happy present. I live 150 minutes away from everyone's house. How long in hours and minutes will it take you to get to my house? For Moose Group—Create 3 questions for tomorrow that indicate what you have learned from today's lesson.
Closure **Time: 2 minutes** (Good replies)	What did you learn today that you can use?

Names of students on team: _____

SECONDS WORKSHEET

1. How many SECONDS in one minute?
2. How do you know?
3. How many seconds in two minutes?
4. How do you know?
5. We have 10 bears. Each one represents 6 seconds. If we put all of them together, what unit of time do we have now? _____ How do you know?

Names of students on team: _____

MINUTES WORKSHEET

1. How many MINUTES in one hour?
2. How do you know?
3. How many minutes in two hours?
4. How do you know?
5. We have six bears. Each bear represents _____ minutes. When we add them all together, we have one hour. How do you know?

Names of students on team: _____

HOURS WORKSHEET

1. How many minutes in an hour?
2. How many minutes in a half an hour?
3. How many minutes in an hour and a half?
4. How many seconds in an hour?
5. If you have to wait 120 minutes for vacation to start, how many hours will you be waiting? _____ How do you know?

FIGURE 1.3 You Find the Time Worksheet

For my group leaders, I selected the following students: Lilly had been problematic because she was struggling with the content, Tawanda seemed to want attention at any cost, and Andre was very argumentative with other students because he felt unlikable. As a result of careful planning, the group leaders were wonderful, and the children worked on their worksheets in their small groups and remained on task during the entire lesson.

Summary

If you read a book that said you need to plan, but did not tell you how, did not show you examples, and simply discussed the theoretical need for careful planning, would you feel prepared to plan a lesson to teach tomorrow? If you were told that you were going to be taught how to make a collage and the activities listed for you for the day indicated that you would be practicing making a collage, but your assessment was a paper/pencil test on renowned collage artists, would you feel your new skills had been accurately assessed? In order to plan with your students in mind, try to remember your last stressful learning experience and remind yourself that learning is both painful and rewarding.

To be sure that this chapter has fulfilled its obligations, let's analyze it using the instructional triangle:

- The *goal* of the chapter was to teach you the basic steps of the planning process.
- The *strategies* included giving a variety of examples and non-examples, providing various templates for generic lesson plans and differentiated lesson plans, and discussing how to use the formats, especially when working with struggling learners.
- The chapter discussed some basics of student *assessment*, but there is no one here who can assess your progress in mastering the skills involved in planning. However, we have included a blank generic lesson plan for you to use (Template 1.3). Your students will let you know by their interest, attitudes, and progress whether or not your skills as a planner are improving.

Template 1.3

Lesson Plan Template—Generic		

Lesson Title:

Lesson Unit:

GOAL	(SC) Curriculum Goal	CCSS Grade level standard
Lesson Objective	As a result of today's lesson, students will be able to	
Materials Needed		
Warm-Up Time:		
Motivation Time:		
Guided Practice Time:		
Independent Practice Time:		
Assessment Time:		
Closure Time:		
Homework		

The terms *at-risk students* and *struggling students* are used interchangeably throughout this text. Although at-risk/struggling students may not be cognitively impaired, it is important to note that this population does not succeed without appropriate interventions, which include differentiated instruction, management that is based on mutual respect, assessments that are transparent, and structure that provides safety, support, and scaffolding. When any of these is missing, these students struggle to learn. The extent to which any or all of these is absent describes the extent of the struggle that schools can prevent.

Identifying Struggling Learners

Nobody rises to low expectations.

CALVIN LLOYD

I n September 1994, using criteria that came from the Maryland State Department of Education's Maryland's Tomorrow Program (retained in grade at least 1 year, poor attendance, and eligibility based on the financial status of a student's family), Joppatowne High School began its own intervention program, which we later named the All Stars Program. Twenty-four non-academically promoted ninth-grade students (19 boys, 5 girls) were grouped with two teachers for three out of four periods a day. I designed Joppatowne's version of the Maryland's Tomorrow Program and made the initial arrangements with all of the outside agencies and organizations with whom we would be working.

My teaching partner that year agreed to teach math and science and follow up on my arrangements. I taught English 9 and geography. Together we taught a class I designed, which I named Life Skills. Each week during one of our Life Skills classes, we visited a soup kitchen in Bel Air or a nursing home across the street from our school, or we read to children who attended a nursery school across the street. In addition, I recruited seniors, who earned a credit for tutoring our students during their academic courses.

After a few weeks of school, it was clear to me that our ninth-grade students and I had vastly different worldviews. I was curious about their constant complaints about anything and everything and their dogged determination not to succeed. Even though in time we were able to overcome their attitudes in my class, their negative outlook initially appalled me. For example, in previous years it was common for me not to have any disagreements with a student until early October, but this year within 30 seconds of my students' arrival, one boy stated loudly: "This place sucks." Since I had spent hours decorating my room to make it look welcoming and less like a traditional classroom, his comment was all the more memorable. I decided to match theory against practice, so I created a journal entry that I required each student to respond to. The questions came from the characteristics of discouraged learners in Sagor's (1993) *At-Risk Students*. Although in later versions I added an assessment to this assignment, the following is the journal entry just as it was handed out in September 1994 and one student's response:

JOURNAL ENTRY

I am curious about the way you look at your world. Very often I have heard you describe life very differently from the way I understand it. Please share your thoughts and opinions on the following topics. You cannot be wrong. You will not be judged by what you say. I just want to understand you better. I am your audience, the form is a letter, the topics are listed, and the purpose is to tell me your honest opinions and ideas. You may select any 5 of the following, but please respond to Item 7!

1. The world is a place over which I have little or no control. Things just happen and there isn't much I can do to change most situations.
   Is this true? Why? Why not? How do you know?

2. When things in my life become difficult, my best defense is to avoid the situation. If I'm not there, I don't have to deal with the problem.
   Is this true? Why? Why not? How do you know?

3. Most adults are not to be trusted. They may act like they care about you, but they really don't. They just want something from you.
   Is this true? Why? Why not? How do you know?

4. My future is not very exciting. I will probably have very little money but very many problems. There is not much I can do to change my future.
   Is this true? Why? Why not? How do you know?

5. School is usually very boring. Teachers do not tell us why we have to do most of their work, and they get angry when I ask them why we are doing a long, boring assignment. When I get really bored, I get into trouble just to keep myself awake.
   Is this true? Why? Why not? How do you know?

6. I learn better if I can see the practical application of what is being taught. I can talk about what I know better than I can write about it.
   Is this true? Why? Why not? How do you know?

7. Effort has very little to do with success. People who do well are just lucky, and people who fail have no control over what has happened to them. Life is a crap shoot. You get up each day and see what happens.
   Is this true? Why? Why not? How do you know?

Male _____   Female _____

The following is an exact replica of a response from a ninth-grade girl in the All Stars Program. As mentioned in the Preface, only some of the stories in this book end happily. This one does not.

Dear Mrs. Porton,

I feel that the world is a place over which I have no control. Things do just happen and there isn't much I can do to change most situations. I've never been able to handle things on my own. I feel like there is no way to coupe (cope) with a problem or tragety without help. Except me, I can't get help with my situations. I know because my problems haven't been solved, they just got worse.

I do usually avoid my problems by blocking them out. If I don't hear them or don't know them then theirs not a problem. The best answer is to avoid a situation cause its never gonna change. I know because I've been there.

I will never trust adults again. All the adults including my parents, that I trusted, lied, cheated or said the wrong thing. They do act like they care and want to help but they stab you right in the back. How do I know? Because my parents & ex friends did the same thing.

I can't talk about stuff better then writing about it. It's easier to write it down and keep it to yourself then to talk about it and have someone tell someone else. I guess you would call it trust, and that's something I couldn't or won't give anyone. My trust in them. I can't.

You never know what will happen next. The future is just like a surprise. People who do good one day, their just lucky. But it makes me mad to see someone brag. Especially since I'm below average. It's not helpful though when your family and friends call you worthless.

I thought this young lady was wonderful. She was bright, she was extremely polite, and in group work, she was helpful to everyone. However, she and a relative who was also in our class were frequently hungry. We called the Department of Social Services to determine if their basic needs were being met, and the investigation revealed that the children were not being fed regularly. Unfortunately, all our interventions were too little and/or too late. The last thing I heard about her was that she and her baby were looking for a permanent place to live.

The story of struggling learners should not be told simply by data. When students speak for themselves, we can hear beneath their bravado the voices of young people who want to do well. However, they cannot imagine themselves as being anything but "worthless." Let us agree that no student who enters a classroom will ever be assigned to the "worthless" category and move on.

For the purposes of this text, any student in one or more of the following categories will be considered a struggling learner who is at risk for school failure:

1. Children who live in unstable families and communities,
2. Children who are unsuccessful in meeting school-based standards,
3. Children who have an external locus of control, and
4. Children who have a limited and/or grim notion of the future.

In this text, being a struggling learner is considered a state, not a trait. Anyone can be at risk for a period of time, but that can be changed with the proper intervention(s). Just like any student who qualifies for an Individualized Education Program (IEP) under the Individuals with Disabilities Education Improvement Act of 2004 (IDEA) or a Section 504 Plan under the Rehabilitation Act of 1973, struggling learners need additional interventions and support, especially those services that promote healthy social and emotional development and address mental health issues (Knitzer & Lefkowitz, 2006).

Children who have been negatively affected because they fit into one or more of the categories under discussion often come to school with challenging behaviors such as aggressiveness and disorganization (Scheeringa & Zeeanah, 2001; Ween, 2003). Frankly, most teacher preparation programs do not provide preservice teachers with the background knowledge needed to understand the root causes of these problems or with the tools needed to address them. Both the students and the teachers are faced with challenges that neither is equipped to handle. In order to plan for these children, we need to delve into each of our four categories systematically.

CHILDREN WHO LIVE IN UNSTABLE FAMILIES AND COMMUNITIES

It might be assumed that this category refers to children who live in broken homes, attend urban schools, and are surrounded by a violent drug culture and gang activity; however, that does not adequately describe the entire population of struggling learners. In this section, lack of stability includes divorce, substance abuse, and poverty. Although neglect and abuse fit well into this discussion, our focus will be on divorce, substance abuse and poverty. However, if you suspect that any child is the victim of either neglect or abuse, it is your legal responsibility to follow your school's protocol immediately. The only attribute of instability missing for students in suburban and costly private schools would be the obvious manifestations of poverty.

Divorce

Evidence from a variety of sources indicates that although children whose parents have divorced often display more academic and behavioral problems than same-age peers, the data do not support the conclusion that this is a sufficient cause for placing a child at risk (EdReform Studies, 1994). In a study on children of divorce and their adjustment, the age of the child during the divorce seems to be a significant predictor on the effects of the divorce on the child. Researchers found that among elementary school students, ages 7 through 12, the students tended to show diminished peer relationships and a drop-off in academic performance anywhere from 2 to 10 years later (EdReform Studies, 1994). Divorce is not limited to any socioeconomic status, race, or culture. Further, the data indicate that when the home lacks stability before, during, and after the divorce, there are likely to be negative effects on children who internalize the stress of their parents' discord. "Since the divorce rate in the United States is now at 50%" (Dallman-Jones, 2006, p. 55), it is only reasonable to assume that many of the struggling learners in any given classroom are trying to deal with their parents' problems without having had sufficient time on the planet to understand the nuances of adults' lives. Children's stress is manifested on the playground with peers and in the classroom with decreased academic performance and/or increased behavioral problems.

Substance Abuse

Long before any struggling learner decides whether or not to engage in substance abuse, he may have lived a life filled with the chaos that substance abuse can create. Research has indicated that parents' substance abuse, antisocial behavior, negative life events, and psychiatric episodes tend to have their most maladaptive and devastating effects on the children (Fauth, Brady-Smith, & Brooks-Gunn, 2003).

As struggling learners grow older, substance abuse becomes a striking indicator of at-risk behaviors. Muuss and Porton (1999) found that the earlier the child engages in risk-taking behaviors, especially the use of addictive drugs, the less likely it is that this is a manifestation of normative adolescent risk taking; instead, it is more likely that such behaviors are a precedent that will result in a lifelong pattern of antisocial behavior. Therefore, an elementary school teacher dealing with a child who is experimenting with substance abuse may be facing a much more serious challenge than a high school teacher is who is working with a similarly engaged student. Nonetheless, any illicit drug use is a serious indicator of at-risk behavior that can have permanent negative consequences. "In 2009, 8 percent of 8th graders, 18 percent of 10th graders, and 23 percent of 12th graders reported illicit drug use in the past 30 days" (Forum on Child and Family Statistics, 2010, p. 2). Since these are self-reported data, they are likely to reveal only the tip of the iceberg. Substance abuse is not restricted to high-crime or high-poverty areas. Sometimes the only differences between schools serving affluent families and those serving more impoverished ones are the "drugs of choice." Money can buy access to designer drugs; however, it does not prevent affluent families from feeling the devastating pain from the loss of a child who is another victim of our war with drugs.

Poverty

Children represent a disproportionate share of the poor in the United States; they are 25 % of the total population, but 35% of the poor population (U.S. Census Bureau, 2000). According to a 2007 UNICEF study entitled "A Comprehensive Assessment of the Lives and Well-Being of Children and Adolescents in the Economically Advanced Nations," among all of the industrialized nations in the world, only the United Kingdom ranks as poorly on six of the seven dimensions of childhood poverty as the United States. For our purposes, it is important to note that children in poverty, even when disaggregated for other variables, demonstrate more behavioral and emotional problems than nonpoor children (Petterson & Albers, 2001). Poor children are twice as likely as their nonpoor peers to have to repeat a grade, get expelled or suspended from school, or drop out of school. They are also 14 times as likely to be identified as needing special education services as their peers who do not live in poverty (Fauth et al., 2003).

When poverty occurs early in a child's life (from 2 to 4 years of age), the negative effects on the child's school readiness and cognitive outcomes appear to be much more powerful, even after controlling for the effect of the mother's education, family structure, and the child's birth weight (Smith, 1997). Young children living in poverty demonstrate lower cognitive ability and appear to present with more behavioral or emotional problems (Azzi-Lessing, 2010) that can compromise their readiness to learn and/or their ability to concentrate in class. The recurrent theme in the literature is compelling: Children who spend their lives in unrelenting poverty score lower on measures of school readiness and cognitive ability than children who have never lived in poverty.

It seems that the damaging, almost drowning effects that are the hallmarks of concentrated poverty and family instability have not changed since Kozol (1991) described the "savage inequalities" that affect learning and achievement in urban schools. In a study conducted on third and fifth graders living in neighborhoods beset by violent crime, female-headed households, and intransigent poverty, the fifth graders demonstrated poorer academic performance than similar peers living in comparable neighborhoods and attending schools with more resources. The results of these and most other longitudinal studies reveal that, as children grow older and interact more with their communities, the relationship between the effects of the community and the children's decreasing academic performance becomes more pronounced. Family poverty is significantly associated with diminished achievement scores in reading and math during middle childhood, and the results remain consistent until adolescence (Fauth et al., 2003).

Poverty is not only the absence of money; it is also the absence of good child-care facilities, good mental and physical health services, and safe living conditions. In such conditions, children are raised by parents who are living with significant stressors that can lead to poor mental health, more depressive symptoms, greater conflicts within and outside the home, and more discordant parent–child relationships (Fauth et al., 2003). In addition, the stresses of living in poverty (i.e., the lack of resources and the absence of social supports) combine to increase the potency and the tenacity of the negative effects on children (Brooks-Gunn & Duncan, 1997; Knitzer & Lefkowitz, 2006; Knitzer et al., 2008; Petterson & Albers, 2001). Many researchers have been interested in the correlations among intransigent poverty, child development, and family stress. According to one model, known as the Family Stress Model, stress that is generated by economic hardship creates parenting that is less supportive and involved and more coercive and harsh, and it frequently results in higher incidences of maternal depression and distress. Further, these lower-quality parent–child interactions brought on by economic factors negatively stimulate mental health issues, resulting in higher rates of behavioral and school-related problems among poor children (Brooks-Gunn & Duncan, 1997; Knitzer, 2000).

Perhaps you have had an experience similar to mine when your students of generational poverty seem very confused by world events. When Bobby Kennedy was killed, I was teaching first graders in the Bronx. My students were the children of generational poverty. The day after the shooting they came to school looking very frightened and telling very similar, but very incoherent stories of a man their mothers knew who lived on Burnside Avenue (a major street near the school). The children said the man had been shot, and they were very frightened. I soon realized that they had no idea of what had happened or to whom. They all saw their mothers crying before they left for school. Either alone or together, they tried to figure out what had happened. Fortunately, when they came to school, I could clarify the situation and calm their fears. We looked at a map of the United States and discovered that California is a long way from New York. We took a walk to Burnside Avenue, and there was no sign of danger. I bought a newspaper on our walk, and when we returned to class, I showed the children a picture of Bobby Kennedy and explained to them who he was and why their mothers were so sad that he had been killed.

I have had many similar occasions in my work with struggling learners because anecdotally I have noted that one feature of the culture of poverty seems to be a lack of communication between parents and children, especially at times of crisis, whether within or outside of the family system. This pattern has reemerged in rural and other suburban settings at various grade levels and throughout my teaching experience. It may help to explain why for many struggling learners the world appears to be a place over which there is very little control and things just happen (Sagor, 1993).

In conclusion, in this as in all other contributing factors that place a child at risk, poverty is a contributing cause, but it is not necessarily a sufficient cause. Disadvantaged parents, neighborhoods, and schools that use appropriate boundary setting, utilize resources effectively, and are sensitive to the needs of students can mitigate some of the effects of poverty.

What Does This Mean for You?

As a teacher, many of these problems are beyond your control. However, the impacts of the child's unstable family and/or community life are evident in every classroom. Therefore, it is absolutely essential that no matter what a child's socioeconomic status, as teachers we must create safety in our classrooms, and we must make our high expectations for each child's ability to succeed apparent and integrate into all phases of instruction.

One of the best teachers I ever knew taught me the wisdom of being the Empress who teaches in the Empire. She taught English 10 college-bound students, and she needed to create safe boundaries for her students. When I heard her refer to herself as the Empress, I immediately "liberated" her idea. Since then, my students knew that when they were in my Empire, they would be safe and they would be treated with respect and courtesy.

Similarly, it is critical to maintain high standards for all students. Many students behave in school very much like those with whom they share a collective sense of identity. They make decisions based on their perception of opportunities available to people who are like them (Holland & Eisenhart, 1988). Teachers need to fill their classrooms and their readings with examples of those who have conquered gender bias, racial bias, and poverty to achieve success. The old adage that "Nothing succeeds like success" does not apply to the population of students who are at risk. For them, success belongs to others. It is the teacher's job to bring success into the realm of possibility by demonstrating that people just like them have accomplished it, and they can, too. Henry Ford said it best: "Whether you think you can, or you think you can't, you're right!" ("Think Exist," n.d.).

While you can establish a few simple guidelines to help keep your students safe in your classroom, they must navigate their own terrain using the rules of their world. It is your job to teach them that there are other worlds with other rules.

How Do You Plan with These Students in Mind?

Struggling learners who live in unstable families and communities crave stability. Since that is missing in their home and community lives, school is often the only place that can provide a secure, dependable environment for them. Struggling learners need to know what is expected of them, and that cannot change from one minute to the next. They need to know the schedule for the class or the day, and that cannot change capriciously. They cannot start to have faith in the integrity of their teachers' commitment to them until they see for themselves that their teachers have made every effort to make consistency and security a priority. Words will not be sufficient. They are very wary of adults. If a teacher wants their trust, it will have to be earned every day, day after day. Since struggling learners need predictability and emotional stability in order to experience the best possible learning environment (Daggett, Cobble, & Gertel, 2007), teachers can use an announcement board or a schedule that gets updated daily to let the children know what they will be doing every day.

In addition, the goals, strategies, and assessments for all lesson plans must match, or the children may be taught one thing and assessed on another. Again, these students are hypersensitive to anything that alerts them to the dangers of misrepresentation. Chaos can be described as a world that tries to look neat, while disguising its mess by diversion and misrepresentation. In the teacher's "Empire," everything must be transparent, stable, and reliable. The only antidote to bedlam is order; it may be the best weapon in a teacher's arsenal, so it must be used consistently and with precision.

CHILDREN WHO ARE UNSUCCESSFUL IN MEETING SCHOOL-BASED STANDARDS

Struggling learners are often in danger of school failure for not meeting school-based standards for a variety of reasons. Some of the variables are under their control, and others are not. In this category, we are going to focus on three issues: attendance, retention in grade, and expectations of those in authority.

Attendance

In many studies performed to predict whether or not students will drop out of school, attendance has been shown to be a highly predictive variable (Allensworth & Easton, 2007; Neild & Balfanz, 2006). Neild and Balfanz (2006) found that eighth graders who missed 5 weeks of school had at least a 75% chance of dropping out of high school. They also found that students' poor attendance in eighth grade was positively correlated with high dropout rates in high school. In Philadelphia, for example, of the eighth graders who attended one school less than 80% of the time, 78% dropped out of high school.

For those working with high school students, the following data are of special importance. Among entering freshmen who had *no previous record of at-risk risk factors*, less than 70% attendance in ninth grade resulted in their earning less than two credits for the year. Therefore, they had a one-in-four chance of being able to graduate with the other members of their entering class (Kennelly & Monrad, 2003). Nothing as nuanced and complex as why children do not attend school can be explained simply, but the result is clear: No child can learn what schools have to teach unless the child goes to school.

Retention in Grade

Attendance and retention in grade are consistently listed in the literature as variables that have the most predictive validity when assessing who is likely to drop out of school. The two are intrinsically linked because a student who does not attend school is not likely to pass. They work in tandem to reinforce struggling learners' beliefs in their own inadequacies, their low self-esteem, and their sense of helplessness (Sagor, 1993).

All teachers need to understand the power of the data. According to researchers Balfanz and Herzog (2005), future dropouts could be predicted as early as sixth grade from a review of elementary school retention records. Further, researchers from Johns Hopkins University found that 64% of the students who repeated a grade in elementary school and 63% of those who were held back in middle school eventually dropped out of high school (Neild & Balfanz, 2006).

Expectations of Those in Authority

In her seminal work describing attempts to modify social behavior between Black and White students in an inner-city middle school, Cohen (1973) made some of the most important findings since work in this discipline began. Her research has enormous credibility among both academics and practitioners, since it was done in the field in an urban setting, and her findings have been anecdotally validated in many classrooms and empirically validated in many studies since they were first published.

Cohen (1973) first asserted that various characteristics, such as race, gender, and class, have status expectations. For example, we expect women to be sensitive, we expect Black males to be athletic, and so on. In the classroom, those expectations have powerful implications. According to the Theory of Status Characteristics and Expectation States, we assume that one group has higher academic competence than the other. Historically in schools, this has led to a single-strand order of success. One person is at the top; one person, therefore, has to be at the bottom.

Unfortunately, due to too many factors to explore within this text, these expectations have led to the expectation that Whites will achieve greater academic success than Blacks. This finding is further validated by Fordham and Ogbu (1986), who found that Black high school students who "acted White" by doing well in school faced opposition from and were negatively sanctioned by their peers (Fordham & Ogbu, 1986). Expectations of peers, who are considered the voices of authority by adolescents, can and do have a powerful effect on student behaviors.

The double dose of the expectation that Whites will be superior and the pressure from Black peers not to succeed has placed a terrible burden on many academically talented young Black students. These students' academic skills and interests often put them in conflict with themselves, their peers, and their own culture regarding the benefits and burdens of scholastic success.

In addition, Cohen's work resulted in another notable finding. While working with an interracial staff in 1973, she noted that the children were keenly aware of the teachers' expectations based on the races of the teacher and the student. In the 1970s, there were not many interracial staffs in inner-city schools; the children involved in the study were experiencing a new social model, and they had a great deal to teach us. According to Cohen (1973), "Expectations of those in positions of authority are often a powerful explanation for behavior of subjects" (p. 867).

Cohen's (1973) findings have been supported repeatedly over the years and have been found to hold true regardless of the nature of teachers' expectation. As recently as 2007, Fauth et al. found that teachers from high socioeconomic levels who teach poor children have a tendency to regard their students from a negative perspective and expect lower academic performance even in the early years. The self-fulfilling nature of teachers' prophecies about children affects the way the children respond both academically and behaviorally. The children act in line with their teachers' thoughts about them.

When a teacher believes that *all* children can learn, the children's behavior, sense of efficacy, and willingness to persist are vastly different than when a teacher's expectations are based on the students' status characteristics, such as race, socioeconomic status, and/or gender. Children are brilliant observers, but lousy interpreters. They may not understand why the teacher expects one child to soar and another to sink, but they do know which is which.

What Does This Mean for You?

Interestingly enough, all of this begins with *you*. Do you think you can teach? You must believe in yourself before, during, and after your time with children, or teaching will be very unrewarding for you and the children you teach. You will not succeed every day and you will not reach and teach every child who is assigned to you unless you have a strong sense of efficacy. No one is perfect, and no one is global; however, you will never know the effect you have on a child unless you have been unkind, been disrespectful, and/or held low expectations for the child. Those results are generally negative and stable over time. On the other hand, if you have an optimistic spirit, hold high hopes for yourself and your children, and do the hard work necessary, at least you will have laid the groundwork for future success.

Do you think all children can learn? Not all children learn the same way on the same day. That is why this text strongly emphasizes differentiated instruction, discovery learning, and cooperative learning strategies. You cannot possibly meet every child's needs. However, if you use all of your resources, including all the children in the room and the positive members on your staff, you will have a much better chance of teaching all your children. Robert Collier, a motivational speaker, must have been thinking of teachers when he said: "Your chances of success in any undertaking can always be measured by your belief in yourself" ("Think Exist," n.d.).

Let me illustrate with a story. I had been teaching for over 30 years when I went into Doris Williams' office one day. I was completely discouraged. I said: "Doris, you know how we always say: 'All children can learn.' Well, I have one that can't!" I told her about my trying to teach Bobby how to respond to a writing prompt and the nine zillion strategies I had tried with no success. Doris listened patiently. She leaned over to look in her desk a few times. I think she was hiding her laughter, but she knew I would lose it if she laughed at me because I was beside myself with frustration. Bobby had multiple disabilities; he had an IEP, but he was in a regular English class. It was my responsibility to teach him my formula for responding to a prompt. All of the special education classes were using my system, so it would not have mattered if Bobby were with me or not; he still had to learn the system. Finally Doris responded. She reminded me of strategies I had not tried, she reminded me of my past victories over difficult obstacles, and she pumped me up again. I felt like the "Little Engine That Could." I went back to class the next day, and because I felt rejuvenated, I tried another strategy. We had a breakthrough!

The moral of this story is that you need to maintain friendships with those who cheer you on; don't listen to those who tell you "these kids can't learn." In order to succeed, you have to surround yourself with people who have high expectations for you and your ability to teach all your students.

When you believe you can teach and the children know you believe they can learn, you are ready to attack their deeply held belief system that school is a place that is unresponsive to their needs and should be avoided. Attending your class has to be important to both teacher and student. Students need to know that teachers truly care about their well-being, their absence is noted, and their attendance in class is meaningful and personally important to the teacher.

In addition, teachers who learn what motivates their students use authentic and consequential incentives to improve attendance. This can result in marked improvements in unexpected arenas. For example, at the end of the day in the All Stars Program, each student received credit for two categories: attending each class and being on task in each class. At the end of every two weeks, students who had missed 1 day or less for 2 weeks and who had earned points for being on-task in their All Star classes at least 4 days each week were eligible to have their names placed in the Big Draw.

We had divided the 24 students into two teams of 12. The A Team had a biweekly winner, as did the B Team. We invited administrators, guests at the school, and any adult the students asked us to invite to come to our class the last period the students were with us on Friday. From the names in the "hat," our invited guest drew a winner from each team. Each winner's family received a pizza, which was delivered to their home that evening, and a large bottle of soda paid for by Maryland's Tomorrow Program.

In that way, we were reinforcing the family's efforts to get the child to school and the child's efforts to do well in school. This simple little system did more good than words can ever describe. Parents who had never received a positive phone call from the child's school before were now being told that dinner would be arriving at 6 or 7 (their choice) and being asked for the family's soda selection. Attendance was not the only variable that improved.

CHILDREN WHO HAVE AN EXTERNAL LOCUS OF CONTROL

Children who have an external locus of control approach school-related tasks very differently than their peers who have an internal locus of control. In this category, we will look at issues related to attributions for success, connections between effort and success, and lack of ownership of failure and success.

Attribution

Attributions are the explanations that people give as to why they were successful or not. There are three sets of characteristics associated with attributions:

1. Is the cause of our success internal or external? Did the factors that determined the outcome start within us or originate in our environment?
2. Are the causes stable over time and likely to get the same results, or are they unstable and, therefore, likely to change over time with different input from us?
3. Is the cause controllable—one that we believe we can alter if we want to—or is it uncontrollable—one that we believe we cannot control? (Vockell, 2008).

Struggling learners do not accept the concept that they are responsible for what happens to them. They believe that they can explain what happens to them as the result of fate, chance, or luck. Good or bad, they do not accept the old adage that "Nothing succeeds like success" because they think life is capricious and cannot be controlled by what they do. They fit under the category best described as "learned helplessness". Researchers explain that people who fit in this group have developed the expectation that nothing they do can possibly lead to success (Vockell, 2008). Schunk and Zimmerman (2006) found that students who have an external locus of control normally ignore praise, since they fail to see the connection between effort and success. However, if teachers use effective praise and connect effort to success and if the students find the praise they receive leads to real accomplishments, the students' belief systems can change (Schunk & Zimmerman, 2006).

Connections Between Effort and Success

Struggling learners who have an external locus of control do not accept the idea that missing assignments, being absent from school for over 15 days during a quarter, and failing major tests are an adequate explanation for their failure in school. According to them, there is no relationship between their lack of effort and the teacher's decision to fail them. They believe everything that happens is external to them and uncontrollable. According to Brabec, Fisher, and Pitler (2004), people who relinquish control over their lives believe that their successes and failures are due to forces beyond their control, which include being unlucky, having teachers who don't like them, and just being "dumb." As a result, they do not see any correspondence between what they do and what happens to them. When asked why they failed a particular subject after having been shown fairly impressive data (e.g., excessive absenteeism, poor test results, and failure to complete assignments), students often have no idea why they failed or what they could have done to prevent their failure.

No Ownership of Failure or Success

Students who have an internal locus of control modify their behavior according to the results of their efforts. If the feedback is positive, they maintain; if the feedback is negative, they change. However, if students believe that nothing they do matters, then feedback is irrelevant. Therefore, students who have an external locus of control do not take pride in their successes or ownership of their failures. If a student does not believe she had anything to do with her success, why should she take any pride in it?

Classroom Applications

Lynch, Hurford, and Cole (2002) found that having an external rather than an internal locus of control is a statistically valid predictor of academic success. Students with an internal locus of control believe they can control what happens to them. They are academic risk takers because they accept feedback, they know how to persist, and they believe they can succeed. In contrast, students with an external locus of control avoid academic risks even when they have been successful because they do not know how or why they did well; they see no reason to persist. Their attributional schema is external and stable, and both success and failure are beyond their control (Vockell, 2008). Beegle (2003) quoted one of the participants in her study of college graduates who were raised in generational poverty as saying, "I never associated studying with success. I just thought intelligent kids did well, and others like me and my friends didn't" (p. 14).

Therefore, teachers working with struggling learners must understand that there is a substantial difference between the way these students understand and interpret the world and the way most teachers account for what happens in life. For the most part, teachers are "internalizers" who are having parallel conversations with their struggling learners who are "externalizers." A typical conversation sounds a lot like this:

WORRIED TEACHER: Beverly, you are in serious danger of failing my class.

BEVERLY: Why?

WORRIED TEACHER: You missed 10 days this quarter, you have not handed in 13 major assignments, and you failed all of the unit tests.

BEVERLY: So?

WORRIED TEACHER: Honey, if you don't make up your work and start coming to school, you will fail.

BEVERLY: I thought you liked me! Why would you fail me? I thought we were friends. That's not fair. I thought you were nice! I guess I was wrong about you!

WORRIED TEACHER: What else could I have done to help her?
(TALKING TO HERSELF)

Teachers have to understand that their students truly believe that their success is just as capricious and beyond their control as their failure. Until that belief system changes, the students will not be active participants in their own success. Since their parents often describe similar views (Sagor, 1993), challenging this perspective requires a great deal of patience on the part of the teacher.

As part of each lesson plan, the connection between students' effort and success must be made explicit. For instance, credit must be given for time on task, staying on task, and other concrete examples that students can easily recognize as features of hard work.

Additionally, students must be given time to demonstrate their learning to the class at the end of independent practice and be able to answer questions from their peers. Their peers recognize those who have been retained in grade, those who rarely made appearances in school in previous years, and so on; therefore, becoming an "expert" can demonstrate to others that this student has had to work hard to become successful. Ultimately, plans should include topics that are interesting to the students. When students are motivated by the topic and are given multiple opportunities to achieve success, more students will try to do the work.

When students' effort is rewarded, students who have an external locus of control may find that the praise they receive leads to real accomplishments, and real accomplishments can lead to internalized self-esteem (Schunk & Zimmerman, 2006). According to further research (Brabec et al., 2010), positive outcomes for effective praise accrue to learners of all ages, ethnicities, and levels of competence; over a range of content areas; and to students living in urban and rural communities.

Teachers can help struggling learners make the connection between effort and success by asking students who have done well and who can tolerate their peers' attention such key questions as these: What did you do to prepare for this test? How long did you study? Is this the first test that you ever studied for? Why did you study for this test? As a final point, a teacher can ask in mock disbelief, "Do you mean to tell me that, if you study, you can do well on my tests?" When I went through this routine with one of my students, a classmate remarked quietly, "She got held back every year that I did. If she can do it, so can I." I could not have had a better witness to the truth: Effort can lead to success.

Throughout the adjustment process, the teacher must plan to make the students aware of the connection between their hard work and their achievement. It is important to make the students articulate that the hard work they did has led to their current success. Again, to effect any substantive change, teachers must be transparent, resourceful, and consistent.

CHILDREN WHO HAVE A LIMITED AND/OR GRIM NOTION OF THE FUTURE

In this category, we will be evaluating the long-term effects of generational crises. Specifically, we will be looking at generational issues related to incarceration, poverty, and the long-term effects of gender bias. These are all policy, psychological, and sociological problems, but first and foremost, they are problems that teachers face every day.

Generational Incarceration

I have to start this segment with another story. Out of sheer necessity, not out of any background knowledge or real competence, I taught All Stars geography the first year we began. I could not read a compass, so together the children and I learned how to do that. We learned how to do a lot together that year. One day when I was teaching Team B, I passed out maps of Maryland to the students, but then I had to step out of the room for a second. When I returned, the boys (Team B had nine boys and three girls) were calling out names to each other, and the other students were trying to locate the names on the maps as they were being called out. The students were really intent on the activity they had created for themselves. Since they were so actively engaged in the maps, I could not complain. Instead, I listened to the names carefully.

They were calling out the names of the prisons where their fathers were incarcerated across the state. No one hid the point of what he was trying to find or why. The boys told me to relax for a few minutes; they would tell me when they were through. I did as I was told.

Unfortunately, the data surrounding generational incarceration are very troubling, and while my boys looked for their fathers, the data indicate they may have been looking into their own futures. "Parental imprisonment has emerged as a novel, and distinctly American, childhood risk . . ." (Eckholm, 2009, p. 2).

As a result of more-severe sentencing guidelines, more than 1.5 million children have a parent, usually their father, in prison at any given time. Amid minority children, the effects are even more devastating. Researchers found that half of Black children whose parents dropped out of school had a father in prison compared to 1 in 14 White children with similar backgrounds. In 2007, the Justice Department's Bureau of Justice Statistics found that 1.8 million children under 18 had a parent in prison. Blacks were eight times more likely and Hispanics were three times more likely than White children to have a parent in prison. According to some researchers, children of incarcerated parents face as much as a 65% higher risk of being incarcerated themselves (Dallman-Jones, 2006). In addition, "an estimated 1,600,000 children in the United States have an imprisoned father, and 200,000 have an imprisoned mother. Most children with incarcerated parents live in poverty before, during, and after their parents' incarceration" (Dallman-Jones, 2006, p. 45).

The results of a parent's incarceration can be overwhelming for any child. Self-reports include feelings of social isolation, depression, or anxiety (at clinical levels); declining school performance; truancy; and drug and alcohol use. Children who participated in a visitation program at a woman's prison reported feelings of depression, poor concentration, poor school performance, and nightmares (Christian, 2009).

Current research indicates that the generational cycle of incarceration is difficult to break. One example is provided by a current prisoner, Mr. Scott, who agreed to be interviewed by a *New York Times* reporter in May 2009 for an article titled "In Prisoners' Wake, a Tide of Troubled Kids" (Eckholm, 2009). Mr. Scott explained that during his adolescence he was depressed and had low self-esteem. At the time of the interview, he was on supervised release from jail so he could receive job training. His ex-girlfriend was pregnant, and he wanted to be there for his baby. However, despite his promise to change, shortly after he spoke to the reporter, he did not report to his probation officer and avoided a mandatory drug test. By the time the article was published, Mr. Scott was in jail awaiting a sentence that could last 3 years or more—meaning that one more child would join the "incarcerated generation."

Generational Poverty

Anyone can lose a job or have a serious illness and become financially impoverished for a short period of time. Ruby Payne (1996) refers to that as situational poverty. However, we will be examining the effects of long-term or generational poverty. "Generational poverty is defined as being in poverty for two generations or longer" (Payne, 1996, p. 2). Although Payne's work has come under scrutiny from several sources, the work cited here has genuine utility and has been validated by other researchers (Beegle, 2003; Peyton, Farrell, Buzbee, & Little, 2005). According to Payne, children who come from generational poverty know a completely different set of rules and norms than set of middle-class rules and norms that govern schools. Having come to school with one set of expectations for behavior, many children learn the hard way that teachers do not accept their behavior as appropriate. It does not take long for kindergarten children to become small at-risk learners who believe early on that schools are unfair, threatening, and even abusive. Beegle (2003) describes her own experiences as a child of generational poverty: "Like others born into generational poverty, I find that thinking of my early educational experiences evokes memories of violence, humiliation, and fear" (p. 11).

Beegle (2003) was able to complete her doctorate and conduct a study of others who had grown up in generational poverty and graduated from college. According to the findings of the study, participants reported feeling shame and humiliation because they were poor. They believed that outsiders blamed them for being poor. They had to overcome physical, emotional, and sociological barriers, as well as the economic barriers, at every stage of their academic careers. According to Beegle (2003), it appears that some barriers have been diminished in areas of race, geography, and religion; however, obstacles related to generational poverty are as impervious to change as poverty itself.

Language usage is also an indicator of generational poverty. Formal or standard usage is the benchmark for all students' spoken and written expressive language in school. Students who live in generational poverty often speak what Payne refers to as "casual register." This is characterized by a much smaller vocabulary, fragments, and many more nonverbal cues. As a result, even the mode of communication the children bring to school can be discredited and the children made to feel personally disrespected in the process.

Goodell (2007), reporting for *The Dartmouth*, described a seminar, "Bridges out of Poverty," conducted by Jodi Pfarr. During the seminar, Pfarr explained the relationships between language usage and class. People from the middle class and those in positions of authority tend to use the formal register at a higher rate. However, people from poverty tend to use the casual register at a higher rate. "Respect is the extent to which someone meets your expectations" (Pfarr, as quoted in Goodell, 2007). Therefore, children who come from middle-class homes are more likely to be treated with respect than their generationally poor peers.

As Lam (1993) observed, one of the more insidious results of racism and classism can be found in the test bias in standardized and high-stakes tests. "The results of the test scores become part of students' files; they provide the basis for high-stakes decisions concerning placement, selection, certification, and promotion. These decisions are made without consideration of the inequities surrounding testing in general and testing culturally diverse students in particular" (as cited in Ford, 2005, p. 1). The paucity of poor and minority students in gifted and talented programs speaks volumes regarding the combined effects of institutional racism and classism.

The disparity that is accorded to children in poverty by those who teach is not lost on the children (Armour-Thomas, 1992; Helms, 1992) and has been reported as making teachers seem like the enemy (Beegle, 2003). As long as the middle-class norms, rules, and language preferences remain hidden, children living in generational poverty will have a difficult time believing that there is any hope for their being accepted or respected in school.

Long-Term Effects of Gender Bias

Normally, when we read about or discuss struggling learners, they appear to be a large, monolithic group, differentiated only by race on some constructs and by class on different questions, but never by gender. Nothing could be further from the truth. Stereotypical thinking based on gender is prevalent from childbirth on, and its negative effects can be permanent. "Women do two thirds of the world's work . . . . Yet they earn only one tenth of the world's income and own less than one percent of the world's property. They are among the poorest of the world's poor" (Barber B. Conable, Jr., President of the World Bank, to the 1986 Annual Meeting of the World Bank and International Monetary Fund, as quoted in Thibos, Lavin-Loucks, & Martin, 2007, cover).

Even in nursery schools serving wealthy families, girls are rewarded for being sweet, helpful, and giving, while their male counterparts are rewarded for their leadership, scientific, and thinking skills. At the age of 5, children are fairly androgynous, and the point of reinforcing gender roles this early is confusing to say the least. In case you think that the list in Table 2.1 was created long before teachers were aware of gender bias, this authentic list was used in an expensive private school in 1990. As you know, Title IX went into effect in 1972—by the time this list was created, schools had been functioning under Title IX for almost twenty years.

TABLE 2.1 Chart of Kindergarten Awards	
Boys' Awards	**Girls' Awards**
Very best thinker	All-around sweetheart
Most eager learner	Sweetest personality
Best friend	Most creative
Most imaginative	Cutest personality
Most enthusiastic	Best sharer
Most scientific	Best artist
Mr. Personality	Biggest heart
Hardest worker	Best manners
Best sense of humor	Best helper

In part, gender differences in learning account for course selection, academic risk taking, and persistence. For instance, females tend to concentrate on failure and internalize it as a highly valid indicator of their abilities, while males tend to overlook failure and behave as if it were irrelevant. Males can persist in spite of negative feedback, but females tend to give up when they feel or fear failure. One of the best explanations for this behavior comes from the work done by Carol Dweck in the 1970s. She and her colleagues followed up on Bandura's work, but in educational settings.

Dweck (Dweck & Leggett, 1988) has shown that women and underrepresented minorities tend to believe that intelligence is fixed and unchangeable and that students who hold this belief are more likely to show academic withdrawal and alienation and decreased academic achievement. Although Dweck's work was conducted over 40 years ago, it is still considered significant because her findings still hold true. For example, although women over time have continued to increase the number of doctoral degrees they have earned, as recently as 2010 70% of all doctorates in mathematics are awarded to men, but only 30% of all doctorates in mathematics were awarded to women (National Science Foundation, 2011).

At-risk females, whether academically challenged or gifted, still face enormous obstacles posed by no other variable than their gender. Since that is typically a permanent state, not a trait, it is no wonder that some young girls, especially those living in poverty, have grim notions of their future.

How Do You Plan with These Students in Mind?

The first thing you have to accept about your role when working with the students in this category is that there are more problems you cannot change than those you can. Your job is to have the courage, the energy, and the empathy with your students to do what you can.

If a child's parent is incarcerated, there is nothing any teacher can do to change the situation. However, providing the child with a time to talk and someone to talk to who will not be judgmental may make a huge difference for him. It may be easier for an elementary teacher to do that, since the children spend the bulk of their day with one teacher, but secondary teachers can make themselves available during planning time and before and after school. A few minutes with a child who needs to be heard can build a trusting bond that may make all the difference between isolation and connection, between acting out and talking it out, and between hope and hopelessness.

Payne (1996) is especially helpful for educators, as she communicates precisely what schools can do to help children from generational poverty. She reminds teachers that these children must understand the "hidden norms" of schools, which middle-class children understand intuitively. Children from impoverished families need to be explicitly taught the new norms and language variations using a methodology that is neither punitive nor disrespectful of the norms they bring with them to school. Perhaps an illustration will help to clarify this point.

During our Life Skills class, we taught the All Stars how to be peer mediators. A peer mediator is a student who has been trained to help other students resolve conflicts in a peaceful and respectful manner. Learning peer mediation skills was a win–win situation for our students. It taught them to think of problems from another person's perspective; it taught them to think of solving problems verbally, rather than nonverbally; and it gave them a means of earning respect among their peers.

One day after I had gone over the routines and procedures for the peer mediation approach we were using, one of the boys in my class raised his hand. He said: "Mrs. Porton, I like what you are teaching us. But in my family, after dinner, if my father and his brothers argue, they go out back and fight. Whoever is standing at the end is the winner. If I used the stuff you are teaching us, they would beat the crap out of me." I said, "Ralph, you are right. I think you need to learn two ways to fight. When you're at home, you better learn how to punch hard. When you're at school, you better learn how to think well." He had correctly analyzed his dilemma. He had to deal with two conflicting loyalties and value systems. My job was to acknowledge the accuracy of his thinking and help him decide how to function successfully in both worlds.

Finally, more teachers have to learn how to make such subjects as math and science more accessible to female students. Too often both subjects are taught without any consideration of multiple intelligences, various modalities of learning, and differences of learning styles. Math does not need to be a subject that one either "gets" or does not. It is the teacher's responsibility to create the scaffolding necessary to provide all students access to success.

Summary

In this text, a struggling learner who is at risk for school failure is one who fits into at least one of the four categories we have been examining. It is important to note, however, that many of these students fall into more than one category. It is the interaction of these multiple pathologies that makes reaching these students even more challenging. We are not going to fix or cure our students; it is our job to teach them about other worlds, other choices, and other norms. The final decisions will be up to them.

Our studies showed us that some of our struggling learners come to us from fragile homes and unstable communities that are struggling with day-to-day survival and crises involving alienation, drug abuse, divorce, and deprivation—not only of the body, but also of the spirit. In addition, some struggling learners start school less prepared than their middle-class peers or their peers who come from families that value education. Very quickly, they find that their schools are not responsive to their needs and their teachers are not willing to understand or respect them.

Early in elementary school, many struggling learners begin to vote "with their feet," and the team of excessive absenteeism and grade retention leads to the high probability that these struggling learners will drop out of school. Cohen's (1973) seminal work would stand on its own as a classic if the only thing her research taught us was that the expectations of those in authority have a powerful effect on the behavior of children.

Finally, coming from a family whose parent is incarcerated and/or that has lived in poverty for two or more generations convinces most children that as it is now, so shall it ever be. When we add the effects of the feminization of poverty and gender bias in education, it is little wonder that so many girls suffer from low self-esteem and select out of the higher-level math and science courses that they have the ability, but not the confidence, to take.

No matter what category they fall into, struggling learners are not worthless. It is our job to teach them to see themselves and their future through a different perspective. In forthcoming chapters, you will be given many ideas on how to make that happen. This chapter has focused on understanding the obstacles your students face so that you can look for effective ways to help them overcome their challenges.

Put a quote in your classroom that inspires you and helps to keep you motivated. Refer to it when you are down. Use it to help you keep up your courage when you are afraid. I love this famous quote by Buxton, "With ordinary talent and extraordinary perseverance, all things are attainable" ("Quote Garden," n.d.).

Effective Grouping Strategies

I never teach my pupils; I only attempt to provide the conditions in which they can learn.

ALBERT EINSTEIN

In 1993, Joppatowne High School (JHS) was chosen to be the only high school in Harford County, Maryland, that would receive training on Dimensions of Learning and Facilitative Leadership. The training was part of a countywide plan to restructure the traditional top-down administration model to create a more inclusive, facilitative leadership team of administrators, faculty, and parents.

We participated in a great many team-building exercises and learned how to rely on each other's skills and how to respect each other's talents and abilities. Our team was made up of two administrators and seven teachers—one math, one science, one computer science (who doubled as a parent/teacher representative, as one of his children attended JHS), one foreign language, one social studies, and two English teachers.

Considering the differences in our ages and backgrounds, normally we worked together beautifully—until we were given an assignment that required only mathematics skills. One of the administrators, the math teacher, and the rest of the teachers who had a math background went to work immediately. The other English teacher was content to sit quietly, watch, and help when needed. At first, I whined loudly. When no one listened, I looked for ways to either help or get in the way. I didn't really care which; I just wanted attention. When I am left out, I get cranky, and I get into trouble. After a few minutes of being told to "Leave us alone," I went away, and after I finished sulking, I thought about the valuable lesson I learned that day. Never create a project that leaves someone like me with nothing to do. No one wants that.

GROUPING STUDENTS

The first law of grouping is to create a project that is inclusive and requires each participant to make a valuable contribution in order for the entire team to succeed. The second law of grouping is to assign the participants so as to create successful teams. This chapter is devoted to both issues.

History of Tracking and Grouping

From the time of the one-room schoolhouse until today, teachers have had to find a way to reach students of different ages, cultures, ability levels, language skills, and learning styles. In 1919, the public schools in Detroit administered intelligence tests; used the results to separate the students into three groups, which became known as the XYZ-grouping type; and used the same curriculum for all three groups. That practice continued in various formats until 1967, when "in *Hobson v. Hanson*, the tracking of students into ability groups in the Washington, D.C. schools was ruled to be a violation of Fourteenth Amendment rights" (Glass, 2002, p. 53). Not only did the law force the end of tracking, but also public sentiment urged its end, in part because it clearly led to a second-class education for those relegated to the lower tracks. According to Slavin and Braddock (1993), grouping by ability has had a long history of failure. It is harmful to many, especially those at the lower end of the spectrum, and has contributed to such unintended consequences as increased delinquency and higher dropout rates among those placed in the lowest track.

Nevertheless, despite the evidence of the long-term harmful effects of tracking—especially on those students we are focusing on, struggling learners—the practice of grouping students based on their academic skills has emerged again. This time it is the result of federal law: No Child Left Behind (NCLB), enacted in 2001. Under its provisions, schools must show adequate yearly progress (AYP) is being made by eight student "subgroups": students in five racial categories, those in special education, those with limited English proficiency, and those who qualify for free or reduced-cost meals.

Schools face a variety of penalties for failure to make AYP, not the least of which is that scores are published in the local newspapers which diminishes the reputation of the schools on the list. Therefore, schools that fail to make AYP over time must offer their students the opportunity to attend more successful schools at the district's expense; principals can lose their positions; and ultimately, the schools face restructuring if change is not accomplished within the given timelines. In addition, schools' scores are published on their websites, and property values in each school's catchment area rise and fall as a result of significant gains and drops in test scores. Therefore, although student placement is no longer referred to as tracking, specific subgroups receive intervention strategies, such as extra time for reading and math, and additional resources, or fewer resources, based on their performance on one test.

The intent of the policy behind the law is admirable. Groups that have been previously underserved are now to be given sufficient resources to close the achievement gap that has existed between more resource-rich peers and the identified subgroups. The stated goals of this current policy, as well as its current implications, are supposed to represent new assumptions, values, and beliefs.

However, the unintended result as schools implement the provisions of NCLB is a renewed emphasis on ability grouping, despite the fact that researchers have clearly demonstrated over time that this approach has only mild positive effects and even those accrue only to more-capable students. For example, "Kulik and Kulik performed a meta-analysis of 52 experimental and quasi-experimental studies on the effects of ability grouping on achievement of secondary school students" (Glass, 2002, p. 59). Their analysis indicated that high-ability students experienced approximately 3 months' growth, but low-ability students declined by approximately 2 months' time when taught in homogeneous classes.

Although no policy is static and a certain amount of shifting is to be expected during the implementation of NCLB, its unintended results have been damaging to the group least likely to defend itself: struggling learners. Having a limited notion of a successful future, not having learned adequate coping mechanisms to succeed in school, coming from an unstable home and/or community, and/or having an external locus of control does not necessarily place a student into any of the subgroups that are likely to receive extra resources as a result of NCLB (except for those who qualify for free and reduced-cost meals or who have an Individualized Education Program). Thus, struggling learners who meet the criteria suggested in this text often fall through the cracks that lie between those who get more resources because their test data drive decisions and those who get less because their data are blended into the total school's scores.

Current Schoolwide Practices in Grouping

The administrator who constructs the schedule creates a class for each teacher based on a number of variables. However, in schools that have not made AYP, assessment scores will be the determining factor in grouping. In schools that have had more success, previous practices will be maintained. As a result, as an elementary school teacher, you might be able to decide, with your other grade-level teachers, if you want to regroup for math and/or reading. On the secondary level, you will get the classes you are assigned. Although no school system will admit to tracking, the old system of the Top Soaring Eagles, the Middle Hunting Hawks, and the Flightless Penguins is still alive and easily observed today.

It may appear obvious that one way to approach this dilemma is simply not to group. It seems like a simple solution on the surface, and certainly, it removes the burdens created by ability groups. Nevertheless, if we believe that learning is a social activity, as Dewey, Piaget, Vygotsky, and Bandura have strongly asserted, not using groups keeps students from making sense out of what they are being taught in a way that is most natural to all learners. Therefore, in this case, we must find better ways of forming groups, not easy ways out of grouping.

Within your classes, the system you choose for grouping your students will tell them what you believe to be true about them. Once you meet your students and have the opportunity to get to know them, you will have to decide which of the many grouping strategies will be most effective for helping *all* your students become soaring eagles in your class.

Grouping and grouping strategies are key functions of the instructional triangle, so let's revisit it. As we noted earlier, the goal is set by the statewide curriculum. The day's objective is a function of where you are on any given day in using the curriculum guide. (What do you want your students to learn or be able to do today?) Grouping decisions are included in the strategies you select to help your students reach the day's goal. (What will you do to help your students reach today's goal?) Of course, your grouping strategies should be designed to help all your students reach the goal and be successful on the day's assessment. (What evidence will you accept that the students have met the goal?)

If the day's activities are significantly different than those on other days, you might want to think about restructuring your teams, but that is rarely recommended. If your teams are functioning successfully, keep them together throughout the unit, and let the groups' positive dynamics help all the members succeed with whatever you have planned for them each day.

COOPERATIVE LEARNING

Although there are many delivery systems that can be used to help struggling learners achieve success in school, cooperative learning includes more of the attributes that help at-risk students feel more comfortable in a school setting than almost any of the others. From the earliest research to the most recent, "documented results include academic achievement, improved behavior and attendance, increased self-confidence and motivation, and increased liking of school and classmates" (U.S. Department of Education, 1992). In a broad meta-analysis across a huge number of studies, "cooperative arrangements were found superior to either competitive or individualistic structures on a variety of outcome measures, generally showing higher achievement, higher-level reasoning, more frequent generation of new ideas and solutions, and greater transfer of what is learned from one situation to another" (Barkley, Cross, & Major, 2005, pp. 17–18).

Definition of Cooperative Learning

One of the earliest and best definitions of cooperative learning still holds true today. "Cooperative learning is a successful teaching strategy in which small teams, each with students of different levels of ability, use a variety of learning abilities to improve their understanding of a subject. Each member of a team is responsible not only for learning what is taught but also for helping teammates learn, thus creating an atmosphere of achievement" (U. S. Department of Education, 1992). This definition provides the foundation for the operationalization of cooperative learning in this text.

CREATING A SUCCESSFUL GROUP

Before the first day of school, create an individual index card for each student. When a new student is added to your class, create a new index card for that child. If you teach in a school that has a highly mobile population, move the cards for the students who transfer out of your school to a separate pile. You will get tired of having to make a new card for a child who frequently moves back and forth into your school district.

During the semester, write notes to yourself on the back of each index card regarding important attributes that you have seen the student display with some degree of consistency. For example, sometimes I remind myself to keep two students on different teams; if that changes, I write the date and reason for the change. If a student consistently persists at tasks and helps others to do the same, I always note that on the card. When I am forming teams based on effort, I create teams that include the following: one hard worker, two average workers, and one student who is normally disengaged. Once I know my students well, I put their "effort" numbers on the front of each child's card. Hard-working students are given a 1, students who can be encouraged to work are given a 2 and a 3, and discouraged learners are assigned a 4. If the hard-working student has high status among his peers, that student will be the team leader. The team leader has a great deal of prestige in my class—and hopefully will have a positive influence on the performance of the other team members.

At the beginning of each new unit that lasts at least 2 weeks, I take out all the cards and arrange them according to the variable I am using for grouping. Again, using effort as the variable for this example, I create as many balanced teams of four as possible. When I have completed making balanced teams, I look at the cards for students I was not able to place on my first try. If your class is made up of predominantly struggling learners, you may have an excess of disengaged students left after you have completed your initial teaming. I do not create teams of nonworkers because those groups are doomed to failure. I keep working until I have at least one hard worker and one student who will support that person's effort on each team. I can teach skills; I can provide missing background knowledge; I cannot create optimism and enthusiasm for learning where none exists. I need my fellow teachers (a.k.a. the other students) to help me create a climate where learning and cooperation are valued and cynicism and indifference are not.

Next, I create daily routines that require each student on every team to respond. I begin by assigning each member of the team a number for the duration of the unit.

Normally, Number 1 is reserved for the team leader, who is usually a hard-working student. Numbers 2 and 4 are reserved for those students who can be encouraged to do the work by an effective team leader. Number 3 is typically used for the most disengaged member on each team. I then ask a drill question, using the placemat shown in Figure 3.1, and each student must write his response on the appropriate numbered spot on the placemat. If every member of the team is present, if the drill is started in a timely manner, and if all supplies are handed out to all members of the team as directed, the team gets an extra point for cooperation. However, each student gets individual credit for his answer to the drill question.

The placemat is relatively easy to create and makes it very simple to differentiate the difficulty of drill questions based on the results of the previous day's assessments. For example, if any particular group of students struggled with the content the day before, I can assign a review question by number to that group.

Next, I teach the routines for working in a group, and the students practice until they have internalized them. Number 1 person is always the Team Leader. It is the Team Leader's job to make sure the team is behaving appropriately, tasks are performed correctly, and missing students' jobs are reassigned so that the team can operate smoothly. Number 2 person is the Team Recorder. This person is responsible for taking notes during team discussions in case the team must report out to the class, keeping a copy of his personal notes for any student who is absent, and writing the team's answers on the board, overhead, or any other device requested. I try to fill that position with a responsible student.

Number 3 person is the Team Spokesperson. This person is the voice of the group. He has to answer for the group, but he does not have to come up with his own answers. If he forgets the group's answers, he can always call for a "Team Time Out" in order to get help. Disengaged learners enjoy this role. They just have to listen carefully in order to speak for the group. It has been my experience that giving disengaged students this opportunity to get positive attention has had many unexpected, positive benefits.

Number 4 person is the Team Supplies person. I always put a list on the board of the supplies each team will need for class that day. In order to get their extra point for cooperation, all supplies must be distributed to each team member when I come to check on each team. Each day I alternate which team I visit first so that no team is unfairly advantaged over the others. My students may forget to carry their books to class, but they are brilliant at remembering which team I checked first every day that week.

The first week of school is devoted to team building. It may seem to be an incredible waste of time, but it pays off beautifully.

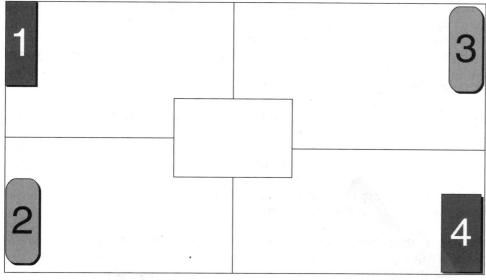

FIGURE 3.1 Drill Placemat

Before Harford County moved away from the traditional self-contained special education model, under the brilliant leadership of the late Dr. Elizabeth Dean, all of the general and special educators who were involved in the first wave of cooperative/collaborative (inclusion) classes received a week of training in this new paradigm. I was fortunate to be a member of the original training group, and I have used everything that I learned, including the placemat, ever since. It was during this professional development experience that I was taught how to do team building for cognitively challenged students. The same principles apply to struggling learners, competent general education students, gifted children, graduate students, and even veteran teachers.

Each team must create its own identity by inventing a name or a motto that says something about each member and the whole team. I will never forget the motto the middle school team created during facilitative leadership training with JHS: "We have upped our standards, so up yours!" Typical middle school!

Next, each team needs to create a product that demonstrates the skills, interests, talents, and goals of each of its members. During this process, I have the opportunity to take my first notes on each student. I am able to get at least some notion of the students' attributes I need to know about: persistence, reliability, cooperation, optimism, distractibility, distrust, avoidance, and difficulty relating well to others.

Finally, the teams are asked to put on a small performance to introduce themselves to the whole class. Their performances are consistently creative and entertaining. We all laugh and clap for each other. I make special certificates for each team, which we place around the classroom for the duration of the semester. Together, the students and I have created a climate of safety and warmth that allows us to express ourselves freely and appropriately. The students have learned the valuable lessons that come from enjoying their work and appreciating each other's qualities.

Their last formal act as a team is to write individual thank-you notes to the team members, thanking each one for his unique contribution to the team's success. In all the years that I used this approach, I never had one student tell me that he had received a negative or mean-spirited thank-you note. I did hear many students comment that they had never received a nice note in school before.

Are Ability Groups Always Harmful?

At the secondary level, you will have students in your class who have natural talent for your content; at the elementary level, you will have good readers, students who have an intuitive understanding of mathematical concepts, and students with various talents and skills that other students do not have. Depending on the objective, grouping by ability, on the basis of recent assessments and for a designated period of time, is a reasonable approach to help students who have similar needs, talents, and skills.

Keeping those groups constant across content areas, over time, and without regard to current assessment data reinforces all of the pitfalls that tracking created. Cohen (1973) clearly identified the hazards of creating a single-strand order of success, which keeps one person, or group, on top, while permanently relegating another to the bottom. Nevertheless, if the data from daily assessments indicate that a subgroup of students needs some reteaching, you must meet those students' needs. Still, all subgroups should be fluid. Many children get "stuck," but once they get past the issue that confused them, they are able to move on with ease. All students must have access to the type of instruction they need when they need it.

Unfortunately, there is a paucity of data on other styles of grouping. The majority of research has been devoted to examining the benefits and burdens of grouping by ability. In practice, there is very little authentic homogeneous grouping except at the two extreme ends of the spectrum. Children who are severely cognitively impaired and those who are gifted far beyond their same-age peers may be the only students being truly grouped by ability. The vast majority of students are loosely grouped with those who perform as they do most of the time on some tests. Under this vague construct, heterogeneous groups are truly the norm.

Even so, inside classes, teachers must use effective grouping practices that will provide equal access to success. For this purpose, I group by effort, and grouping by interests, talents, or values also has excellent utility. Finally, I remember that there are gender issues to be aware of here, as in all other matters related to struggling learners.

GROUPING BY EFFORT

Cooperative learning has been found to be an effective teaching tool (Barkley et al., 2005). Although many proponents of cooperative learning suggest groups of four students, their model uses ability as its variable for grouping. Research and experience indicate that this variable has much less utility than effort in creating an effective cooperative learning team. Research (Bandura, 1989; Ormrod, 1999) shows a positive correlation between students who have high ability and those who have high prestige in a heterogeneously grouped class; however, there is also a positive correlation between students who have high prestige and those who have terrible work habits and abilities.

According to Bandura's Social Learning Theory (Ormrod, 1999), people learn by observing the behaviors of others, and those who are held in high regard have more influence on the behaviors and choices of their age peers than those who are not. If the observer watches and repeats the behavior of the model and if the model positively reinforces that behavior, the behavior is likely to be maintained. The observer can also be reinforced by a third person—in this case, the teacher. If the teacher notices the improved work habits being displayed by the observer and compliments and supports the observer, the behavior is further reinforced. The combination of rewards to the individual, rewards to the group, and the strengthened prestige of the original model helps to solidify the targeted behaviors among all members of the team.

One of the belief systems we wish to target for change among struggling learners is the concept that there is no relationship between effort and success. In order to help students see that they have control over their own lives and that, by having a more internal locus of control, they can determine what will become of them, it is vital to show them explicitly the effects that effort can have on their daily success.

This is not a hidden agenda on my part. It is part of the daily extra-credit cooperation point. The square in the center of the placemat is reserved for the addition of the extra point. It is concrete evidence of the difference that can be made by doing what is necessary to achieve success. There is no luck involved in starting the drill, having the supplies distributed, and having all students on the team in school. In order to eliminate any confusion regarding the effects of luck or chance, if any team has an outlier (i.e., any student who rarely comes to school), that team is excused from the last criterion in order to earn the extra point.

Typically, I create teams based on effort. I make sure that the racial and gender makeup of each team is balanced. I try to make sure that students who work well with others are evenly distributed. I am more concerned with social issues than with academics because it is the social variables that have the most impact on how well students learn during the turbulent adolescent years.

As I have observed my student teachers who are working toward elementary certification, I have found that those who struggle with classroom control have resisted using cooperative learning strategies the most. However, once they divide their classes into cooperative learning teams, they begin to relax and enjoy their students more. In order to be able to identify their team leaders, they need to know their students better. After they learn that they can rely on their team leaders to do the micromanagement that the students truly enjoy, the student teachers' management begins to improve; they enjoy teaching; and their children become more productive, independent, and effective learners.

GROUPING BY TALENTS, INTERESTS, OR VALUES

There are many grouping techniques that are useful for professional development activities with teachers. For example, you can place icons in four corners of the room representing four different approaches for managing students. You can then ask teachers who find themselves attracted to the GI Joe/Jane doll or the teddy bear, for example, to discuss among themselves why they feel that these icons best represent their management styles. The discussions are very interesting and revealing. Fortunately, children are equally as talented at classifying and categorizing themselves by different variables. However, as a classroom teacher, you need to classify your students for the purpose of creating effective teams; therefore, if you want to use a variable other than effort, try creating teams based on students' talents, interests, or values.

Talents

One of the more intriguing members of the All Stars was an "entertaining" young man named "Jermaine." Despite the fact that he was legally blind, his family virtually left him to fend for himself for years. He started using drugs long before high school. Therefore, he fit into the category of children who come from an unstable home. Nevertheless, he had a strange gift: The child was an outstanding artist. I don't understand how he could visualize that which he could not see, but he could. I learned to group by talents because of him.

As a result of his disability, I had to make large-print copies of every book we read. But my friend Jermaine did not like to use large-print copies of our books because they are not cool. I didn't know the protocol under the Individuals with Disabilities Education Improvement Act regarding the number of times any teacher has to make a copy of the same book for the same child, but after I had made the third copy of *The Miracle Worker* for him, I had had enough. In a sickeningly sweet voice, I said: "Sweetie, if you tear up this copy, I will find a way to make you put it back together." He said, "Mrs. Porton, I believe you. I just don't want to use those nasty copies. Don't make another one!" We looked for another solution. His Individualized Education Program included having someone read to him for all his tests, so that meant Jermaine could have a reader for his class work, too. When I grouped for talents, each team that worked with Jermaine had to have someone who would read quietly to him. Someone else always had to copy information from the board for him, since he could not see the board, but when I grouped for this variable, I always added an artistic component as an option for assessments.

Sometimes students have terrible burdens that are beyond their control; however, a lot of these children also have benefits that they can bring to the team. If the teacher can find a way to balance the benefits with the burdens, grouping by this variable can add equilibrium to the team just by devising an avenue for our many talented but physically and/or cognitively challenged children to demonstrate their creativity.

Interests

In some projects, it is possible for teachers to use students' interests as the variable for grouping. If the subject is broad enough and there is sufficient time, a variety of approaches can help students who rarely work together get to know and appreciate each other.

For example, after the statewide assessments have been given, English teachers might allow students to select short stories based on a theme. If the theme is "unusual characters," for example, there are a number of short story writers who excel at characterizations. At the high school level, students could select the type of character they wish to read about from stories by authors ranging from Poe to O. Henry to Thurber. At the elementary school level, students could select from various tall tale characters. A list of activities and assessments would be crafted for every group. At the end of the unit, each group would present its favorite unusual character to the class. Using the same expectations for team roles and norms, students would follow the procedures they have learned in order to fulfill their obligations.

Values

Let me illustrate the benefits of grouping by values with an example from a seventh-grade social studies class. The teacher is concerned that her students still have a very elementary-school style of looking at history, and she thinks they are capable of seeing that history is more nuanced than their texts would lead them to believe. At the beginning of the unit on the Revolutionary War, she tackled the problem with a concrete example: the Boston Massacre. She divided her class into three teams based on their choice of any one of the following positions: the British soldiers, the revolutionaries, and those who tried to remain neutral. During the first week of the unit, the students read their textbooks and took notes based on their group's perception of the truth or travesty of how the American textbook reported the event. Next, the teacher provided texts from other countries that described the Boston Massacre from their perspectives, including excerpts from the United Kingdom, China, and the Soviet Republic. Again, the students were asked to respond to those texts from their own group's perspective. The last readings came from an actual transcript of the trial of several of the British soldiers who were tried for shooting at unarmed civilians.

Finally, using paper for snowballs, the class reenacted what the American textbook reported about the Boston Massacre, and the teacher videotaped the reenactment. After the reenactment, a "person on the scene" reporter asked various participants to describe what they saw. Each person reported seeing a vastly different version of the same event. When the students watched the video of the reenactment and the "on the scene" interviews, they were astonished by the difference between what they saw on tape and what they thought had happened.

The final assessment included a thought question to see whether or not each child had learned that each history text is written from a perspective that advantages one position over another. No telling of history is ever neutral or completely credible. Although the class included students of varying cognitive abilities, all of the students were able to articulate that after having looked at the Boston Massacre from a number of different perspectives, they really knew only a little bit about what had actually happened. The goal of having students learn to question the reliability of any history book had been reached.

Using grouping by values helped students bond by self-selection, by perception, and then through emerging insights. If the teacher had told the students what she believed, the truth would have been hers. However, because the students discovered the lack of accuracy in their textbook together, in a group that started out believing they all thought alike , their thinking was transformed by the process.

GROUPING BY GENDER

For our purposes, when we look at gender issues in grouping, we must be sure that we use gender as a variable only to students' advantages. Contributions made by all members must be acknowledged and valued, and gender equity must be one of the norms of all team experiences.

Current brain research clearly indicates that there are distinct differences between male and female brains. "Male and female brains can be distinguished on the basis of how particular structures are organized at gross, cellular, and even molecular levels" (Norden, 2007, p. 122). Neuroscientists refer to the actual structural and probable functional differences in the way male and female brains are organized as *sexual dimorphism*. The corresponding differences result in males and females having different areas of strength. Females show enhanced language skills, empathy, the ability to read and accurately interpret emotions in others, and superior emotional memory. On the other hand, males are clearly superior in spatial ability and their ability to build systems. Baron-Cohen (2003) of Cambridge University explains the difference well. Females are hardwired for empathy, which is the drive to identify another's emotions and thoughts and to respond to those with an appropriate reaction. The male brain is hardwired to analyze and explore a system—which could be a car, a computer, a pond, or a math equation—and to extract the underlying rules that govern that system's behavior. Neuroscientists do not say which brain is better; they say only that the brains are different (Norden, 2007).

When teachers ignore issues surrounding gender differences and assume that struggling learners can be treated as a monolithic group, they fail to acknowledge one of the critical variables that affect students' learning styles, preferences, and strengths/weaknesses. It is ironic to listen to faculty room comments about "girls with grudges" and "forgiving boys" and watch the same teachers expose all their students to the same learning experiences and expect the same results.

Single-Gender Teams

If there is a good balance in numbers of boys and girls in your class and if the relation-ships within the class permit it, creating groups by gender can work. As a teacher, you must know your content very well so you can decide when to use gender as the variable for teaming.

One of my eleventh-grade English classes was reading Steinbeck's *Of Mice and Men*. The class consisted of 16 boys and 12 girls. The single-gender teams I created were well balanced by race and ability level. During the course of the unit, the students dis-cussed the various themes of the novel. At the end of the unit, I decided to hold a mock trial for George to see if he should be convicted for killing Lenny. The girls felt that he had no right to kill Lenny, but the boys accepted Slim's judgment that he really had no choice. The class was divided again, but this time into roles played in a courtroom drama. Students played George, his defense attorney, the prosecuting attorney, and so on. The jury was divided equally between boys and girls. It was during the prosecuting attorney's closing argument that the jury heard one of the best lines ever. Ms. Attorney for the State said: "The Bible tells us Thou shall not kill. And there ain't no *but* at the end of that sentence!" The jury decided that George was guilty, and unlike Steinbeck, who spoke through Slim, they found that George was guilty of first-degree murder for killing Lenny.

Gilligan (1977) found that women construct moral problems differently than men. Because women are relational, they look at moral dilemmas from a different perspec-tive than men. By teaming by gender for the unit on *Of Mice and Men*, both boys and girls could discuss freely the moral decisions they make and how they make them from their unique perspectives.

Valuing Contributions Made by All

When I first started using cooperative learning strategies, my students taught me another valuable lesson about gender equity. I had a terrific class, and the students normally worked together very well. However, I made a novice's mistake and placed only one girl on a team. She was very bright and made many good contributions to the team's efforts. However, on one occasion, the boys on the team blocked her from par-ticipating. I watched as she raised her hand to be recognized by the team leader, moved her seat to be seen better, raised her voice to be heard, and finally just gave up. At that point, I intervened. I told the team leader he would lose his position if he ever allowed the team to disrespect any member of the team again. He truly did not know what I was talking about. The boys did not even realize that they made their female colleague "disappear." The next day, instead of the Warm-Up, the class had a "Learn This or Die" lecture from me. I am not subtle.

One of the norms that had to be added to team behavior came as a result of what I saw happen in that class. I had to teach the dominant culture, male, that ignoring any female on their team was unacceptable and would result in shared negative con-sequences. I had to bring this behavior to their attention because they did not realize what they were doing. Nevertheless, as a teacher, I had a unique opportunity to correct this problem in very concrete and beneficial ways. Now at the end of each class, I ask team members to rate each other's contributions on the basis of effective support to the team. I give the students copies of the chart shown in Table 3.1 and tell them to put an X next to their number and rate each of their teammates according to the scale provided. Students who consistently receive high scores from their teammates are given extra credit or other incentives that are meaningful to them. Whether a student makes sub-stantive contributions, therefore, is a matter to be determined by what a student does, not who he is.

This chart also helps to get rid of that dreaded member of any cooperative learn-ing team: the freeloader. Most children are reluctant to point out the child who does little or no work until the added work becomes a burden on the rest of the team. The daily chart makes it clear who is and is not working. It is up to the teacher to handle the

TABLE 3.1	Member Contributions				
Using a rating scale of 1 = No help to 4 = Best help, rate each team member on the following questions.	Did the team member give good answers to team thought questions?	Did the team member find answers in the text to support team answers?	Did the team member complete his/her share of the work?	Did the team member help clarify points so that all of the team understood what was being discussed during one-minute pause-and-discuss reflections?
Member 1				
Member 2				
Member 3				
Member 4				

situation quickly and fairly. One solution is to offer the student in question the option of working alone, since being a member of the team does not seem to be valued. If that is the student's choice, the student gets all of the work to do on his own with no other penalty involved, and the team continues on with its work.

I have never believed that schools mistreat girls, but treat boys well; I have always believed that schools mistreat girls differently than they mistreat boys. As teachers, we must work against mistreatment of any child for any reason.

Summary

Grouping, like everything else in teaching, is both an art and a science. It requires an ability to make a reasonable decision about the best type of grouping for a particular topic within the content area and an intuitive eye for who will be the best leaders, followers, and helpers on any given team. The most important caveat for anyone involved in creating teams is that nothing is written in stone. People can always be moved.

Ability is not normally the primary variable used in successfully grouping students because the data are very compelling regarding this issue. Longitudinal data have made it clear that only very gifted children profit, if at all, from being homogeneously grouped. Children on the lowest tracks appear to move backward, something they can ill afford to do, after having been trapped in groups with similarly cognitively limited peers. The data show that unintended consequences such as high dropout rates, delinquency, and negative social problems are positively correlated with sustained placement in the lowest-track classes.

Despite the problems clearly related to tracking, it has been part of American education since the days of the one-room schoolhouse. It has emerged again, this time as a result of a federal law, No Child Left Behind, which uses statewide assessments to sanction schools in which eight identified subgroups of previously underserved students are not making AYP. Nevertheless, grouping students can have a positive impact. Within their classes, teachers have the ability to create cooperative learning teams based on effort, talent, interests, gender, values, or any other constructs that can motivate students regardless of their ability and give them access to challenging goals, strategies, and assessments. It is up to the individual teacher to plan so that each child can achieve success and become a soaring eagle.

Practices of Reflective Planners

The whole purpose of education is to turn mirrors into windows.

SYDNEY J. HARRIS

I can always tell when a group of people has not seen a real child in the last hundred years. They romanticize children, weep freely, and talk about their own duty to save the "darlings" from their dreadful destinies and come to their rescue. Usually, I turn green and get out as soon as possible from whatever "workshop from hell" they are conducting.

One time when I was very lucky, I attended just such a workshop with one of my best friends, who was an excellent teacher and a gifted staff developer. The teary-eyed leaders gathered around a faux beach scene and read about the lone starfish that had just been tossed back into the water by the kind-hearted Good Samaritan. The leader spoke about a teacher's mission to save suffering children. They actually had to stop the seminar because so many people were crying after the demonstration.

I looked at my friend and said, "It is clear to me that no 13-year-old has come up to anyone in this group recently and told them to go to hell." She agreed. What I love about my friend's staff development presentations, and all those that are truly credible, is that students are discussed as they really are: people who can be in your face, challenging you to do your job and demanding that you prove to them every day that you can. Any relationship between a real child and a dying starfish is spurious, at best.

Teaching is very hard work. It must be done with skill, patience, and persistence every day. Finding the answers to problems demonstrated by struggling learners is neither convoluted nor costly. The answers are obvious and free: It takes hard work and unwavering dedication to help struggling learners overcome their challenges. It takes committed teachers and administrators who are willing to set high expectations for their students (Bohn, 2006). In order to become a successful practitioner, you must think about what you want to do (planning), what you are doing (instruction), and whether or not what you did was successful (assessment). The practice of reflective teaching is, therefore, recursive and demanding.

In this chapter, our first goal will be to look at reflection during the planning stage. According to Hartman (2010), the most important practices associated with successful teaching are planning, monitoring, and evaluating. "They can be thought of as considerations before, during, and after teaching. They involve both reflection on action and reflection in action" (p. 19). Having completed the part of the text on planning, we are looking at the questions we must ask ourselves about what we *want* to do. Following the part on instruction, we will be asking ourselves questions related to what we did *during* our lesson. After completing the part on management, we will be asking ourselves if we treated our students with respect and created a safe climate where students learned to be trustworthy because they were trusted. Finally, in the reflection chapter after the part on assessments, we will be asking ourselves questions about what we *did* that worked so it can be sustained, what we did that didn't work so we can learn from our mistakes, and what we should do next.

The second goal of this chapter is to offer some scenarios that tie together the essential points made in the previous chapters on planning. Share your answers with other teachers, your mentor or college supervisor, or someone else you truly respect to see how well your ability to plan using this format is developing. It is always helpful to practice reflecting about your plans, so try as many of these as you can.

WHY SHOULD TEACHERS BE REFLECTIVE?

In 1987, Donald Schon wrote *Educating the Reflective Practitioner*, which has become a classic text among educators. His work has encouraged us to become more proficient teachers by learning how to think carefully about what we do while we are doing it. According to Schon, "I have come to feel that [the] only learning which significantly influences behavior is self-discovered, self-appropriated learning" (Commonwealthpractice.com/reflective practitioner review, p. 1). Although his findings, like those of every other theorist, have come in for some criticism, when we take reflection *in* action (while we do something) and *on* action (after we have done it) together, we find that, for the most part, Schon's theory has enormous utility. Moreover, Daniels (2002) found that adult learning theory supports Schon's findings, including his conclusion that self-learning from experiences in natural settings is an essential element of adult learning. In addition, research on effective practice has shown that reflection is highly correlated to inquiry, effective teaching practices, and continuous professional growth (Daniels, 2002).

Reflection can occur in a variety of modalities. There are those who prefer written reflections, those who advocate the use of a coach or a peer and those who promote the use of action research for more formal reflective practices (Daniels, 2002).

For our purposes, we will be discussing written reflections and the use of coaching to accomplish effective reflecting practices. Hillocks (1995) found that "our inquiry results in a construction, an account of our observations and the transformations we impose upon them. When we write, that construction is very likely transformed again with the written product" (p. 4). Researchers (Costa & Garmston, 1994; Henry & Sutton, 1999; Hillocks, 1995) have found that teachers' practices change when they see a clear need for change and that is possible only through reflective practices.

LET'S REFLECT ON WHAT WE HAVE LEARNED SO FAR

When we first met, we learned about the instructional triangle. This triangle explains, in a very concrete manner, how the three fundamental questions of teaching and learning are connected. Our first question is always, What do I want my children to learn or be able to do? This question is answered through statewide curriculum guides, which are driven by statewide assessments and federal laws that have classroom implications. Nevertheless, teachers make many instructional decisions when following these curriculum guides, including which objectives are appropriate for their students each day.

However, the majority of the planning decisions that teachers make revolve around the strategies they choose to help *all* their students reach success on the daily goal. Following the instructional triangle, they must ask themselves, What can I do to help all my students learn or be able to do what I am teaching today? It is the strategies chosen that most reflect each teacher's awareness of and sensitivity to her students' cultural, academic, gender, ethnic, racial, and attitudinal differences. In contrast to nonreflective teachers, reflective teachers have a richer understanding of themselves and their students; their assumptions about their students' motivations, beliefs, and values; and their own definition of what determines academic success (Hartman, 2010). Teachers who reach students who are at risk of school failure normally use motivational activities and an assortment of strategies that are designed to help *all* students have access to success. Teachers who learn what experts in the field have done to help struggling learners can develop their own repertoire of useful strategies for a wide range of learners. Using students to help other students learn and make meaning out of their content by developing effective cooperative learning groups is an extremely effective system for sharing the wealth of knowledge that exists in every classroom and the amount of work that teachers normally believe they must shoulder alone.

According to McKeachie's *Teaching Tips* (Svinicki & McKeachie, 2011), when teachers are creating strategies for their students, they brainstorm as many activities as possible that could have utility for teaching in engaging ways. They use the Internet, they talk to other teachers who have worked with the content before, and they try to use activities that their students have enjoyed in other projects to help keep them actively engaged. They provide activities that engage auditory, kinesthetic, and visual learners. They think about potential problems that arise when their students become frustrated while doing challenging tasks, and they create plans that will prevent their students from becoming overwhelmed.

Teachers working with struggling learners need to make the work accessible; struggling learners have to achieve success early and often, and they need to see the practical applications of what they are learning. All of these factors must be considered when creating the strategies for any discipline.

The last question posed by the instructional triangle assesses the success of both teacher and learners: What evidence will I accept that my students have reached my goal? If no one is successful on the teacher's assessment, the failure does not accrue to the children. However, normally that is not the case. Assessments reveal those who understood the content, those who understood some of the content, and those who did not or could not do the work. The essential task of reflection at this phase is to analyze whether or not the assessment you created measures real progress. In other words, does your assessment capture whether or not the students who were successful learned anything new; whether the children who made progress could have made more; and whether those who failed did so due to lack of understanding or lack of effort—and if the latter, whether that lack of effort came from the students' sense that there is no connection between effort and success.

To help facilitate the reflection process, I have created the following Template 4.1 for your use:

Template 4.1

Guidelines for Reflection

As we move through the reflection process during the planning phase, please keep the following suggestions in mind:

1. Keep a journal or notebook.
2. After you write your plan, reflect on whether or not your plan demonstrates the guiding principles of the instructional triangle.
3. Check your plan to be sure that you have provided access to success for *all* your students.
4. Review your plan again to be sure that you have provided yourself with some alternatives in case you need them.
5. Use your journal when you have completed your unit plan, when you have created a new activity or exercise, or when you are making a difficult decision.

LET'S PRACTICE REFLECTING TOGETHER

You and I have been assigned to teach a unit on writing to a group of ninth-grade students. We will have to follow the state curriculum guide so that our students will be able to pass the English 9 High School Assessment (HSA). First, we have to review the guide so that we both understand the task at hand.

According to our guide, the students have to understand a writing prompt by recognizing the following features: form, audience, topic, and purpose (FAT–P). All of these features can be found in the first paragraph of the prompt. Next, they need to be able to analyze the second paragraph of the prompt to determine how many paragraphs they will have to write in order to create a well-elaborated response. They have to be able to understand that the last paragraph simply restates the purpose of the prompt and use that to make sure they have included a clear statement of the purpose for writing in their response.

The curriculum guide requires that all students in our state understand the concept of being graded using a rubric. Therefore, our students will need to be taught how to do self-assessment using a rubric. Our class consists of 10 boys and 8 girls. All of our students have been grouped together because our feeder middle school expected them to have difficulty passing the HSA they will be taking this March. There is an extended response portion on the test, and the unit we are teaching is intended to prepare the students for this portion of the test.

We have many decisions to make. First, we should decide on the type of team that will serve our students' needs best during a long and stressful unit. We know that our students are reluctant readers, but they would rather read six books than write one paragraph. You are right—we have to team by effort. Effort is the only thing that will keep us going during this unit. We must recognize it, reward it, and reinforce it every chance we get. Now we have four teams of four and two teams of five. That will be fine because we have two outliers who rarely come to school. If we assign one to each of our five-person teams, we can function perfectly well. We will make the Number 5 person answer in the center spot of the placemat and be responsible for all of the extra types of papers that are used during the unit.

Our next big decision deals with how we want to plan to cover the unit in the time we have available. I like to do a backward map. We have 3 weeks to complete the unit. We should never take more than 3 weeks on our writing unit, or we will never complete the curriculum guide for this year. Our unit begins on the 4th and ends on the 22nd. On Friday, the 22nd, we will collect the final draft of their last structured writing assignment. By that time, they will have learned how to do the following:

- Identify the FAT–P
- Break down the second paragraph of the prompt so that they know how many paragraphs they must write
- Understand what they must include in order to earn a 3 (passing score on the HSA) or better on their writing assignments
- Be able to earn a 9 or above, on a scale of 10, as a peer editor
- Write at least a six-paragraph response to any prompt

This translates into the following products:

- FAT–P identified
- Prewrite
- Rough draft
- Peer edit of rough draft
- Final draft

We need to agree on a time allotment for each phase of the unit in order to be able to cover all of our content by Friday, the 22nd. As we reflect on how to best use our time, we must remember that we will need a variety of strategies that will keep our students engaged and on task. We need to think of games that will help them find the FAT–P in the first paragraph so that we can move beyond recognizing form, audience, topic, and purpose. After all, we have only 3 weeks to get our students writing at least six paragraphs. Next, we have to use discovery learning to help all the students unlock the second paragraph of the prompt. Even though the test designers have never admitted this, if a student fails to respond to any of the cues in the second paragraph, she loses one full point on her response. It is critical that all the students be able to find all the cues for themselves so that they can respond to each cue on any prompt—no matter what! Our students are terrified of a blank page, and when I have faced students in this situation before, I have taught them to take the first words of each cue and use them as part of the topic sentence for each of the middle paragraphs of their responses to the prompt. If you agree, when we teach them how to do a prewrite, I would like to use that formula.

I have always found that it is easier to find mistakes on anyone else's paper than it is on my own. The same is true for students. In addition, when students carefully check each other's work, they learn to become more skilled readers, and they learn such important skills as analyzing errors and reading to perform a task. Therefore, we need to plan to teach our students how to become skilled peer editors, once we have taught them the basics of writing to respond to a prompt. When our students hand in their final prompts, we must plan to evaluate the quality of their peer editor's comments to determine if the editor helped the writer upgrade her rough draft in order to write an improved final draft. This strategy combines reading and writing skills with understanding the use of a rubric for scoring a prompt.

Now that we have laid out our schedule from the 4th to the 22nd, let's reflect on what we will do tomorrow when we begin the unit. To do that, let's look at the lesson plan format (Template 4.2).

Template 4.2

Planning Template—Reflection	

Lesson Title—Introduction to Structured Writing Assignment SWA
Lesson Unit—SWA

Reflections	Lesson Component
This comes to us from the guide.	GOAL (SC) Statewide or local systemwide goal or goals taken from appropriate CCSS standards. Lesson Objective As a result of today's lesson, students will be able to find the FAT–P.

Reflections	Lesson Component
According to the guide, we hand out a lot of materials. Do we want to do this? I think that will put them off. After we show them what a prompt looks like, I think we should make copies of only the top paragraphs. We will need visual aids for our visual learners. They like color coding a lot. We can make our FAT–P color coded to help our visual learners.	Materials Needed Make the list. Check to see that all items are present. During the lesson, if you find you need something not on the list, write the item in the margin.
Time: 10 minutes We can use the drill to find out how much they know about the HSA and the writing process (i.e., prewriting, writing a rough draft, peer editing, and writing a final draft).	Warm-Up Use this to activate prior knowledge.
Time: 10 minutes I think we need to think of ways we can help our class believe that we can get every student to pass. What about bringing back students from prior years to talk to them about their experiences?	Motivation What will you do to engage students in today's topic? How will you help students understand the importance of today's lesson?
Time: 15 minutes Model how to find the FAT–P. We have to decide if we want to teach all of it together or one piece at a time.	Guided Practice Introduce the topic. Model how to construct meaning/organize information/store new learning *or* how to perform the task/create the product/share the performance.
Time: 15 minutes We have to create activities that will make finding the FAT–P interesting. Perhaps we can create some competition between the teams for finding the FAT–P.	Independent Practice Working with their teams, students practice the new learning. During this phase, errors are eliminated, strengths are praised, and students learn from each other. Using differentiated group assignments will help students with the wide variety of skills, interests, and abilities they need to succeed. Discovery learning is the essence of this phase.
Time: 10 minutes We have to create an assessment that will allow us to see how well each student was able to reach today's goal without frustrating the students so that they become discouraged immediately.	Assessment Each student must supply evidence of the extent to which she mastered content or skill development as described in today's goal. Use data from this assessment for tomorrow's instruction.
Time: 5 minutes We need to think about a quick closure for today that will help students leave class feeling positive about themselves.	Closure Ask students a question about key attitudes and learning in today's lesson: What did you learn today? What was the best part of today's lesson? What did you learn from each other today? How are you going to use today's lesson?
If they are ready, they will do Homework A: Write an opening paragraph of a prompt that includes a FAT–P. If not, they will do Homework B: Define each of the letters in the FAT–P.	Homework Make homework relevant and practice oriented. Avoid drill and kill exercises!

OUR REFLECTION JOURNAL

Dear Us,

We reviewed the plan we wrote together, and we think it can work. Our goal is to have our students find the FAT-P because the state said so. Bringing in students who had me last year and passed the HSA using my formula should be motivating because the kids know each other and the older students have credibility with this class. Our strategies do not follow the state's guidelines because that would not work for our kids. We think we should show the kids the whole prompt and then concentrate on the first paragraph only. We are going to color code the FAT-P for our visual learners to help them identify the form, audience, topic, and purpose. We will model how to find the terms, one at a time, and then by letting them work in their teams, the kids can find each term. When we think they are ready to move on, the teams can compete for finding each term. We will play one round of listening baseball to get them to move around the classroom. At this point, the auditory, visual, and kinesthetic learners will have been engaged meaningfully in the task. We are going to keep our eye on David J. because he frustrates so easily, especially on writing tasks. If he starts to go up, Mrs. P. will work with him one-on-one. We will use the results of today's assessment to determine what to do tomorrow.

If the kids are ready, they will get Homework A. If not, they will get Homework B. We think this is a good plan because we have all the elements of the instructional triangle, we have provided access for all our learners, and we have alternatives planned where we think we may need them.

Summary

There are no plans here for passive starfish waiting to be rescued. Instead, we have thought carefully about what we can do to help real students, who will not want to do the task ahead of them, to approach the future with confidence and the knowledge that they will be taught with respect and high expectations for their success. We may not write reflections every day, but we will use our reflection journal to help record our thoughts when we plan our units, when we plan new activities and exercises, and when we need to reflect on difficult decisions.

YOUR TURN

In this section, you will have the opportunity to respond to a variety of scenarios. There are no correct answers in the back of the book. Children do not come with a set of instructions; teaching is the art and science of judgment, expertise, and sensitivity. In elementary school, teachers make sure that the soil is rich and fertile. In middle school, teachers plant the seeds. In high school, teachers help the early buds to blossom. Few of us get to see the fruits of our labor. We just do our best.

SCENARIO 1 LOVELY LISA B.   Lisa B. was a very hard-working, well-intentioned student teacher. Her mentor teacher had very little success with her second-period Spanish class. The students had become intimidated by a group of four "mean girls" who were in charge of the class. The mean girls determined who would be allowed to ask questions without being laughed at, they decided who could hand out the supplies, and they kept the rest of the students from attempting to speak by their facial expressions, eye rolling, and other forms of ridicule. The mentor teacher gave in to their pressure, and the student teacher felt helpless when she first started working with this group.

Since none of the other students was willing to hand out supplies, Lisa found that there were no routines in place for distributing materials when she first started working with the class. She found it almost impossible to motivate other students to participate and attempt to answer in Spanish because they were so afraid of being mocked by the Fearsome Foursome.

Lisa's plans reflected her indecisiveness about how best to address the problems she was having with the class. They lacked focus because she was so distracted by the miserable climate in her classroom. Her goals were not clear. Her strategies were unlikely to help most of the students reach her goals. Her assessments did not measure whether or not her students had reached her goals.

Make a list of suggestions for Lisa:

- Tell her what she needs to think about to address the climate in her class.
- Tell her what she could do to establish routines.
- Tell her how she can plan to diminish the power of the Fearsome Foursome.
- Discuss ways she will know whether or not her plan is successful.

Talk to her about how to strengthen her plans and why you think that is essential to resolving her problems. Remember that you are her coach; the learning needs to be hers. Guide her in her thinking so that she can become more self-aware of what she is doing *in* action and *on* action.

SCENARIO 2 CLUELESS CONNIE C.   You and Connie C. have taken two courses together, and you are friendly, but not friends. You have just found out that you will be doing your student teaching at the same elementary school where she will be starting as a first-year teacher. She has been told she will be teaching fifth grade.

Connie has told you that after she graduated from college and earned her teaching credentials, she got married, started her family, and did everything she could to keep her certificate current. When she was ready to begin her teaching career, 20 years after she had graduated from college, she needed to take only two courses to renew her certification and then find a job. However, a great deal has changed in the intervening years, but Connie did not keep pace with all the new technology and terminology that have enriched the world of teaching in the last 20 years.

You have been sitting next to Connie at the orientation session for new student teachers and first-year teachers, and you have just realized how clueless Connie really is. During the orientation, Connie has appeared confused and very concerned about being able to maintain control over her students. She has ignored the discussions about planning and only wants to discuss how to discipline unruly students. The leader of the orientation has asked you to work in pairs to decide on the most important first step a new teacher should take to get ready for her students the first day of school. Connie is arguing vigorously that the rules for the classroom should be posted, distributed, and explained the first day of school. You believe that a good lesson plan that includes putting the students to work immediately may be better than spending a lot of time on a list of rules for establishing classroom decorum.

In the next 5 minutes, prepare your argument.

1. Remember what you have learned about the instructional triangle.
2. Review what you have learned about struggling learners.
3. Review what we have said about getting to know your students.

You will have to convince Connie that you believe the children need a lesson plan that is engaging and gets them involved in the content, rather than a list of rules, when they come to class on the first day of school.

SCENARIO 3 ENERGETIC ERICA L.   Erica L. is that rare combination of youth, talent, and enthusiasm. However, self-discipline is not among her gifts. When she was in the classroom, her students loved her; however, they did not learn much from her. She was entertaining and engaging, but she thought planning was boring. As her supervisor, I saw things very differently. She was doing her student teaching at a magnet school for gifted and talented students. They already knew a lot of what she was saying to them. They were polite at first because her personality was so engaging, but as time went on and she resisted my requirement that she work on her plans, the students became less tolerant. I finally told her that she could not move to her next assignment until her plans moved from being lists to being well-elaborated lesson plans.

Erica L. consistently found herself losing control over her students for the following reasons:

- Her students had problems transitioning from guided practice to independent practice; independent practice to assessments.
- Her students felt betrayed when they saw their daily assessments.
- Her strategies were so competitive that some students could never achieve success, and some of them stopped trying.
- Some days there was no model of what was expected, and her students seemed confused.
- No daily goal was ever posted for the students, and they never knew what they were supposed to accomplish by the end of class.
- After her students had completed the day's activities, they questioned the purpose of the work they had done that day.

Using the skills and knowledge that you have acquired so far, email Erica before my next formal observation, and tell her what she must do to improve her plans so she can move to her next student teaching assignment. Be specific. Start with the instructional triangle, and talk to her about what she is missing in her plans and what she should eliminate from her plans. Encourage her to maintain her faith in herself because she does have some good qualities (tell her what they are), and be clear. Remember that your goal is to be an effective coach and help Erica become an effective, reflective practitioner.

SCENARIO 4 EMANUEL G.   You and Emanuel started teaching at Joppamop Elementary School last fall. His evaluations have not been as positive as yours. When the two of you talk, he complains bitterly about the children, but he does not listen to your ideas and never brings in interesting materials that could keep his students actively engaged in his lessons. The administration does not seem to know all his issues, but you know he is really struggling with classroom management because his plans are so weak. The last time he was observed, he read to the children to keep them quiet. He is going to be observed next week, and he has come to you for help. He has been told that the administrator who is coming to evaluate his lesson wants to see the children more actively engaged this time. Even though you are also a first-year teacher, you understand the relationship between effective planning and successful management better than Emanuel. He is frantic.

Plan an approach that you can use to help Emanuel. Remember that you have to calm him down before he can process what you have to say. This time you have to triage the problem and prioritize topics for your meeting with Emanuel from the most to the least important.

SCENARIO 5 FIX THIS PLAN   It is your job to review this lesson plan and tell the student teacher what must be done before any supervisor ever sees this plan.

Lesson Title: Intro to Directing
Lesson Unit: Directing
Objective: The learner will participate in a script selection process in order to understand the role
of the director.
Materials Needed: Scripts, analysis worksheets, monologue evaluation forms
Procedure:
1. Review vocabulary words of the week
2. Observations, class announcements
3. Review objective
4. Review class activities for the day
5. Have two helpers hand out materials
6. Review analysis worksheets
7. Review types of plays
8. Review due dates
9. Discuss the role of the director—how to read and analyze a script, the directing process
10. Allow students to review scripts
11. Have students complete calendars
12. Exit ticket: List two plays that you are interested in and explain your interest

SCENARIO 6 WHAT'S WRONG WITH THIS?   Not too long ago I visited one of my student teachers who was working in a first-grade class. She and her mentor had divided the students into three teams, and they believed that each team was receiving differentiated instruction that was appropriate, meaningful, and respectful. After I describe the basic structure of the class, write a letter to the mentor describing what you agree with, what you disagree with, and why.

Ms. Pinhead was an experienced first-grade teacher who agreed to accept a student teacher for the fall. She showed the student teacher how to divide the class into three ability groups. The groups were static for reading and math. In math, the top group was called the Eagles, the middle group was called the Falcons, and the bottom group was called the Penguins. In reading, the children remained in the same groups, but the groups had different names. The top group was called the Swans, the middle group was called the Geese, and the bottom group was called the Pigeons. Differentiation in math frequently followed this pattern: After whole-group instruction, the Eagles were able to create their own math problems based on the independent practice exercises; the Falcons were given 10 problems similar to those given during independent practice and could select any six to complete; at a back table, which was usually filled with odds and ends, the Penguins worked on drill and kill exercises.

REFLECTIONS ABOUT PLANNING

At the end of each of the four parts of this book, you will find a chapter on reflections that covers the broad topics presented in that part. Each reflection chapter includes a unique template that will become more sophisticated as your understanding of the teaching–learning process develops (see Template 4.3). When you complete each additional part of this book, you might want to go back to previous templates and add more erudite answers.

Template 4.3

Template for Reflection on Planning

1. Review your lesson plan and write down the following:
   a.   Goal:
   b.   Strategies:
   c.   Assessments:
2. How do you know that your strategies will help the students reach the goal?

3. How do you know that the assessments measure the goal?
4. What will you do with the results of the assessments?
5. Where do you expect the students to face challenges during the lesson?
6. What provisions have you put into place to help your students overcome the challenges?
7. What enrichment activities do you have planned for students who already have mastered your goal?
8. What strategies do you have in place for students with psychosocial issues? What would trigger their use?
9. What evidence will you accept that this lesson was a success?
10. What have you learned from reflecting *in* action and *on* action?

Summary

We started the first part of this book by learning how to plan, and we ended by learning how to become reflective practitioners. Do you see the relationship between effective planning and reflective practices? I knew you would. If you don't think about your plans, you may never know whether or not the plans were effective. You will have no way of tracking the instructional decisions you made and your reasons for making those decisions. By the end of the week, you will have forgotten most of the salient details that went into your planning (trust me), and you will remember only a few high points and low points during instruction.

Current and classic research in the field of reflective practice supports its use as a way of helping new and in-service teachers find consonance between themselves and successful veterans. Schon (1987) believes that reflective practice occurs when novices compare their experiences and knowledge against what the professionals in the discipline recommend to them. In addition, if you keep a journal during your planning and after you have made the challenging decision regarding how to help *all* the children master each day's goals, you will have a record of what you were thinking and why. Your past reflections will help to improve your future planning. You will be the kind of teacher who can repeat success, avoid failure, and control a lot of what happens to the students in *your* Empire.

Part Two

Management

Successful Management Skills:
Rules, Routines, and Boundaries

Better three hours too early than a minute too late.

WILLIAM SHAKESPEARE

My first teaching assignment was at a junior high school in the Bronx. I was 22, I weighed about 100 pounds, and I maintained then, as I do now, that I am 5' 1" (don't believe me!). My plush student teaching placement had not prepared me for the realities of life in the Bronx in 1966, but life's circumstances have a way of making us face life's challenges. I learned by the grace of God through the "grace" of Mr. Liebson, the school's principal, that height is meaningless as long as you work hard, plan ahead, and use good judgment and effective routines to help you manage your students.

The 1960s were turbulent years, and not only in terms of civil unrest. As true then as it is now, crime in the streets comes into schools. In order to protect his teachers,

Mr. Liebson required that we leave the building with our students at the end of the day. Although that may sound like a simple request, it is not. It means that the students must have all their belongings ready when the final bell sounds; it also means that the teachers must have all their belongings ready as well. For a new teacher, that means that a lot must be done in a short period of time.

Mr. Liebson walked by my room enough times to know that I was having a great deal of difficulty managing all of the steps of the routine well enough to get the students and me out of the building in a timely manner. As a result, the students were disorderly, and our day ended in chaos. None of this was effective management, and it did not establish a good climate for successful instruction.

As a principal and an instructional leader, Mr. Liebson decided to salvage the situation and me. For 2 weeks, he came by my room and coached me by breaking a huge routine into smaller steps that were more easily accomplished. At the end of the 2 weeks, the students and I completed the entire routine without any assistance. As we left the building, the students were cheering and Mr. Liebson was beaming. I will never forget the sense of victory we all felt that day. Routines are the heart and soul of management, and I had learned how to use them.

In this first chapter devoted to successful management skills, we have to cover rules, but then we are going to examine routines. Boundary setting will follow because many struggling learners require clear and explicit boundaries so that they can be successful in school. Next, we will discuss teacher–student relationships as they relate to successful classroom management skills. Even before the first child arrives in any class, the room arrangement can add to the climate of safety and security, so room arrangement and physical environment will be addressed. Then we will talk about the importance of teachers' having positive energy when intervening with their students before a problem arises. The presence of recurring defiant episodes signals the existence of a systemic problem. We will examine the nature of defiance and strategies to create a psychologically healthy climate so that defiant behavior is the exception, not the standard (Turner, Meyer, Midgley, & Patrick, 2003).

DEFINING RULES, ROUTINES, AND BOUNDARIES

Before we move on to our discussion of successful classroom management, I think it is important that we understand some key vocabulary: *rules*, *routines*, and *boundaries*. In this section, we will discuss only the definition of each term. In later sections, each term will be discussed in terms of its relevance to the population we are studying: struggling learners. Although some people use these terms interchangeably, they have unique meanings and applications. However, rules, routines, and boundaries all must be carefully planned and developed appropriately at each instructional level. They will not show up on most teachers' lesson plans, but without them, students would live in a world of chaos. In general, effective teachers have a few rules, lots of routines, and safe boundaries that provide physical and emotional security for their students.

Rules

A rule is a statement of what to do or what not to do; it is a governing principle that every member of the community is expected to follow. Teachers should never have more than a few class rules. Experienced teachers almost never add a new rule during the school year. When a student breaks a rule, he must face consequences in the form of escalating punishments. It is preferable to use rules phrased in terms of what will be done, rather than in terms of what will not be done. We had the following three rules in the All Stars Program:

1. We will respect each other's property at all times.
2. We will speak respectfully to each other at all times.
3. We will treat school property appropriately at all times.

The consequences for breaking any rule normally followed a three-step pattern. The first offense resulted in the student's being sent to time-out. I used the time-out room to discuss the situation with the student so that we both acknowledged that the student had broken the rule and decided what the student would do to rectify the situation. According to Long, Morse, and Newman (1996), having a cool-down area for distraught students allows them space to take a break, relax, and compose themselves prior to trying to speak coherently to their teacher. The second offense resulted in a phone call home. At that point, the parent or guardian and I would decide what the student would do to rectify the problem. At the third offense, the student was sent to the office. Since I rarely sent students to the office, the school's administrators were very severe with my students. If the offense was sufficiently serious, any step could be skipped at my discretion. Sprick, Borgmeier, and Nolet (2002) found that effective teachers have a wide array of consequences for misdemeanors that prevent students from being sent to the office frequently.

In order to understand how rules function, I will use an example from one of my classes. "We will respect each other's property at all times" is a rule that I used with the All Stars. Let's say that Brenda borrowed Tanisha's pen without asking. When Tanisha returned to her seat, she saw that her pen was missing. We investigated and found that Brenda had Tanisha's pen. Brenda broke our classroom rule. She did not respect Tanisha's property and took something without asking first. There are two issues that need to be resolved: justice and consequences. Brenda did not intend to steal Tanisha's pen; she said she had it as soon as she was asked. When I spoke to the girls, I made it clear Brenda had violated a rule, but she had not committed a felony. Both ladies agreed. Brenda and I had spent some time in time-out recently, and I found that she responded better when her grandmother was involved, so I called Brenda's grandmother to report the incident. We agreed that Brenda should write a letter of apology to Tanisha, taking responsibility for her behavior and promising to ask for permission before taking anything that does not belong to her. If Brenda repeated the behavior another time, I would be less lenient because I would be less likely to believe it was an accident. The consequences would be more severe, and Brenda would understand that the nature of her offense changed as a result of its being duplicated.

Routines

Routines are the daily procedures that children follow in their classrooms, such as walking in the hallway and in various parts of the building each day. Routines help students feel secure because they are designed to help the students understand their teachers' expectations. As a result of careful implementation and consistent follow-through, routines have been positively correlated to higher rates of student engagement, feelings of security, and attentiveness to instruction (Center on the Social and Emotional Foundation for Early Learning, 2007). Routines cover such issues as how to line up for lunch, what to do when class starts, and how books and papers are distributed. Teachers need a lot of routines, and new routines are added as needed.

Routines differ at each level of schooling. For example, at the elementary school level, children frequently move from their chairs to a carpet. Unless there is a routine in place for moving from chairs to carpet, the activity can create disruptions and cost instructional time.

When students do not demonstrate that they know how to follow the routine, they practice the routine again until it is done well. Practicing the routine again is the only consequence of failing to demonstrate that the routine has been internalized.

One of my favorite routines included having my students start the drill before I came in from hall duty each day. I expected to see each team working on its placemat with all of the day's materials distributed to each team member. The consequence of not having the class ready for me to begin my lesson was that we got to practice leaving my room, walking down the hall, taking our seats, starting our drill, and then leaving my room, walking down the hall, ad nauseam. The All Stars really hated doing that. Oh, well—life is like that. If we don't remember our routines, we get to practice them until we do.

Boundaries

There are multiple definitions for the term *boundary* in the dictionary. In one dictionary, a boundary is something that indicates limits. It is also referred to as a frontier. Its synonyms in many dictionaries are *border* and *frontier*. *The Oxford Dictionary of English*

(2011) defines *boundary* as a "limit of something abstract, especially a subject or sphere of activity." If we blend all these concepts together, for our purposes, a boundary represents a limit marked off by a "theoretical line" that by its existence creates a perimeter that allows students to feel safe inside its borders because they are safe. When we establish clear limits for our students, we are saying: "You can go here, but no further. If you stay within our borders, you will have all the freedom you will need and all the safety I can provide." The goal of any useful boundary must be for an external source to provide the freedom we need to succeed within the perimeters needed to be safe. In school, boundaries provide students with the information they need prior to making important decisions that can jeopardize their safety, security, and well-being (Bluestein, 2008).

Many struggling learners come to school believing that rules and boundaries are created for "suckers" and that they do not need to abide by the same guidelines as everyone else. Unfortunately, failure to stay within a boundary can result in emotional and/or physical danger. Therefore, students must be told exactly what can happen to them if they fail to stay within the boundaries that have been created to protect them. Truman Capote once said, "The problem with living outside the law is that you no longer have its protection" ("goodreads," n.d.)

One boundary that was clearly essential in the All Stars involved not threatening anyone. Some of my boys had spent time in adjudicated juvenile facilities where they had learned fairly sophisticated bullying tactics. If I even heard or sensed any bullying in my classroom, I stopped all instruction, and I, the daughter-in-law of a Holocaust survivor, told the story of what hate and fear have done to the world. My students understood the reasons for all our boundaries, and as Bluestein (2008) suggests, I experienced very few power struggles in my classes.

WHY SUCCESSFUL CLASSROOM MANAGEMENT IS SO CRITICAL

We are working with students who normally function at the risk end of the risk-to-resilience spectrum; our goal is to move them closer to resilience. In order to do that, we must create and maintain a psychologically supportive classroom environment (Turner et al., 2003). The attributes most likely to be found among resilient youth include social competence, a sense of purpose, problem-solving skills, and the ability to accept alternatives (Bernard, 2004; Henderson & Milstein, 1999). Classrooms that run smoothly and that are free of most power struggles between teachers and students and antagonistic interactions between students don't just happen by chance. They are the result of careful thought, planning, and teacher sensitivity. Classroom harmony requires active learning on the part of all the members of the learning community (Long et al., 1996).

Resilient students know how to become independent thinkers who are capable of hard work and self-restraint in order to reach their goals. However, we need effective management methods to teach at-risk children self-restraint. Research in the field (Nelson, Smith, Young, & Dodd, 1991) indicates that the development of self-regulatory skills is an area of real promise for students with emotional or behavioral disorders. Successful classroom management is the art of teaching all children the critical role self-control can play in their lives.

ROUTINES: YOUR BEST FRIEND

Most effective classroom teachers spend a considerable amount of time in the beginning of the year teaching their basic management strategies. However, good teachers do not teach all their routines at once; instead, they begin by teaching the routines that are absolutely necessary to run their classrooms. Then step-by-step they introduce a new routine, practice the new routine until it is mastered, and move on to the next routine as needed.

Establishing Routines

Routines require slow, regular, and consistent implementation. The new routine must be justified, modeled, and practiced during a "shaping period" in which errors are eliminated and signs of correct implementation are reinforced. During this phase, students are not punished for failing to follow a routine; they are required to practice the routine until it is implemented correctly. Only rules can be broken and punished; a routine needs more practice if it is not implemented correctly. Using the following steps, you can establish routines that allow the day to run smoothly for you and your students.

1. Mentally walk through the routine to be sure that it is effective and possible for your students to implement.
2. Relate the new routine to previous behaviors, and explain the purpose of the new routine.
3. Model the routine for your students.
   a. Do it yourself correctly.
   b. Let a boy follow the routine.
   c. Let a girl follow the routine.
   d. Ask the class to try the routine.
   e. Reinforce, by reward, any student who is successful at using the routine.
4. Check for understanding.
   a. Be sure the students understand the routine by allowing them to restate the steps in their own words.
   b. Give step-by-step directions as students gain confidence in the routine.
   c. Provide for successful practice by giving cues, adjusting behaviors, and having students model the routines for each other.
5. Provide opportunities for independent practice.
   a. Let students practice the routine on their own.
   b. Constantly monitor the routine during practice.
   c. Have students provide positive and negative feedback to each other.

Let's try a simple example. I want my first graders to be able to move from their chairs to the carpet when I call their teams to work with me.

1. I walk my way through the routine and make note of all the steps that are involved.
2. I explain the routine to all of the students, making sure they all understand the purpose of the routine and when and how we will be using it.
3. I model the routine for my students.

   a. I do it and talk about each step I need to follow.
   b. I ask a boy to follow the routine and talk about each step he is following.
   c. I ask a girl to follow the routine and talk about each step she is following.
   d. I call my first team to the carpet and follow each step of the routine.
   e. I call every team to the carpet and follow each step of the routine.
   f. I give a small reward to the team that does the best job at following every step of the routine.

When I want my children to move from their teams to the carpet, I make sure that I review each step of the routine, correcting errors, praising students who do well, and reminding students that all routines take time to be learned.

The goal of all routines is to have a plan in place for all activities that happen daily so that the children, without instruction, know what to do, where to go, and how to follow the daily procedures of school life. By following each routine well, each child is practicing self-restraint.

ESTABLISHING CLEAR BOUNDARIES

Boundaries always need to be age appropriate; therefore, younger children need more boundaries that deal with their personal safety. As children become more aware of the hazards around them, the boundaries must expand to include their more sophisticated decision making. More than anything else, boundaries must be teaching tools to help students understand the reasons for having the boundaries. Teachers must use past experience and common sense as they anticipate and explain both the purpose of the boundary and the consequence(s) that can accrue for violating the boundary (Bluestein, 2008).

At the alternative middle school where I served on the administration team, our faculty agreed that saying "Shut up" would result in an immediate office referral. Students who had been sent to our school from their home schools had committed serious violations of school board policy, such as bringing a gun to school, calling in threats to blow up the building, and hitting staff members. Nevertheless, the data on school violence are clear: From small nasty conversations, big altercations often spring.

Our beliefs were predicated on research in the field. In one study, researchers found that students' exposure to low-level aggression, such as rude language and mean-spirited comments, relates to psychological functioning that is similar to more serious forms of aggression. Therefore, as the faculty at an alternative middle school, we realized that we could not allow the climate of our school to be one of high levels of anxiety and low levels of perceived safety (Boxer, Edwards-Leeper, Goldstein, Musher-Eizenman, & Dubow, 2003). Arnold Goldstein's (1999) *Low-Level Aggression* did a great deal to inform many of our decisions regarding how and when to intervene to protect the emotional climate in the school. It was Goldstein (1999) who recognized that "verbal abuse may well be the prime example, among all forms of low-level aggression, of behavior that is both frequent and frequently prone to escalate to higher rungs on the ladder to violence" (p. 47).

We believed that, if we drew the line in the sand at "Shut up," the language in the school would not escalate. We explained our reasoning to parents/guardians during their initial meeting with the guidance counselor when they came to enroll their children in our school; both parents/guardians and students were required to sign a copy of our school's behavior policies; also, we discussed our policies regarding appropriate language at the opening assembly each semester.

Although there was no end to the complaining about our "stupid" policy, mostly from our students, we rarely had to deal with cursing or, more importantly, with fights that stemmed from students' using curse words to provoke fights with each other. This preventive boundary helped students understand the power of language in creating a positive climate for learning, especially since they attended a school where 100% of the student body had been removed from their home schools for very serious violations of school board policies.

Some Benefits of Boundaries

Struggling learners usually know all about the dangers that come from ignoring boundaries. They have often lost friends and/or relatives to reckless behavior, but because of the externalizing nature of their thought processes, their explanations are simple: "Uncle Jasper wasn't lucky when he rode his motorcycle at 95 mph, so he died." It is through utilizing clear, reasonable boundaries and explaining their purpose that we can help struggling learners understand the benefits that come from staying within their confines.

Boundaries allow everyone to explore freely and safely within the limits that have been created for them. Moreover, boundaries that are clear, do not change, and provide for everyone's safety offer access to success for all.

STUDENT–TEACHER RELATIONSHIPS AND MANAGEMENT

When I was working with the All Stars at Joppatowne High School and noticed that one of my students seemed to be having a difficult time managing himself, I calmly walked behind the student and said quietly so no one else could hear: "It looks as if you are having a bad day. Why don't you go outside to get a drink of water? I can see you. When you feel better, come back in and join us." I moved away, and when the student felt that he could look as if it were his idea, he would raise his hand and ask to get a drink of water.

One day I must have been very grouchy, and Tyrone noticed that I was having a lot of trouble. As I was putting something on the board, he walked up to me very unobtrusively and said, "Mrs. Porton, it looks as if you are having a bad day. Why don't you go outside and get a drink of water. You can see us. When you feel better, you can come back in." I nodded, and when I could, I got my drink of water, laughed, and went back into class, and I did feel a lot better.

The point of this story is that management is not really about controlling children; it is about recognizing the importance of developing positive student–teacher relationships. If the students do not believe you care about them, they do not care about you or what you have to teach them. They are not intrinsically motivated to learn; they do not see the value of an education; they only value their relationships with their teachers. According to Pianta, Hamre, and Stuhlman (2003), student–teacher relationships deeply influence how well students function both academically and psychologically in school. No instruction of value will take place until students believe you value them.

In one very interesting study on this topic, researchers asked a third grader to comment on the topic of teacher–student relationships. According to Cushman (2003), one of the children said that teachers should remind their students that they expect their children to do their best, provide helpful feedback, and don't compare one group of children to another. The child said that it is important to the children that their teachers are sommitted to their success. Sometimes if we are very lucky, we get to hear from some of those we helped along the way. This is part of a letter I recently received from one of the original All Stars: "You impacted my life at a time when it needed impacting, and I will always be grateful. I think of you often . . . I would love to see you again, I am probably your biggest fan." Trust me, when we shared our classroom together, I don't think either of us would have anticipated this letter; however, I consider myself truly blessed to have received it.

Develop a Positive Rapport with Your Students

To develop rapport with your students, find out what interests them, attend their activities, let them tell you about their pets, allow them to help you set up your classroom in the morning, talk to them, share your own stories with them, and let them get to know you as a person.

My mother died when I was young. I always kept a picture of her on my desk. The students knew that I treasured the picture and her memory. They were allowed to pick up any other picture, but not that one. When anyone came into my classroom and looked at my pictures of my children and my dog, Rocky, the students told the visitors the names of all my family members. However, if people looked as if they were going to reach for my mom's picture, at least four or five students would shout out in unison, "That's her mom. Don't touch her mom; she's dead!" I didn't say my students were polished, just devoted. And I was equally devoted to them. It was the strength of our relationship that built the foundation for our classroom climate.

Children need to know and be shown that it is their well-being that is the driving force behind all management decisions. We create rules, routines, and boundaries not for our benefit, but for theirs. We must make that clear on the first day of school and demonstrate that fact all year long.

A Sense of Humor Is a Valuable Asset

Another feature that will help to create a positive relationship between students and their teachers is the teacher's sense of humor. Children say a lot of very funny things. You can spend a lot of your day laughing with your students. They are very funny people. According to Berk (2003), students who have teachers with a good sense of humor tend to learn more. Laughter in the classroom increases a positive student–teacher relationship, decreases anxiety, provokes imagination, and promotes motivation.

As long as the teacher never laughs at the child, only with the child, any student can be a source of delight and humor. Sometimes a teacher's reaction can change a student's naïve comment from a nasty confrontation into a moment of shared humor. It is always better to assume that there was no ill intent and act accordingly than to assume that an innocent comment was meant as an attack.

Benefits, but No Burdens, Come with Positive Relationships

There are infinite benefits and no burdens from appropriate student–teacher relationships. It is the best model for respectful, restrained relationships that many of our struggling learners will ever know. Researchers continually emphasize the influence positive teacher relationships can have on children's and adolescents' development of academic skills and behavioral and emotional growth (Davis, 2003; Midgley & Ederlin, 1998; Pianta, 1999; Pianta et al., 2003). An effective teacher's message is always this: "No matter who you are, no matter what you have done, you are a valued person who will be treated with respect at all times." Since the goal of management is to teach self-control, modeling effective interpersonal relationships is an outstanding vehicle for showing children what the benefits of self-restraint can be.

CREATING A PRODUCTIVE ROOM ARRANGEMENT

"The arrangement of the classroom is a factor in children's successful learning experiences" ("Classroom Arrangement," 2011, p. 1). Even for artistically challenged teachers, classroom arrangement does not need to be a nightmare. There are only a few principles that you must always keep in mind, and then you can use your own imagination deciding how to use your space effectively.

You Must Be Able to Reach Any Child Quickly

Never create a room arrangement that makes it impossible for you to stand near any child in your room. Always set up teams in arrangements that allow you to stand next to or behind every student in your classroom. If you are not tall enough to be intimidating by height, you can use proximity to quiet a chatty child who does not see you coming. Proximity is a highly effective management tool; if you can't get close to a child, you lose your ability to use it.

Even in a graduate school class, proximity can be important. When I was in a class with my friend Sally (she is now a principal, so I cannot use her real name), we often wrote notes to each other. We were excellent students, and we did all of our work with great care, but we were still very playful. One of the students in our cohort was very smart, but when he spoke quickly, he could be very difficult to understand. One night when I had a head cold, I wrote Sally a note saying: "I have a cold and can't understand a thing Eugene is saying. It all sounds like blug flug flug blug to me." Sally wrote back and said, "Don't look at me." We were both laughing so hard the teacher had to come over to where we were sitting to use proximity to get us to settle down. We were contrite and regained our self-control, but that evening taught me that no one is ever too old to be beyond the need for a teacher's calming influence.

Every Child Must Be Able to See and Hear You When You Are Teaching

It is important that you are able move around as you teach. Do not get stuck behind any piece of equipment or at the board. When you have finished your "draft" of your classroom, ask a friend to come in and walk around the room to be sure that you can see and hear your "teacher" from every seat in the house. If there is a problem, you have to change the arrangement because a child who can't see or hear you can see and hear his friends, and we can't have that.

You Must Be Able to See All Your Students All the Time

No matter where I am in the room, I want to be able to look out and easily see all of my students. If I can't see them, they will know that quickly, and in some cases, management problems can quickly follow. I know that my students need me to be able to see them because their faces reveal how they are feeling about what they are doing; however, it is also true that when the work gets challenging, some of my students would rather hide than work. In any case, I need to be able to see my students, and so do you.

It is also true that I never send anyone for a time-out or a drink of water unless I can see the student easily. This is not only a trust issue, but also a matter of courtesy to the teachers in surrounding classrooms and safety for my students. Students who wander the halls tend to disrupt other classes, and my students by their very nature are highly suspect. If I know where they are, no one can blame them for doing things I know they could not have done. Unfortunately, my students did not have positive relationships with many other teachers, and they were easy targets for blame when things disappeared. More than once I had to stand up for one of my students and report that the student in question had never left my sight.

The most important fact that you must remember is that you are responsible for each student you are assigned to teach every minute that child is assigned to be with you, so you must keep your students in your line of vision at all times. If anything happens to a child and you cannot account for the child's whereabouts, you may be held responsible. If a child does not report to your class and is not listed as being absent, you must follow your school's protocol for reporting the child's absence from your class. If you have given a child your permission to leave the room and you know when the child left and where he was going, you may be fine. However, you are not fine if you have told a child to stand outside your classroom and you cannot or do not keep the child in your line of vision.

There are excellent courses on school law, and I strongly advise you to take one as soon as possible to learn as much as you can about your rights, responsibilities, and liabilities. You are the adult in charge, and the rights you enjoy outside the schoolhouse gates are not all the same as those that accrue to you once you enter those gates and take on the responsibility of being a teacher.

Decorate Your Classroom so That It Is Welcoming

I think I may have an inactive IQ when it comes to creating anything artistic, so I don't try. However, I know how to decorate my room so that it looks as if it were my living room, and that is what I do. My front desk is filled with pictures of my family. I bring in prints of my favorite artists and posters from some of the places that I have visited. I love *Peanuts*, so there is usually a Lucy in the room reminding the students, "Save time and do it my way." I love fresh flowers and I usually have some on my desk.

When the students begin their work, best examples of student work are posted in the back of the room under the title "Shining Stars." I also have a bulletin board filled with pictures of former students entitled "My Pals." My students love to look for their friends among those pictures. When I started the All Stars, I began taking pictures of the students on our trips to the nursing homes, nursery schools, and soup kitchen. Those pictures went on a wall I called "Caughtya Being Great!"

Most of my students did not come from homes filled with Chagall, Monet, and pictures of Muir Woods. They delighted in a classroom that had fresh flowers and family portraits. Our "living room," as one of my colleagues named it, became a special place for all of us. Naturally, some of the All Stars thought it "sucked" at first, but even they became accustomed to a classroom designed to make them feel important and special.

Provide Easy Access to the Technology in Your Room

Today technology needs to be integrated into class activities and every phase of instruction. You must have access to a storage area for all of your handheld devices. You should place your computers where they can be easily accessed, but out of the flow of traffic in your room. They should be in an area where there is enough light, but away from windows and other sources of glare, and where they are far from liquids, dust, and food, but close to electrical outlets ("Classroom Arrangement," 2011). This may be a 21st-century problem, but it is certainly one worth having.

YOUR ENERGY IS THE KEY TO STUDENTS' WELL-BEING

Right now you might believe that it is up to the students to decide whether or not they will listen to you and behave: *wrong*! Your students will listen to you and behave as well as they can most of the time, depending on the energy you use, from the minute you meet them until you say goodby to them in June. Some people have a naturally calm demeanor. When they are with students, their children calm down and imitate the quiet energy of the teacher. Some people have a frantic energy. Their classrooms are always busy, and the children are always moving; it feels like organized chaos in those classes, but it is always safe and orderly. Some of us have a fairly maternal/paternal energy, and the children relate to our nurturing style of management. The children know that we are deeply committed to their well-being, and they respond well to our redirects because they trust us.

I would like to tell you the story of two teachers I admire. Both of them teach in schools that are considered low performing. Most of the children they teach fall into at least one or more of our categories for being at risk. Many teachers in their respective schools struggle daily with management, and the school's scores reflect instructional "challenges" (i.e., neither school has made adequate yearly progress consistently in the last several years).

Teacher A is the special educator at an alternative school. She is frequently assigned to teach the school's least academically competent and the most behaviorally challenged children (whether or not those children have an individualized education program). She has the calmest affect of any person I have ever known. Following the school's protocol, her students stand outside her room until she asks them to take a seat inside. The children wait quietly for her and take their seats. They follow her rules, but when they don't, she addresses them in a calm and kind manner and asks them to think about the choice they have just made. I have seen explosive, clinically ill children respond to her as if they had no cares in the world, apologize for the poor choice they made, and return to work. This is not magic; it is her use of her quiet, firm energy that allows her children to remain calm.

Teacher B is a fifth-grade teacher at an urban elementary school. She is very tall, loud, and full of energy. She laughs a lot and her classroom is always hopping. Her students are taught using the discovery learning method of instruction. Projects for learning about science and social studies fill the room. Officious fifth graders ask to be excused to go to the library to get books they need for their work. Students are on task at all times. Student leaders are obvious in every part of the room. Teacher B has her eye on everyone and everything. Every once in a while you can hear her robust laugh when a child says something that amuses her. She delights in teaching and in her students. In her chaos, there is order. The children know it, the teacher knows it, and an observer who is paying attention sees it immediately. Both teachers' schools have had disturbing assessment results, except in the areas in which Teachers A and B teach. Not surprisingly, the special education scores in Teacher A's school and the fifth-grade reading comprehension scores in Teacher B's school were well above the rest of the school's scores. Not everyone can replicate Teacher A or B, but for those of you who see yourselves in these teachers, good for you.

Your first task is to do a quick self-examination. What kind of energy do you exhibit around children? Your students will respond to your authentic energy and will follow your directions as long as your energy is positive and you are making your decisions in their best interests. This is natural and intuitive for you and the children. However, there are many skills required of you as the classroom manager that are not natural. Knowing how to intervene quickly and effectively may be very new to you.

A Quick Intervention Is Worth a Lot

One of the benefits of having a good team leader for every team is that the students are always more aware of undercurrents than the teacher. If you have a good relationship with your team leaders, you may be able to count on them to alert you to possible problems. However, if you see a student who is beginning to act out or two students who are having problems together, it is always better to act quickly and efficiently than to wait and see what can happen. Left to their own devices, some students, enjoying the attention of the crowd and/or lacking the self-restraint we have been discussing, can escalate a small problem into a major confrontation in a nanosecond or less.

However, if you can provide a prudent but subtle signal, the entire event might be avoided. Sometimes just a simple nod, a gentle hand on the shoulder, a wink, or some other acknowledgment that lets the child in question know that you see him trying to show restraint is enough to encourage him to keep trying (Wright, 2011).

On other occasions, asking a child to help you do a small task can keep a little disagreement between that child and another from developing into a real fight. After the two have been separated from each other for a few minutes, asking the two children to speak to you after class to resolve their disagreement more appropriately can help both of them learn a better way to resolve their conflicts.

Clear the Field

Most children like to have small objects they can play with, and struggling learners normally choose to be distracted rather than to be on task. Therefore, make your students clear their desks of everything before you start the next part of any lesson. For example, once the warm-up is complete and I am going to begin my motivation, no one needs paper or pencils on his desk. I ask team leaders to be sure all desks are cleared. If I am working with a class that has not yet internalized this routine, I may give a reward to the team that gets its desks cleaned off first. If the routine has been internalized, I reward the behavior only intermittently to maintain it. Nevertheless, my point is that, if we are having a discussion, no one needs to have any paper or pencils available.

Decide what materials are needed and when they need to be available to your students. Flying pens and pencils are distracting to everyone. Watch carefully to see who has control over objects and who does not. Place the pen throwers next to the team leaders so that the team leaders can help maintain the materials. For children who must tap because of their own hyperactivity issues, ask them to tap on their thighs. Their needs are met, and so are yours.

Handle Defiance Without Confrontation

The evidence of defiant patterns in any classroom tells us that something has gone very wrong. One fundamental strategy for correcting this pattern is to establish and preserve a psychologically secure and supportive environment (Turner et al., 2003). In order to create a secure classroom environment, the teacher must intervene quickly when a student appears to defy authority and politely ask the troubling student to follow the simple direction that was given. It is not advisable to get into a discussion about the merits of the request or turn the event into a contest for power.

For example, if I ask a student to move, I don't get too worked up if the move is done with some grumbling. As long as the student moves, I say, "Thank you," and we continue on with the lesson. I always stay calm; students do not see the need to defy my authority. A psychologically safe classroom environment is noted for the caring relationships between the teacher and students, the high expectations for students' behavior, and the opportunities students have to learn problem-solving skills and experience autonomy—all of which are the core attributes of resilience (Bernard, 2004; Henderson, Milstein, & Bernard, 1997). In the Empire, there is no question about who has the final authority—that would be me.

When I started teaching, I did not have the skills I have now. I remember vividly a dispute that I should have handled differently—and would have handled with much more grace if it had happened last week. Again, I need to tell you another story to illustrate my point.

One of my students who had some social problems and cognitive limitations joined a neo-Nazi group. At first, he kept his membership to himself, but after some time had elapsed, he wanted to talk about his new friends. One time in class, he shared with me that the "Holomecaust" never happened. I knew the child was limited and was easy prey for the White supremacist group that had found him, but I really felt no sympathy for him or his group. Instead of maintaining my self-control, I responded on a personal and emotional level. I should have used that as a teachable moment to help the youngster understand the incredible lies that he had been told. Instead, after my outburst, the defiant youngster tried to goose-step all the way down the hall to the office. When he returned to my class, we did have a long talk about the reason for my response; however, I was responsible for the boy's feeling that, if he did not stand up for himself and his beliefs, he would be considered weak in front of his peers. When teachers lose control, the results are always counterproductive.

I have learned from experience and research that in order to avoid defiant confrontations, teachers need to offer students face-saving strategies so that they can "de-escalate with dignity" in front of their peers (Wright, 2011). Not every defiant episode is a calculated event, and just by projecting calmness and relaxing before responding (Braithwaite, 2001), teachers can help students compose themselves before the small event turns into a major confrontation. Other researchers have found that teachers can help students who have become defiant by validating their emotions and listening with empathy. However, when a confrontation occurs, it is up to the adults to act like adults, think in terms of everyone's safety, and always use a calm, neutral tone of voice (Wright, 2011).

If you are concerned by any child's persistent problems with authority, seek help from the school's counselor, social worker, or psychologist. The psychological literature is filled with intriguing discussions regarding oppositional defiant disorder and conduct disorder, as well as the critical symptoms that may indicate future serious dysfunctions among students with mild to severe disorders (Loeber, Burke, Lahey, Winters, & Zera, 2000). As teachers, it is our task to handle a defiant student in a calm, efficient manner. Learn as much as you can so you can do your job well, but your vocation is to teach. The clinicians will do their jobs; you do yours.

As I watch some young teachers and some veterans get into "life and death" struggles with a child over who will pick up a pen, I am convinced the foolishness of the issue knows no bounds. Nevertheless, once the battle has been engaged, the two seem to perform at the same level. Neither one seems capable of rational thought. If you find yourself getting close to that type of engagement with a 7-year-old, get out of the dispute immediately. Use the rule or routine that is most closely aligned to the issue to end the quarrel. Don't make it personal. Remember that you are the adult. This is what you say to the child nicely: "I know you think that Billy should pick up the pen, but I saw you throw it, and our rule says that we all have to pick up what we throw. You have made so many good choices today. Why don't you pick up the pen, and we'll keep working? Thank you." Let the rules and routines do the work. Leave the child alone. He will pick up the pen, but he does not need an audience. If you have gone too far and you are reading this to see what to do next, apologize to the child tomorrow. It is your mistake. I don't care what the child did. If you acted like a child, you did not model appropriate adult behavior. You must "own the problem" and create the solution.

Summary

In this first chapter on successful management strategies and practices, we have explored a number of issues related to helping students learn how to use self-control. I hope you have been able to see the close relationship between planning and management. Many management decisions are made when you are doing your initial planning. Let's review the instructional triangle now (Figure 5.1) specifically as it relates to management.

In our work on management, we have learned that we need to determine the rules and the routines we will need in order to be sure that instruction will take place in an orderly manner. We have to consider how we can create appropriate boundaries for our students to keep them safe and yet give them the freedom they need to explore and learn. Before the children even come into our rooms the first day of school, we must create inviting classrooms that are so well arranged that we will have easy access to each child, and each child can see us and hear us easily as we teach. Using what we know about ourselves and about the developmental trajectory of our children, we will start planning to develop positive relationships with our students.

Once we have decided on each day's management goals, we have to select the strategies we will use to help our students reach the goals. Some strategies can be implemented only if we have routines that our children know how to follow. If we need to introduce a new routine, our lesson plans must include the steps needed for teaching the new routine. We need to have a record of when we started the routine, what its purpose is, and how the routine is expected to support the children's acquisition of the new learning.

The only part of management that cannot be planned is that which happens during instruction. So much of management is the result of good planning—the better the job you have done preparing for your instruction, the less management will be a problem during instruction.

It is the use of your natural, authentic energy when dealing with your students that allows them to respect you, accept you as you are, and respond in kind. Children

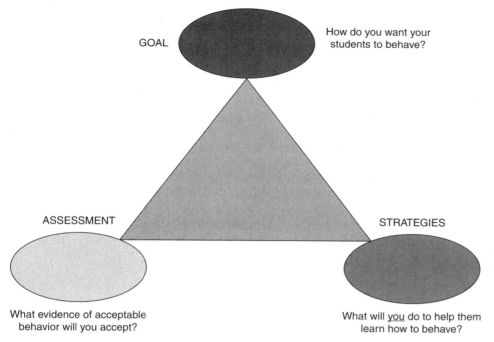

FIGURE 5.1 Instructional Triangle—Management

respond to adults with different energy levels every day, and they make the internal adjustments naturally and easily. They do not adjust well to people who do not or cannot control themselves.

Defiant behavior is frightening to everyone. It creates a feeling of disorder and insecurity that can be very damaging. When the teacher remains calm, treats every student with respect, and maintains the safety of all the children, the participants and witnesses learn that they are under the guardianship of someone who has clear boundaries and good sense. The benefits of rules, routines, and boundaries accrue to everyone, and more students are willing to accept and respect them.

6

Guidelines for Effective Classroom Management

The highest form of wisdom is kindness.

THE TALMUD

Teachers who have mastered effective management can take their class outside for a fire drill quickly and efficiently and have the students resume their work swiftly when they return to class. That may be the ultimate test of a good classroom manager. The tension exists, of course, between keeping the students under such tight control that nothing they do feels enjoyable and having the students enjoy themselves so much that they do not respect the teacher as the authority figure in the class.

In this part of the book, we are discussing the attributes that can be found among teachers who are firm leaders who take pleasure in teaching and helping their students enjoy learning, rather than classroom managers who are either tyrants or pals. In this chapter, our second on how to become a successful classroom manager, we are going to refine the broad brushstrokes of rules, routines, and boundaries and unpack them so you have the specifics you need to create a safe learning environment for *all* under your leadership. We need to emphasize *safe* because of a new reality that we are facing.

THE NEW REALITY IN OUR CLASSROOMS

In today's world, we are all confronting a reality that did not exist, or at least was not recognized, forty years ago: children who are enraged at adults. It has been a long time since children were "seen, but not heard." However, pint-sized felons are now found in many American schools, and the anxiety they cause and the fear they bring with them create new challenges for everyone.

Why Are Today's Children So Angry?

In too many families today, young children have been "parentified," meaning that they have been given the responsibilities of a parent while they are still children. In addition, at the ripe old age of 4 or 5, they have had to learn how to fend for themselves. Finally, and most importantly, young children have been exposed to danger at their parents'/guardians' hands. The pathologies that grow out of these situations have yet to be fully understood, but we do see some of the results in schools all over the United States today.

According to Kerr and Schneider (2008), there has been much less research on children's and adolescents' expression of maladaptive anger than on such expression by adults, but the current data provide some confirmation that youth who deal with their anger inappropriately are at risk for future negative interpersonal relationships and poor general and mental health outcomes. In a longitudinal study of victimized children and adolescents, Turner, Finkelhor, and Ormrod (2006) found that exposure to violence, either directly or as a witness, increases levels of depression and/or anger/ aggression. Their research suggests that cumulative exposure to numerous forms of victimization over a child's life creates a substantial mental health risk. As teachers, we see many of the manifestations of poor anger management and the cumulative effect of victimization on children in our work every day.

As a result, classroom management has evolved, becoming more of an idea that a caring and knowledgeable adult is in charge who can and will take care of every child than simply a system for teaching self-restraint. Some children will be very cynical about their new teacher's willingness or ability to protect children from the dangers that surround them. However, if the teacher is clear about the extent of the coverage (how big the Empire is) and the cooperation that is needed, most students will give their teachers a chance.

How Can You Help?

In order to understand how much children count on a teacher's empathy, guidance, and firm but fair management, please participate in the following exercise.

Let us suppose, for example, that you're 8 years old; you're in bed thinking about tomorrow, the first day of school. You are going to be in third grade. What are you most concerned about? Answers may differ by gender and life experiences; they usually do. That's fine. We are hard-wired differently. Write down the top five worries on your 8-year-old worry list.

Here is Harriet's eight-year-old worry list (I skipped second grade so I was going into fourth grade):

1. Will my teacher like me?
2. Will my teacher make us do a lot of math?
3. Will I know people in this class?
4. Will I know how to find my classroom? (I was then, and I still am, able to get lost going down a straight hallway.)
5. Will my sister Susie know how to find me to walk me home?

Which of these worries can be handled by my teacher's planning for effective management before school begins? If you selected items 1, 3, and 4, you are correct. When the children are lined up outside of the building on the first day of school, my teacher can plan to walk slowly, point out features of the building that we pass on our way to the classroom, and assure us that someone will help us if we get lost getting to our classroom during the first week of school. When we get to our room, she will put us in teams to help us feel comfortable and safe in school.

We will go into more detail throughout this chapter, but you can see that making specific arrangements in light of the ages of your students can make a tremendous difference in their willingness to believe in you. Therefore, in this chapter we will begin with a discussion of what you can do to help your students see you as a benevolent but firm leader from the minute they meet you. This first meeting, as in all other relationships, can set the tone for what is to come between you and your new students.

Next, we will examine Brophy's (1981) extraordinary descriptors of effective and ineffective praise. In this section, we will discuss effective praise, especially as it relates to Ginott's (1972) groundbreaking work on relationships between students and teachers. In our next section, we will examine new findings from brain research. We are fortunate to be teaching at a time when brain research has brought forth so much clarity regarding how people learn and especially how children learn during different phases of their development. We will apply some of these findings to enlighten our discussion of what teachers can do to improve their classroom management skills. Finally, "Harriet's Helpful Hints" is a list of 10 specific ideas for developing a healthy emotional climate in your classroom. Children of all ages need to know they are emotionally safe in order to learn and grow.

"I've come to the frightening conclusion that I am the decisive element in the classroom. It's my daily mood that makes the weather. As a teacher, I possess a tremendous power to make a child's life miserable or joyous. I can be a tool of torture or an instrument of inspiration. I can humiliate or humor, hurt or heal. In all situations, it is my response that decides whether a crisis will be escalated or de-escalated and a child humanized or de-humanized" (Ginott, 1972, p. 13).

"IF IT IS TO BE, IT IS UP TO ME"

If I were reading this from your perspective, I would be thinking two things simultaneously: "What do you mean it's up to me?" and "Yes, I can do something about classroom management!" As I recall, I vacillated between fear and confidence a lot. However, the more you believe in yourself, the less fearful you will be. Years ago I told one of my graduate classes a story. I had been talking to a new student who had been sent to me to get ready for one of the now-retired functional tests, and he was really struggling. I asked him, "Do you believe I can teach?" He said, "Yes." I asked, "Do you believe you can learn?" He answered, "Yes." I said, "Together we can do anything!" One of my graduate students loved that story and turned it into a sign she placed in her classroom (Figure 6.1). Since she had been a cheerleader and was in charge of the cheerleading squad at her school, her sign matched her personality.

Teacher makes major announcement!
I know I can teach!
I know you can learn!
Together - <u>we</u> can do anything!

FIGURE 6.1 "Cheerleading" Sign

The Importance of Dressing Like a Professional

There is no other job that can make our claim: "Teaching is the one profession that teaches all the other professions" (Author Unknown, "Teacher Appreciation/ Quotations," n.d.). When you put effort into looking professional, your students will know that you consider yourself a qualified expert in your field. They will be more likely to respect you because you demonstrate self-respect. Remember that classroom management is, in part, the art of teaching self-restraint.

There is a strong positive correlation between self-respect and self-control. According to Lowenstein (1983), "Self-control can be learned, and when it is learned it leads to increased self-confidence and self-esteem. Children with poor control are likely to be poorly adjusted to the adult world. This is because they continue to practice a demeanor which may have been necessary for their early survival but is inappropriate in later circumstances" (p. 229).

Struggling learners are in real need of positive role models who can teach self-control and model self-respect. Your appearance is a nonverbal cue regarding your feelings about your own importance, as well as that of your job and your students.

How Do You Stop the Noise?

There are times in every classroom when the noise gets out of hand. From Mr. Yourpal's to Mrs. Tyrant's room, there is always a noise level that is too loud. Some teachers raise their voices so they can be heard over the noise. Some teachers say, "Shhhhhhhhh." I don't do either because I know neither one works. In the first place, 30 children from ages 5 through 18 can always make more combined noise than one person can overcome. In the second, my desire to sound like either a snake or a tire that is going flat is slim to none. Therefore, I stand in a centrally located place in the classroom, look at the clock, give my hand signal for silence, say "1," and wait. It's called "the fine art of waiting." I will give you the specific directions for my hand signal in my "Helpful Hints" and also the counting system that I use, but I will tell you now that they are incredibly effective.

We said that every student must be able to see you, but there is always one spot in your classroom that is clearly visible to every student. Go to that spot and stand very still. Someone will see you and someone will hear you because these are routines that have been practiced a lot. Once the routine has been started, the system of getting quiet begins, and the class is ready to start listening to you in a matter of seconds. However, I am going to share a secret with you. Promise not to tell, OK? I still don't know what the students think I will do to them if I ever get to 2 when I start to count, but they must have imagined very terrible things. Whenever I say, "1" and silence does not follow my expectations, I say, in a very stern voice, "Don't make me say 2!" and you can hear a pin drop.

GUIDELINES FOR EFFECTIVE PRAISE

Praise can be a very effective tool for inviting students to use their best cooperative and positive behaviors, but it has to be meaningful in order to be effective. Brophy (1981) provides us with a list of attributes of both effective and ineffective praise. There is a lovely congruence between Brophy's (1981) effective praise and Ginott's (1972) suggestions to teachers for successful management techniques. Table 6.1 is a complete list of Brophy's guidelines for effective praise.

Ginott (1972) believes that in order to provide an environment that is conducive to learning, teachers must remain aware of the needs of students and communicate with them in a sensitive manner. According to Brophy (1981), effective praise "is delivered contingently" and "specifies the particulars of the accomplishments." Therefore, to be effective, global phrases such as "You are doing a nice job," which do not mean anything, are replaced by comments that are based on specific accomplishments that children can recognize as being their own. Brabec, Fisher, and Pitler (2004) found that students whose teachers used praise effectively increased their efforts and set higher goals for themselves. The teacher's comments are made either publicly or privately,

TABLE 6.1	Effective Praise

1. is delivered contingently
2. specifies the particulars of the accomplishment
3. shows spontaneity, variety, and other signs of credibility that suggest clear attention to the student's accomplishment
4. rewards attainment of specified performance criteria (which can include effort, however)
5. provides information to students about their competence or the value of their accomplishments
6. orients students toward better appreciation of their own task-related behavior and thinking about problem solving
7. uses students' own prior accomplishments as the context for describing present accomplishments
8. is given in recognition of noteworthy effort or success at difficult (for this student) tasks
9. attributes success to effort and ability, implying that similar successes can be expected in the future
10. fosters endogenous attributions (students believe that if they expend effort on the task because they enjoy the task and/or want to develop task-relevant skills)
11. focuses students' attention on their own task-relevant behavior
12. fosters appreciation of, and desirable attributions about, task-relevant behavior after the process is completed (Brophy, 1981, p. 26).

depending on the comfort zone for each child. Sprick, Borgmeier, and Nolet (2002) found that using specific, contingent praise, even with defiant students, in a manner that does not embarrass the students can have a calming and positive effect on their behavior and academic performance.

For example, if Antwon was working hard and finding a lot of examples in the text to help his team do its work, you could say, "Antwon, you must have read very carefully to be able to do such fine work today. I can tell how much you are helping your team find good answers this morning. Two people have called for a Team Time-Out to get help from you." If Antwon would rather eat dirt than accept public praise, your praise would be said privately, and Antwon would certainly continue his hard work and see you as his advocate.

Ginott (1972) tells teachers that constructive communication encourages students' cooperation and appropriate behavior. To this end, Brophy (1981) suggests that teachers use "students' own prior accomplishments as the context for describing present accomplishments"; praise "is given in recognition of noteworthy effort or success at difficult (for this student) tasks" and "attributes success to effort and ability, implying that similar success can be expected in the future." As you know, these three guidelines have particular utility in dealing with struggling learners, who need to be reminded as often as possible that they own their success. Brabec et al. (2004) similarly found that praising effort and work strategies can result in students' tolerating and then accepting more challenging tasks. Let's go back to Antwon.

Last semester Antwon had to sign a contract stating that he would show more persistence in completing his work, be less argumentative with his peers, and ask for help when needed. You are now seeing indications of Antwon's commitment to his own future. When you speak to Antwon privately, you might remind him of the difference between the old Antwon (but don't dwell on the past) and this new and amazing Antwon. Acknowledge that the reading is difficult, but that he has been an insightful reader who has been able to help his teammates see some very subtle features of the characters and that this is a particularly impressive accomplishment because it was done in such a short period of time. Since no one sprinkled magic dust on his head (make sure he promises that no one has done that), he must be responsible for his newfound success.

Researchers (Brabec et al., 2004; Brophy, 1981; Sprick et al., 2002) further suggest that teachers ask students to explain their work to them because effective praise "focuses students' attention on their own task-relevant behavior" (Brophy, 1981). If Antwon can do well now, there is no reason to believe he will not do well all quarter. He knows what he did to succeed, and he may recognize that it was his effort and ability that garnered your attention. Your praise is not manipulative or false; it is real and has integrity. Nevertheless, it is your belief in Antwon that will help him to believe in you and ultimately in himself.

Your praise has credibility, it is contingent on the student's accomplishments, and it is given in a sensitive and discrete manner so that the student can process it. Hopefully, your goal of becoming a fair but firm classroom manager who has appropriate positive relationships with students is more obvious to you now.

CURRENT BRAIN RESEARCH

During a recent lull in my activities, I decided it was time to learn something new, so I purchased a wonderful CD and text from The Great Courses™ called *Understanding the Brain*. It is written for nonscientists to help us understand how the brain learns. This whole field of research can provide teachers with a great deal of critical information that can inform our instructional decisions and result in improved classroom management. This is not the text and I am not the right teacher to cover all that neuroscience has to teach you about how the brain learns, but we can explore some of the more interesting ideas you might find useful, whether you are an elementary, middle, or high school teacher.

Elementary School

To begin, it is important for all teachers to understand that children's brains develop over time, and during each phase of development, students need different types of stimulation and recognition. For example, from 6 to 12 years, children are in what is known as "developmental grace. Many skills and competencies are gained more easily during these middle years. . . . The most conspicuous cognitive ability that children have during the middle years is the ability to learn languages" (Wolfe, 2010, p. 79). We know, for example, that foreign language learned before adolescence is spoken without an accent, but that, even when accounting for linguistic skills and/or effort, foreign language learned after adolescence is almost always spoken with an accent. In addition, complex physical skills and music must be mastered before age 12, or they will almost never be mastered to their full potential.

Researchers have learned that children remember more of what they are taught as they get older. Part of the reason for that lies in the fact that younger children do not practice or rehearse recalling the stimuli until they are about 10, and by that time, they tend to rehearse the information spontaneously (Flavell, Friedrichs, & Hoyt, 1970). Therefore, when we practice routines before our students are 10, we can explicitly teach rehearsing/practicing skills to help them develop their ability to memorize information. Such intentional behavior works to improve both instruction and management.

When working with young children on management strategies, a teacher can use foreign language, musical cues, and short physical exercises. Here are a few helpful suggestions:

1. Teach children to count to three in various foreign languages. Use the "language of the week" as your counting strategy, but always hold up your fingers to help children who may not remember the new words for one, two, three.
2. Sing a brief song with the children while they clean up their area. At other times, when the children are working quietly, play classical music very softly. The management cue is that, if they cannot hear the music, they are making too much noise.
3. When the children get restless, do a few baseball swings or pitches, run in place, or try some similar activity. According to Jensen (2008), classroom movement raises

the chemical output in the brain used for thinking, focus, learning, and memory (noradrenaline, dopamine, and cortisol). Jensen suggests allowing students to participate in a variety of exercises and then to self-select an activity because forced activity may cause an overproduction of cortisol.

Middle School

Researchers have discovered something that parents and teachers have known for some time: For most adolescents, emotions trump rational thinking. However, now we understand this behavior in terms of brain development. "The emotional center matures before the frontal lobes" (Wolfe, 2010, p. 86). Early in adolescence, the levels of dopamine, a naturally produced stimulant, are low, which may help to explain teenagers' tendency to act without thinking. As middle school teachers, we often ask a student, "What were you thinking?" only to have him honestly tell us that there was no thinking at all, ever: he just reacted to the situation. We cannot say, "Well, I know you are experiencing low levels of dopamine, so you don't have to face any consequences for your behavior." However, at least we can understand that until they grow older, young teens are going to make decisions based on impulse more often than by careful consideration.

If you are going to count on middle school students to think before they act, you are likely to be very disappointed in your students. As a result of what we now know, a result, the boundaries in your Empire must be clear and carefully considered. You also need to make decision-making skills an explicit part of your management objectives and reward students who are trying to show self-restraint because it is much harder during early adolescence than it is at any other time.

High School

Until fairly recently, scientists believed that one of the most active periods of brain growth and reorganization began by age 2 and was completed by early adolescence. As a result of brain-imaging techniques now available to us, neuroscientists have found that the teenage years are also a period of significant changes in the brain's anatomy and neurochemistry. Therefore, assuming that an adolescent has the same capacity to function as an adult is not only false, but also unfair to those whose brain is not fully operational until they are 20 to 25 years old (Wolfe, 2010).

This information is relevant to teachers because the frontal cortex—what some neuroscientists call the CEO of the brain—is the final part of the brain to mature. The frontal cortex controls executive decisions—that is, moral, ethical, and behavioral decisions. "Individuals with damage to this part of the brain often know what they are supposed to do but are unable to do it" (Wolfe, 2010, p. 85). Among struggling learners who may have few role models of appropriate self-restraint, the task becomes even more difficult. They are delayed in their own development by the dearth of responsible parenting they may have experienced, and they are expected to behave as adults long before they have the developmental neurological functioning of those who have fully matured.

In order to counteract this double-edged sword, it makes sense for decision-making skills, especially those involving moral and ethical issues, to be a priority in every classroom, across all disciplines. Courses in literature, history, science, business, and journalism provide easy access for such instruction. Thoughtful, carefully prepared lessons can be helpful in demonstrating the consequences of individuals' ethical and moral lapses in judgment. This is closely related to classroom management because at the high school level, students make choices about their behavior and need to understand the relationship between their choices and the consequences of their behavior in a much more sophisticated manner. Classroom management must include providing students with reasonable explanations for rules, routines, and boundaries. Students should also be given some responsibility, when possible, for determining how to resolve the problems they have created.

In addition, as anyone who has taught a first-period high school class can tell you, high school schedules work against what brain research has to tell us about adolescents' need for additional sleep. Sleep researcher Carskadon (2002) confirmed what every high school teacher has known for years: Adolescents need more sleep than small children. However, their body clocks are set to stay up late and get up later in the morning. This is a problem we may understand, but we are unlikely to change. However, if you teach a first-period class, make sure you include a lot of active, interesting activities, or you will have to live with the unintended results of transportation policies that leave your students apathetic and sleepy.

HARRIET'S HELPFUL HINTS

This list comes to you in no particular order because I don't know what you will need to know first. When I was a student teacher, I was told not to smile until Christmas. I actually heard that repeated at an orientation for new teachers recently. However, I am going to tell you what I tell my own student teachers, "Beat the Christmas rush, and smile now!" I can't imagine anything more deadly than working with children from September until December and not smiling once. Smile at your students when you meet them. Would you glare at anyone else you were meeting for the first time? Of course not.

1. Count to three slowly.

Whenever I need my students, whether K through 12 or graduate school, to settle down because I need their attention, I stand in a designated spot. I show the signal for Time-Out, and I say clearly, "1." According to the routine, when the students hear me say "1," they get quiet and help their teammates to settle down. I give them a brief, but reasonable time to quiet down, and then I proceed. If I am not satisfied with the speed at which they are getting quiet, using a stern voice I say, "Don't make me say 2!" As I have mentioned, there is no noise after that. The key is to teach, practice, and reinforce the routine. After that, use the routine and no other to get the class from noisy to silent. I do not yell. I don't like to be yelled at. I like the Time-Out signal because it reinforces the counting routine. Even my most frequent visitor to adjudicated facilities felt that this was a respectful way to get students to adjust themselves without a lot of micromanagement from the teacher.

2. Praise the one child who is doing what you want.

Sometimes I get a good chuckle when I read the literature about classroom management written by some researchers. I remember reading an article by someone who said that praising a child for appropriate behavior is so manipulative that no one above the age of 8 would ever buy into it. In the real world, not the theoretical model, effective praise is a very valuable teaching tool. When I taught at one school, I had a youngster who did not have many skills, but he knew how to sit up straight when I was ready to start my lesson. I used to say, "Thank you, Irving. You are always ready to learn. You are such a pleasure for me to turn to when I am ready to teach. You sit up straight, your books are on your desk, and I can tell you are ready to begin our work today." Well, Irving had lots of issues, but he could sit up like a champ. Because the praise Irving received helped all of the students know how to meet my expectations (Sprick et al., 2002), every child in our class knew how I wanted them to sit by looking at Irving. In the wonderful world of classroom management, honest, specific praise can be incredibly valuable.

3. Use a child's name when giving praise—*never* when giving corrections.

If you want to praise a child publicly and the child is comfortable with public praise, it is perfectly acceptable to use the child's name. However, if you need to redirect a child, correct a child, or reprimand a child, *never* use the child's name in delivering those instructions.

For example, in the morning Lucy was doing an outstanding job during the math lesson. She was attentive, she was helpful to her teammates, and her assessment results indicated that she achieved mastery on the day's goals. You can pull her aside or speak to her in front of others and praise her for the specifics of her accomplishments and use her name.

Later in the day, Lucy became cranky and difficult. She talked during instruction. You stop talking, since you never talk when any child is talking. This time you look over at Lucy's team and say, "I am waiting for everyone at Team 2 to quiet down." Lucy's team leader may signal to her to stop, or since Lucy knows she was talking, she may stop on her own. In either case, you have accomplished your goal to get Lucy quiet without damaging her sense of well-being that she had worked so hard to achieve in the morning.

Praise is always connected with a child's name, since it is contingent on the child's effort and ability. Corrections should be emotionally neutral, and that can happen only if no one personalizes the content of the correction. Ginott taught us "Children are like wet cement. Whatever falls on them makes an impression" ("Thinkexist," n.d.). When we use the child's name, we are making the correction personal, and the child can interpret our correction as a specific attack on her.

4. Give three chips to your constant talkers.

As you may remember from your psychology courses, theorists from Pavlov through Hull to Skinner have postulated that positive and negative reinforcements can be applied to learning principles (Berk, 2000). The operant conditioning model has been very helpful in improving classroom management. As a result, its token economy system has been used extensively in schools.

In many classes that I have taught, and in lots of classes that I have observed, there are children I refer to as "talking addicts." They seem to be obsessed with either talking or calling out. I do not always know the function for such disruptive behavior; as the Empress, my goal is to change the conduct. I have "healed" many students with the three-chip "cure." First, I talk to each student privately, and we discuss the reality of the situation. I explain that I am not in the business of fixing blame; I only want to fix the problem. The students are often relieved, since they have struggled with this behavior for years. Next, I explain the process we will follow. When class begins, I put three poker chips on the desk. There are no consequences for the behaviors as long as the child has not called out or talked out of turn more than three times during class. Each time she does the targeted behavior, I take a chip off the child's desk. I do not tolerate arguments or discussions at these times. When I remove the last chip, the child is on notice that, if I speak to her about another incident of its kind, a punishment will follow. In this way, students learn how to control their own behavior. Thompson and Jenkins (1993), suggest offering troubled students face-saving devices for de-escalating problems; since one goal of management is teaching students self-restraint, this is an ideal system for helping students learn how to manage their chronically disruptive behavior.

5. Be creative.

I loved each one of the All Stars differently and for very diverse reasons. One of my boys has to be one of the most comical characters I ever met. My pal Larry had no love for a chair, any chair. During middle school, he was often found wandering the halls, the office, the gym, or the cafeteria; any open doorway was an invitation to Larry. When he came to high school, he thought it was just a larger version of the playground he had just left. Researchers (Mayer & Ybarra, 2004; Walker, Colvin, & Ramsey, 1995), suggest looking for alternatives to replace prior maladaptive behaviors.

In order to help Larry make the adjustment to life in the big city, I offered him a bargain. I bought a plant at the local grocery store. It was on the shelf of dying plants, so it cost only a dollar. I brought in a watering can, and I told Larry that he could water the plant whenever he could no longer sit still. However, if anyone got wet at any time for any reason, the deal was off. Larry understood why he was being allowed to water my dying plant. He never abused his privilege, and I learned that when all else fails, be creative.

No one really expected him to graduate from high school. When Larry crossed the stage at graduation with his cap pushed rakishly to one side, I thought, "What a ride you gave us, but you have been worth every second!" I hope you are still making folks laugh, Larry. I will never forget you.

6. Whenever possible, use humor.

Some students come to school looking for a fight. They may have had an argument at home; they may have a difficult temperament; they may be the target of a dysfunctional family; there are any number of variables that are beyond our control that contribute to some people's need to quarrel. Effective teachers use humor to illustrate a point, diffuse tension in class, and maintain classroom control (Stigler & Hiebert, 1999).

There are students who are experts at dragging others into their nightmares and who enjoy the frustration and fury that they can create just by quibbling over nonissues and refusing to accept reasonable responses. Intelligent adults can be turned into blithering idiots by a small child who has outwitted them.

When I see one of the "regulars" start tuning up for another round of "I bet I can make you crazy," I have a decision to make: I can allow the child to take over my class, or I can maintain my posture as Empress, use humor, control the exchange, and move on. The conversation often sounds like this:

CHILD: Mrs. Porton, why are we reading *The Odyssey*? (Sounds innocent, but it isn't because we discussed our purpose for reading the epic before we started the reading and the purpose of each episode every day.)

ME: As you know, Henry, I am up for Mean Teacher of the Year, and I am hoping to get your vote. I thought asking you to read this poem was a surefire way to get you not only to vote for me, but also to campaign for me. OK?

CHILD: Why do you want to be the Mean Teacher of the Year?

ME: It's always been my dream. Now we have to get back to O. because he is in a lot of trouble, and he needs us.

CHILD: Whatever.

ME: I knew you would see it my way. Thanks!

I don't want to argue with this child about a nonissue. I did what I had to do; I told him that I wasn't going to discuss silly stuff with him, without humiliating him or losing control of my class to him. By using diversions or humor, good teachers can keep from jumping in a child's pool, which was designed to watch them drown and keep the class from working.

7. Talk to your kids when bad things happen.

Doris Williams was the first African-American woman to be named principal of a high school in Harford County. When she was assigned to Joppatowne High School, she decided she would change more than just the color of the front office. Her vision of a principal was that of an instructional leader—not the chief executive of a small corporation, which is what former principals had been. She wanted to build a staff devoted to taking educational risks on behalf of children.

Harford County had been a rural community in the 1950s and 1960s. Bel Air, the county seat, boasted two cows on Main Street. Large farms and old money dominated the politics of a very conservative, very traditional landscape. Things changed slowly over the years, and there were many stories of well-meaning but culturally insensitive comments made by White school leaders during school integration. After 30 years, Harford County was still slow to accept real change, and some folks had their own "unique" ways of showing their resistance to the 20th century.

One day early in the fall of Doris' first year as principal, we came to school to find "Go home, Niger" spray-painted across the building. The children of color were devastated. Many of the faculty of both races felt shocked and mortified that our new principal would be greeted in such a shameful manner.

When I walked into my first class that morning, it was clear that instruction would have to wait. There are times when the emotional climate has been filled with such toxins that you must address the issue because no one can or will learn anything else until that is done. Knowing that my students did not have a history of successfully adapting to stress, I believed I had to intervene. "Healthy adaptation to stressful experiences seems to be facilitated by a history of successfully coping with stress and challenges (Garbarino, 1993), something that at-risk students often do not have" (as quoted in Auger, Seymour, & Roberts, 2004, p. 228).

I asked the class to sit in a large circle. I started with the children of color, and I apologized to them for having to come to their own school and being insulted in such an outrageous manner. They knew I did not write those horrific words, but they knew I was truly sorry for the assault on their sensibilities. Next, I asked all the students to talk freely about how they were feeling. I don't remember what each child said, but I do remember their body language. They were all miserable. They didn't know what to do with themselves. They wanted to take their anger out in some physical demonstration, but that was not going to solve anything. Perhaps all we could do was talk about our frustration and rage, but it was better than ignoring it. Finally, one student said, "You know it was a moron who wrote it, he couldn't even spell Nigg-r correctly!" We all laughed, and by the time the bell rang, we felt better.

It is important to know that when bad things happen, and they do, you need to stop what you are doing and talk about it with the children. They may not be in tune with their emotions, but they do know how you are feeling. It is a lie to tell them that everything is OK when it is not. Be honest, discuss the situation at an age-appropriate level, and let them process it with you. If you want to help them manage their feelings appropriately, you have to show them how it is done.

8. Keep them so busy that they can't get into trouble.

There is enormous support in the literature (Ginott, 1972; King Rice, 2003; Marzano, Marzano, & Pickering, 2003) for the proposition that teachers have the most powerful influence over the dynamics of classroom life. We know that careful, reflective planning results in effective instruction and management. Therefore, it is reasonable to assume that, if you have planned a busy schedule of meaningful activities and provided access to success for all of your students, they will not have time to get into any real trouble. They will be too actively engaged to find time to do anything else.

Technology is an extraordinary tool for keeping children engaged, even in challenging assignments. One of my student teachers created an outstanding lesson plan last spring on physics for her fifth-grade class. She combined high-interest materials with a lot of hands-on activities and experiments and taught an exemplary lesson. She used the following materials to help her students discover how light travels in a straight path and how it bends: a PowerPoint presentation, a YouTube video, mirrors, flashlights, a CD, combs, and a variety of worksheets to help her students process somewhat difficult information.

In prior lessons, she had experienced difficulty keeping this very diverse group of learners on task. The class included children with physical disabilities, a child who needs a one-on-one para-educator due to her cognitive limitations, several children who have behavior challenges, and a few extremely bright children who became unruly because they didn't like to wait for others. However, in this lesson she was able to use technology, a very engaging lesson plan, and enough hands-on activities for all levels and types of learners that she only had to redirect, not correct any student. At the end of the class, for her closure, she said, "Define light and tell me one way we can make it bend." Many hands went up to answer her question. The children were excited about what they had learned, and they had mastered the material well. Instead of spending her time on management, she spent her time on instruction, and the results were obvious.

9. Call home with good news as quickly as you call home to complain.

One day I received a note in my mailbox saying that someone from my bank said I should call immediately. With my heart in my stomach, I made the call. I started off with my typical line, "If I didn't have any money in the first place and you are charging me money for not having money, how do you expect me to pay fines with money I don't have?" The lady from the bank started laughing and said, "Harriet, I am not calling because you are overdrawn. I am calling because the bank wants to make a donation to your Reading Incentive Program." I said, "I am sorry, but whenever I get a call from the bank, I immediately feel miserable." The lady from the bank said, "That's how I feel whenever I get a call from my son's school." I felt as if someone had just kicked me in the stomach. I realized that teachers, at least at the high school level, almost never make positive phone calls home. From that day on, I made myself a promise to make at least one positive call home each week. Sometimes it was a stretch, but lots of times I could make two or three calls each week. In either case, the payoff was fantastic. Parents who had not heard a nice thing said about their child since the child was in third grade received a call complimenting the child—and through the child, the parent—about good manners or hard work or excellent achievement.

Now let me make the connection to management for you. When I had to call the same parent at a later date to ask for help because the same child was acting out in my class, the parent remembered that I had called to say something nice. The parent who might have been very defensive about the child was now on my side, and that parent was not going to allow the child to misbehave for me because I had shown respect for the child and the child's family.

If all you ever do is complain to parents about their child's behavior, it is difficult for them to see you as their child's advocate. However, if you are seen as an unbiased source of information that is as quick to compliment as to complain, you have much more credibility and parental backing.

It is especially important to let parents/guardians of struggling learners know when their child has demonstrated improved effort and performance. Researchers—too many to mention, but notably Feiler (2010)—believe that parent–teacher relationships can create a framework for success for students, even among those parents who have been the most difficult to reach. When teachers reach out to their students' parents with respect, Feiler (2010) believes that schools can facilitate, not impede, the communication process that is so necessary for children's success in school.

10. You become a master teacher by paying attention to the little details and the big picture.

Never, ever, ever talk over a student's voice. Never, ever allow children to play with objects while you are teaching. Keep your eyes open at all times for what students are doing, where they are sitting, and what they are looking at. *You* must be the center of attention while you are providing instruction. I learned a lot teaching first grade, and the only strategies I didn't go on to use in high school were finger plays and little songs.

At all times, every student's eyes must be on me while I am giving instruction. I can tell if that is happening because I am in constant motion and I am looking all over the room while I talk. If a student talks while I am talking, I stop. I make a neutral comment about the team that is not quiet, wait for the talking to stop, and then begin. I am never rude. I am not above the law. One of the rules in my classroom is that we must always treat each other with respect. If I expect children to treat me with courtesy and respect, I must model courtesy and respect all the time.

Effective classroom managers know that in order to help children learn, the students must be taught how to learn. Children have to be quiet, attentive, and thinking about what they are hearing in order to learn. A good classroom manager makes sure that the classroom climate, layout, and community work together to help every child learn.

Summary

The reason for all the rules, routines, boundaries, and now guidelines we have been discussing is that we need to create a world where everyone is safe, where children learn self-restraint, and where instruction is the clear purpose of the day. One of the primary reasons that children are so very angry today is that too many adults in their lives have stood by and watched them experience danger and have not intervened to protect them. In the Empire, no one is allowed to get near dangerous situations. The rules, routines, and so on are in place to protect all of the children from physical, psychological, and other forms of danger so that the Empress/Emperor can guard students from harm.

We began our discussion by examining the tension between tyranny and anarchy. In a classroom where the children are afraid of the teacher, instead of making the children feel safe, the teacher becomes the greatest object of fear. Obviously, that is not what we want. However, it is no more desirable to have a class where there is no control. Too many struggling learners grow up in families where their parents are their "pals"; children need both same-age friends and adults who are in charge and act their age.

Therefore, our goal is to create a fair, but firm, benevolent leader who is clearly in charge, but who makes all decisions using a single lens—what is in the best interest of the children. To help us reach this goal, we blended Brophy's (1981) guidelines for effective praise with Ginott's (1972) expert advice to teachers. The two gave us a unique way of praising students that is contingent on their specific achievements and correcting them without demeaning them. Brophy's and Ginott's work has been repeatedly validated by current research, and teachers who are wise enough to take advantage of their insights continue to profit from their wisdom.

Current brain research has helped us to unpack some of the behaviors we have been able to describe accurately, but not explain. Recent researchers have indicated the natural trajectory that brain growth follows; we can plan our management goals more appropriately to fit the developmental stages our students are experiencing. Since our focus is on struggling learners, it is critical that we know what interventions and support systems our students might need in order to provide them with the specific strategies that can help them meet success.

Finally, after more than 40 years of experience, I created "Harriet's Helpful Hints," which is a list of 10 suggestions that I offer to you to help you make difficult decisions on a daily basis. Read them before you need them. Ultimately, it will be your own good judgment and common sense that will determine how well you manage your students. Treat your students as you would want another teacher to treat your own child and you will do well.

7

Mistakes in Management

Good teachers are costly, but bad teachers cost more.

BOB TALBERT

When I was in the ninth grade, I was 14 years old. My brother Bob was 21 and completing his Ph.D. in physics at The Johns Hopkins University. My sister Susie, who was on a full scholarship to one of the premier private schools in the state, recently had been accepted into the Peabody Institute's program for talented children. While they excelled at many things they did, I prayed nightly to the Great D god to get me through ninth-grade math.

One day my math teacher, Ms. Cobb, started her lesson by saying, "Harriet, you won't understand this." Ms. Cobb didn't know that I had a whole chorus at home, except my mom, singing that exact song with several verses for good measure.

Well, I said to myself, I may not be good at math, but I am terrific at being bad, and the battle between Ms. Cobb and me was on.

If you really want to injure a child, if your goal is to set up a negative relationship with someone who struggles with your content, I can think of no more effective way to begin your lesson than by announcing to that student in front of the class that he does not have the ability to understand what you are planning to teach. Apparently, I hold a grudge. It's been a while since I was in the ninth grade, and I have not forgiven Ms. Cobb. Chances are good that I never will.

Years later I taught a class in character development at the alternative middle school where I served as a member of the administration team, in part because I had instituted a schoolwide character development program. I am a firm believer that, if you are going to ask teachers to do something, you should be able to do it yourself. Besides that—you know me—I wanted to teach. Every once in a while, one of the children would ask me how I understood what they were going through so well. Normally, I just said, "I have your T-shirt. I didn't want it, but I got it. It taught me a lot." If they probed, I answered with age-appropriate details from my own experiences that let them know that, even though I look like a person who has a nice life now, that has not always been the case. Our mutual experience with life's challenges helped me to understand them. As a result, I wanted to show them there are many paths to success—and that education is on each one of them.

In this chapter, we are going to explore what *not* to do while you are working with children. The first section deals with mistakes that are made as a consequence of innocence, lack of experience, and good intentions that result in poor outcomes. Everyone makes mistakes that fall under this category. Frankly, we never stop making mistakes; the trick is to continue to learn from our errors and move on. These are errors that we refer to as fixable and forgivable.

The next section deals with mistakes that are made deliberately and happen when a teacher is more concerned with his own well-being than the welfare of the children. These are egregious flaws in judgment. In such cases, children's safety has been put at risk, their emotional security has been assaulted, and the teacher's need for releasing his anger by selecting a target has been met. In each situation, the teacher's desires have been coped with, but at the expense of a child's well-being. Finally, the worst of all possible failures occur when the teacher does not care enough to plan for or manage what happens to his students. These are unforgivable errors; they are made willingly and knowingly. People who repeat any of these behaviors frequently need to consider a different occupation.

In the final section, we will discuss Brophy's (1981) guidelines for ineffective praise. Since we have a good working knowledge of effective praise, it makes sense to become aware of the type of praise that does not have a positive effect on children so we can avoid its use.

EVERY MISTAKE IS NOT A FELONY

Why Is It Important to Have a Neat Classroom?

Some teachers are less sensitive to their surroundings than others. Messy desks, sloppy bulletin boards, and cluttered counters do not seem to bother the adult in the classroom. However, there are many children who are sensitive to chaos and disarray. The lack of organization makes them physically uncomfortable. When there is an untidy classroom, it is best to assume that the teacher has not had time to straighten up or is not sensitive to what a disorderly classroom can do to those children who need order. Normally, a few minutes of planning time spent cleaning the room will fix the problem. A classroom that has been arranged well provides another effective management tool because it establishes a climate that is conducive to learning (Hoffman Kaser, 2009).

Children should be required to clean the tops of their desks at regular intervals. This reinforces the importance of the shared commitment to excellence through effort. There are always youngsters who are very good at arranging materials and who would love to tidy up the counters so that materials can be accessed easily. Finally, a few minutes of stapling bulletin boards can do a lot of good in terms of grooming shoddy-looking classrooms.

There are those who would argue that a neat classroom is a minor detail when there are so many more-important factors to consider when dealing with classroom management. However, researchers (Bettenhausen, 1998; Cummings, 2000) have found that a messy environment creates a sense of disorder, which can be detrimental to student achievement. Therefore, teachers do not need to be overly zealous in their housekeeping, just neat and organized so they create a safe and orderly learning environment.

Many struggling learners return to a very chaotic home each day; therefore, it is imperative that school provide a place of security, reliability, and order. One demonstration of order is classroom appearance. The message of a tidy classroom is as follows: "We care about each other, and our surroundings. I will keep you safe, but you must cooperate by keeping your materials neatly organized inside your desk. You must keep the top of your desk clean, and we must all work together to maintain an orderly environment." Children don't feel comfortable with rigid rules, people, or standards; however, they do appreciate the comfort of a nice, neat, and cheerful learning environment.

What Went Wrong with My Lesson?

I can't tell you how many lesson plans I have written that looked wonderful on paper, but were total disasters when I implemented them. I followed all my principles—I really did—but the students simply didn't respond the way I had expected. When I reflected on my errors, I found that my mistakes usually fell into one of the following two categories: (1) I didn't do enough to access the students' prior knowledge, so they never knew what I was talking about, or (2) I needed routines in place for the plan to run smoothly. In each case, the mistakes were mine. I took responsibility for my mistakes in front of the students, went home and rewrote the plan based on my assessment of my problems, and tried again the next day. My students were very forgiving and usually encouraging. "We'll try again, Mrs. Porton. Don't worry." No wonder, we had such faith in each other. We all tried, made mistakes, and tried again.

Look at one of my lesson plans in Table 7.1. Doesn't that look like a good plan?

Well, that plan was a complete flop! I will tell you when and how I knew the plan was a disaster. When the students were reading the interview with Mel Brooks, I was the only person in the room who was laughing. I was hysterical. The students looked at me as if I had lost my mind; my looks at them mirrored the same feeling. I kept asking them, "Why aren't you laughing? This is really funny!" Their response: "No, it isn't!"

Look back at the plan. Where did I make my mistake? That's right. In my warm-up, I accessed only prior knowledge about drama. I never provided the knowledge base they would need to understand how Mel Brooks would sound to those who had never heard him speak. I needed to have a recording of him so that they could "hear" his voice as they read the interview. (Remember this lesson was written for and implemented in 1973.) Since Brooks and other Jewish comedians had been a part of the fabric of my life, I assumed my students would be able to do what I could do: "hear" Brooks deliver the answers to the questions of the interview as I read the words to myself.

We didn't get too far in that lesson. I stopped it, and we discussed how difficult it is to write comedy. For example, if there are no shared experiences, there is no comedy. The next day I brought in a recording of Mel Brooks doing one of his comedy routines, and then the students laughed as they read his responses to the interview questions.

Where Is the Routine?

Poor Griselda Mirelda, one of my aliases—she never remembers to think through some of her more ambitious plans to see if she will need a new routine. Griselda Mirelda really got herself into trouble one very bad day. Let me tell you what happened.

Griselda thought she could read a compass. Now, wouldn't you think that, having taught since the earth was cooling, she would check out that assumption with

TABLE 7.1   **Lesson Plan on Comedy**

Date: March 5, 1973
Lesson Title: Comedy
Lesson Unit: Understanding Drama

Goal	Lesson Goal–English 11 Students will study 20th-century American dramatic literature
Objective	Lesson Objective As a result of today's lesson, students will be able to write a short essay explaining the difference between comedy and tragedy by comparing the features of classic tragedy to 20th-century American comedy.
Materials needed	Materials Needed: Interview with Mel Brooks
Warm-Up	Warm-Up What are the features of classic tragedy?
Motivation	What makes you laugh? Why do you think it is funny? Do you think comedy writers have a more difficult job than other writers? Why?
Guided Practice	After students read the interview with Mel Brooks, they will respond to the following prompt: You have just watched *Oedipus Rex* and then gone to see Mel Brooks perform. Write a brief essay comparing the two. Be sure to include the features of a classic tragedy and compare each to Mr. Brooks' performance as an example of modern American comedy. How are they alike? How are they different? What does each one say about the time and culture they were written for?
Independent Practice	After I have discussed the prompt, each team will read the interview silently and then, using each student's notes, work together to create a response to the prompt.
Assessment	Each student must provide his/her notes for the prompt so that I can determine whether or not the student understands what is expected.
Closure	Did you like Mel Brooks' interview?
Homework	Watch something funny on TV and explain in a few sentences why you think it was funny. What does your show say about our culture?

her pals who teach geography? Not our Griselda—she decided that she was right, with no evidence beyond her saying to herself, "I can do this!" Then our little friend decided that she could take 12 nonacademically promoted ninth graders outside and away from Joppatowne High School (JHS) and, using only the compass, they would find their way back to school. Oops! Next, she had no routine in place for taking the class for a walk, but she didn't even consider that problem because she was so wrapped up in the instructional triangle and her excitement at having created her first geography lesson plan, which she *knew* would succeed.

After 40 minutes of wandering in some area somewhere, one of the students said to Griselda, "Mrs. Porton, you don't have a clue where we are or how to get us home, do you?" Griselda (a.k.a. Mrs. Porton) said, "No. I thought I knew how to read the compass, but I don't know what to do." One of the students said to the rest of the class, "She's lost. Follow me. I will get us back." In about 3 minutes, we arrived back at JHS. The principal and assistant principal were waiting for us. The class came in first; I walked in behind them, looking and feeling like an idiot. I thought Doris and the assistant principal would split a seam trying not to laugh at me in front of my class. "Nothing like a wandering Jew," Doris whispered to me as I walked slowly past her. Only she could make me laugh on a day like that.

In Griselda's defense, and she doesn't deserve much, the class was never in danger. JHS is located in a very safe community. Apparently, we had just walked in a circle in the woods behind the school. At no time would I have tried this plan if I had been working in a school where getting lost could have meant that the children's safety was an issue.

However, you can see that I made lots of mistakes. I was teaching new content, and I needed help, which I was foolish not to get. After that fiasco, I did all my planning for geography with people who actually knew the subject. I thought through every plan in terms of routines. Because the content was new to me, I needed to be much more reflective about when I would need a routine and how I should introduce it. I also invited my students to be a larger part of our discovery, since they knew this was a content area we were learning together. Please understand this did not weaken my authority. I was the Empress, but in geography class, I didn't pretend to know as much as I do about English. It's the truth, and after our compass walk, let's be real.

What Should I Do About Mean Girls?

All teachers make mistakes. It's part of the job; it's part of life. However, there are subsets of students that make it very difficult for even veteran teachers to be successful. I think three or four mean-spirited girls in a middle or high school class can create a toxic environment for almost any teacher.

They are frightening to the other students, male and female, and it seems that their main target can be the teacher. Common mistakes that teachers make include using sarcasm, retaliating in kind, trying to get the girls to like you, and attempting other inappropriate methods that are doomed to failure.

One of my most impressive student teachers had just such a group of students. One of her classes was "run" by a small group of mean girls. After several heart-to-heart post-observation conferences, she started to set up clear boundaries, she instituted effective routines so that these girls could not control who did what and when, and she enforced her own rules with her own consequences so that she was clearly in charge. From the first time I visited her class to my last observation, the climate in her class changed dramatically. The first time, a small group of female bullies made many decisions in that class. By the last visit, my student teacher ran the class with a firm hand, and the rest of the students felt safe for the first time all year. No group should ever be able to hold a class hostage, but it is easy to relive your own problems with bullies when confronted by them again.

My advice to new teachers is to remember that this is now. The opening line of Hartley's (1953) book *The Go-Between* is one of the best opening lines in literature: "The past is a foreign country: they do things differently there" (p. 1). When you were a child, you were vulnerable to bullies. Now you are an adult, and it is your job to protect children from bullies. When a student teacher is struggling with "mean girls" or other types of bullies, it is important to remember to use all the tools available to keep the bullies under control. They have no place in school, and it is the teacher's job to keep their behavior under control in the classroom. It is difficult, and it takes time. If the student teacher struggles with this issue, it is not a felony; it is a learning curve that is steeper for some than for others.

MISTAKES THAT CANNOT BE FORGIVEN

If you are looking for a text written by an experienced educator who has never made a mistake, please look in the fiction section online or in your local bookstore. Anyone who has taught real children for more than 1 day has made mistakes. However, if you find yourself being described in this section, think seriously about your choice of careers. Teaching is not a good match for every person, and there are many other careers that may be a better fit for you. However, if you know that you would never deliberately choose your own convenience or comfort over the well-being of children, just remember that everyone makes mistakes.

Wall of Shame

From kindergarten through middle school, hallways and classrooms are routinely decorated with pictures and samples of students' work that demonstrate excellence and mastery of skills and goals reached. It is wonderful to walk through schools to see children's work artfully displayed. However, one can see in more than one classroom, almost always in a secondary school setting, a clearly labeled Wall of Shame.

In each case, a student's work, with that student's name clearly visible, is displayed with the reason for its being displayed noticeably written across the top of the paper.

Student's Name	
Date	
Class	PAPER PLACED HERE DUE TO CHEATING!
XXXXXXXXXXXXXXXXXXXXXXXXXXXXXXXX	
XXXXXXXXXXXXXXXXXXXXXXXXXXXXXXXX	
XXXXXXXXXXXXXXXXXXXXXXXXXXXXXXXX	

I have asked teachers why they put up a Wall of Shame, and their answers have been frighteningly similar, even though the schools they are teaching in can be found in every community that has a public school. They have all assured me that this is done to *help* the children learn the dangers of cheating, handing in poor quality work, and so on. "How does it do that?" I ask. "Simple, my students don't like to see their papers displayed on the Wall of Shame. Once that happens, they believe that I will keep my word. I do a lot to reduce cheating in this school!" I often wonder—after I listen to the teachers' accounts of how they have, for example, reduced cheating or improved handwriting—how much data they have to validate their claims.

On the other hand, the data against using shame are very compelling. Shaming is a form of punishment, not a reasonable consequence of unwanted behavior. All punishments are likely to have short-term impacts in terms of reducing undesirable behavior, but the long-term effects are counterproductive and rarely result in changed behaviors. For our purposes, the worst of the unintended consequences is that shaming intensifies students' external locus of control because the teacher has all the control (Shindler, 2010).

One other point we know for sure is that a Wall of Shame is the creation of a bully. If you wonder where bullies learn or refine some of their skills, all you have to do is look in classrooms taught by teachers who believe that shame is a better teacher than encouragement. Although the teachers in question may claim victory and report that their system works, their attribution is a misinterpretation of what is really working and often conceals a more serious set of unwanted consequences (Shindler, 2010).

Targeting a Child

Have you ever been the target of someone's disapproval? Has the person who targeted you had more power than you? Did you feel helpless? Hopeless? Frustrated? Angry? All of these? Now imagine that you are a child and the person who has targeted you is your teacher. Your parents have taught you to believe that your teachers want only what is best for you, but you know that this teacher does not like you and treats you poorly. The balance of power is clearly not in your favor, and you have very few outlets for your feelings of powerlessness, rage, and despair. The paucity of research on this topic is disturbing. Fortunately, McEvoy (2005) conducted a study specifically on the effects of teacher bullying. He defined the construct of "bullying by teachers (or other staff, including coaches, who have supervisory control over students) . . . as *a pattern of conduct, rooted in a power differential, that threatens, harms, humiliates, induces fear, or causes students substantial emotional distress*" (p. 1). Goldstein (1999) estimates that "10% of teachers regularly engage in bullying behavior" (p. 74). Teachers who are bullies have a powerful and negative influence on their victims.

Such is the life experience of every child who has been selected by a teacher to be the target of his rage and scorn. The selected child cannot do anything right. The child might try to keep quiet to stay under the teacher's radar, but if the teacher needs to vent some rage, he will poke and prod the child into doing or saying something that will prompt a tirade against the child.

Usually, the other children in the class are aware of the dynamics, but for various reasons, they accept the teacher's position. "She brings it on herself," the children say to each other. Once targeted, the victim is treated in a manner that sets her apart from peers. There may be frequent references to how this student differs from the rest of the students, who presumably are more capable or valued. As a consequence, the student frequently becomes a scapegoat among peers (McEvoy, 2005). According to Lerner's (1980) "just world perspective" (as cited in Goldstein, 1999) the other children increasingly see the victim as deviant, worthless, and "almost deserving of being bullied" (p. 76). According to researchers (Salmivalli, Lagerspetz, Bjorkqvist, Oserman, & Kaukianinen, 1996, as cited in Goldstein, 1999) looking at a child who is bullied by peers, "it becomes part of the social norm not to like him or her" (p. 77).

The spiral downward from graceful and competent to clumsy and bungling may take longer for some than for others, but the trajectory is inevitable. As Cohen (1973) stated, "Expectations of those in positions of authority . . . are often a powerful explanation for behavior" (p. 867). And so my fourth-grade teacher was able to change me from a child who loved school, was popular, and excelled in everything except math to an anxious, miserable, lonely child who frequently missed school in order to escape my daily dose of misery. Until fourth grade, school was my sanctuary; during fourth grade, it was my prison.

My mother went to meet with my teacher, who was the first to call to complain—and certainly not the last—about my poor work habits. According to my mother, the teacher complained that I was immature, annoying, and below grade level in math. My mother explained that I had skipped second grade and was less mature than the other children. She promised the teacher that my brother Bob would help me with the math and she would work with me at home to improve my handwriting. The older children had better fine motor skills than I did, and their handwriting was neater than mine.

I knew the real problem. The teacher was working with several of her friends on a huge mural. Have I ever pretended to have artistic skills? I didn't pretend to have any artistic skills when I was in fourth grade either. However, every other child was able to work on the mural, and I wanted to be able to help, too. My teacher didn't like me—she shared this information with my only friend in the class—because I asked to work on the mural too often.

By the end of the year, my skills and my self-confidence were both hovering around the "No longer in existence" level, and the teacher suggested that I should be retained in grade. Fortunately, my mother knew me well enough to know that when I was with a teacher who believed in me, I always did very well. Mom was right. The following year I had a wonderful teacher who believed in me, and a lot of my confidence returned. However, I did not forget how I had felt just a few short months before, so when I looked on the playground for a little girl from the fourth grade that was standing all alone. I asked if she had Ms. Mean, and when she said she did, I promised her that I would be her friend because I had been last year's target and I knew how it felt. It's funny—everyone else loved Ms. Mean, but I knew what she was really like. I have taken her with me all my life. When I observe someone who targets children, I try to counsel that individual out of teaching.

I Had to Move My Car

Unless you ask me how much I weigh, I don't lie. This is an honest description of a situation that happened several years ago. A student teacher—let's call him Mortimer—had been hired by a large urban elementary school to teach special education students, grades 1–3. Mortimer had no teaching experience, but he was willing to take courses in order to earn his teaching certification. By the time I met him, he was ready for his "student teaching" experience. At this point in his program, he had to be observed by a supervisor and pass his state-mandated credentialing examinations in order to become a certified special education teacher.

One day his principal came to his classroom to observe him, but no one was in his room. According to the schedule, he was not supposed to be anywhere else in the building. She waited for him to return to his classroom. After about 10 minutes, he and his students came back to class. When she asked where they had been, he said, "I realized that there has been a lot of street crime around here lately. I took the class with me. I told the students to stand still on the sidewalk and wait for me to return. I walked to my car and moved it so that I could see it from my classroom, and now we are back." If I had been the principal, I would have started the procedures for his termination immediately. He left children with special needs standing alone on a city street known for its crime so that he could move his car and park it in a safer spot.

Justice has a unique way of operating in the universe. Although his principal did not have the sense the Lord gave a twig and did not start the procedures to have him terminated, Mortimer was never able to pass his credentialing exams and to my knowledge has never earned his credentials to teach. Mortimer could be a fine employee as long as he is never responsible for the safety of young children. If I have any control over the career of someone like Mortimer, I strongly suggest that he work with adults, but *never* children.

Teachers Who Ignore Their Students

Jack Kerouac once said, "If moderation is a fault, then indifference is a crime" ("Brainyquote," n.d.). He used the right words to describe the worst offense any teacher can commit: the crime of indifference to the welfare of students. If not doing much to help is a fault, doing something is better than doing nothing; teachers who ignore the well-being of their students have committed the "crime" of indifference. Teachers who are oblivious to children sleeping, children stealing from each other, children wandering in and out of the classroom, and children fighting in the classroom put their students' emotional and physical well-being in jeopardy every day.

During one phase of my career, I was the Coordinator of Reconstitution-Eligible Schools for the State of Maryland. It was one of the most interesting appointments I have ever had, and I will forever be in awe of the former state superintendent of schools, Dr. Nancy Grasmick, after I saw firsthand her incredible dedication to the students in Maryland. It was through this work that I was exposed to some of the most depressing displays of "nonteaching" I have ever seen. I was also deeply moved by the strength and courage of some of the principals and teachers whose schools were nestled in the heart of pedophile rings and gang and drug wars. These educational heroes were living proof of one of the best definitions of courage I know: "Courage is not the absence of fear, but rather the judgment that something else is more important than fear" (Ambrose Redmoon, "Quote Garden" n.d.).

Reconstitution-eligible schools are those that had performed so poorly on statewide assessments that they were eligible to be taken over by the state. In this transition period, a group of state monitors visited these schools regularly to see if they were making any progress in improving their instructional practices.

The person I am going to describe exists, so I am going to refer to him by his attitude, not his name. I am going to call him Mr. Apathetic. Mr. Apathetic was assigned to a special education class at one of the reconstitution-eligible schools. One of our monitors, who had been a successful principal prior to her retirement, reported back to me that this was the poorest teacher she had ever seen. She asked that I accompany her to visit Mr. Apathetic.

Our visit was planned, and the monitor and I came to the school as scheduled. The room was messy and included pictures on the wall displaying White children playing on a playground in a suburban setting. This school served an urban population of 100% African-American children, but there was no reflection of the students in this classroom in any way. Obviously, Mr. Apathetic found some old pictures, tacked them up, and forgot about them.

Mr. Apathetic pretended to teach a lesson to a small group sitting in front of him based on what he had "taught" them the day before. Only the children were not going to let him get away with it. "You didn't do nothin' yesterday, Mr. A," one child said loudly after the teacher tried to review what they had "learned" yesterday.

There were several small groups of children sitting in other parts of the room. All of the children in the class had Individualized Education Programs (IEPs), and Mr. Apathetic was working toward his certification as a special educator. One child sat alone staring into space. When I asked the child what he was doing, the little boy just looked at me. Mr. Apathetic called across, "He just finished his work. He is waiting for me." In the meantime, the child sat quietly with absolutely nothing to do. Four children who were working with the teacher's aide were learning about parts of speech. Those children were getting some instruction, but this multigrade group should not have been working on the same topic without differentiation by grade and accommodations according to each child's IEP. In addition, the children were subjected to ridicule if they didn't answer correctly or quickly. I wrote down one of the aide's comments to a student: "Jermaine, you taking too long to answer my question. You too slow. I ain't gonna wait for you."

Finally, Mr. Apathetic brought all the children together for a lesson. The children in the class belonged in grades 1 through 5; however, Mr. Apathetic chose a lesson plan from the first-grade curriculum guide entitled "Let's get ready to read!" He did not attempt to differentiate instruction, and within a few minutes, the older children did the following: Two put their heads down on their desks and fell asleep, one little boy went into the closet, two girls looked at magazines, and two boys started a fight. At that point, the monitor and I stopped the fight and took the boys to another room to help them resolve the conflict. I don't think Mr. Apathetic saw us leave.

I knew I had seen enough. When we spoke to the youngsters who were involved in the fight, they said that Mr. Apathetic used to send them to the office a lot, but he got into trouble for writing too many office referrals, so now he just lets them fight.

Let's review what was missing in Mr. Apathetic's class. There was absolutely no meaningful instruction at any time for any of the students. There were no routines in place. During each transition from small-group to large-group instruction, each child had to be told what to do. The only management technique that I saw or heard was a constant "Shhhhhhhhhhhhhhhh" from Mr. Apathetic or a loud "Shut up" from the aide. The children ignored both equally well. The only reason there was a name and an objective for the lesson plan was that the curriculum guide provided both for the teacher. This was a room that should have had this sign posted on the door: "No learning takes place here." Actually, that's not entirely true; some children learned how to sleep at their desks, others improved their fighting skills, and the girls were getting better at looking at magazines.

The principal asked us about what we had just observed; we gave her a frank accounting of our concerns. She shared with us that during her conferences with him, he was just as indifferent with her as he was to the welfare of the children. He didn't want to lose his job, but despite his many promises to do better, there were no signs of improvement. This situation and many others like it were some of the root causes of the accountability movement. I am sure you can understand the need for making teachers, principals, schools, and school systems accountable for how students are taught and how they are treated.

FIXABLE VERSUS UNFORGIVABLE ERRORS

At this point, you should be able to see the essential difference between fixable and unforgivable errors. On the one hand, a fixable mistake is a part of the learning process. It is an honest mistake, made with good intentions, but whatever the teacher expected to happen came with unexpected negative outcomes that were easily remedied. The teacher just needs to be honest, accept responsibility for the mistake, fix it, explain to the students what happened in an age-appropriate manner, and move on. Even trampling around the woods can be seen—maybe only in hindsight—as a pretty funny experience that taught everyone something.

However, an unforgivable flaw involves a decision made in the best interest of the teacher without regard for the well-being of the child or children. No child should be the target of a teacher's personal stress. There is never an excuse for displaying a Wall of Shame in any classroom. Research and experience tell us that tactics such as these only teach new techniques for intimidation and bullying. When teachers put their students' safety at risk to take care of themselves, they have not only failed to act as professionals, but also violated their students' trust, and they may be liable for resulting harm to students under their care. We review these issues in order for you to understand the full magnitude of the possible repercussions and to remind you that there are many fine people who can do wonderful work, but who should not become teachers.

Should You Become a Teacher?

Teaching is not a 9 A.M. to 3 P.M. job for folks who like summers off. We work long hours, and those who don't work in the summer may have a tough time eating in the winter. This is not a career for those who don't love children and enjoy being around young people. If you are not able to see a situation from another person's point of view and you are not flexible, perhaps you need to rethink your career goal. Flexibility and empathy are attributes that every teacher must have. If you feel confident that you can "go with the flow" and you have empathy, continue.

Spend some quiet time and ask yourself the following questions:

1. Are you still playful?
2. When you are around children, are they drawn to you?
3. Are you animated when you explain something you really care about?
4. Do you like helping other people learn?

The importance of your answers will differ according to your teaching goals. For example, if you plan to teach A.P. physics, you might not need to be very playful, but you had better be good at explaining complex information to others. If you are planning to teach kindergarten, you should be animated. Whatever your plans are, think about yourself honestly and realistically. Do you feel at ease in the world of teaching and learning? Do you feel comfortable in the world of young people? If so, welcome aboard; we need *you*.

GUIDELINES FOR INEFFECTIVE PRAISE

According to Brophy (1981), ineffective praise

1. is delivered randomly or unsystematically.
2. is restricted to global positive reactions.
3. shows a bland uniformity that suggests a conditional response made with minimal attention.
4. rewards mere participation without consideration of performance, processes, or outcomes.
5. provides no information at all or gives students no information about their status.
6. orients students toward comparing themselves with others and thinking about competing.
7. uses the accomplishments of peers as the context for describing students' present accomplishments.
8. is given without regard to the effort expended or the meaning of the accomplishment.
9. attributes success to ability alone or to external factors such as luck or low task difficulty.
10. fosters exogenous attributions (students believe that they expend effort on the task for external reasons—to please the teacher, win a competition or reward, etc.).
11. focuses students' attention on the teacher as an external authority who is manipulating them.
12. intrudes into the ongoing process, distracting attention from task-relevant behavior (p. 26).

In order to put these into perspective with all that we have learned, we are going to analyze these guidelines through three lenses. First, we will look at what damage ineffective praise can do to children normally referred to as general education students.

Next, we will examine the guidelines according to what we know about struggling learners, and finally, we will try to see how much damage using ineffective praise can do to girls.

General Education Students

This group is the "vast majority" of America's schoolchildren. These youngsters neither need nor qualify for special services. However, ineffective praise can have a confusing effect on any child. Recipients of ineffective praise are left with no meaningful information to help them maintain or improve their performance. Ineffective praise is useless because it is given in a manner that is both random and unsystematic and it provides "no information at all" to the students about their status. Ambiguous global praise provides no clear feedback for students regarding the specifics of their performance.

Every child needs to be able to learn from praise; however, ineffective praise has the opposite effect. A teacher who believes that by saying, "Sam, you are doing nicely," he has helped Sam has just repeated Robert Abernathy's famous quote: "I know that you believe you understand what you think I said, but I'm not sure you realize that what you heard is not what I meant" ("Think Exist," n.d.).

Struggling Learners

As you know, struggling learners are more vulnerable to the vagaries of praise than most other students. Their externalizing thought processes leave them susceptible to any ideas that support their belief that their failure to thrive has nothing to do with their unwillingness to try. Therefore, ineffective praise that "attributes success to . . . external factors such as luck" only serves to reinforce their general worldview and must be avoided.

Gender Issues

In Gilligan's (1977) article "In a Different Voice: Women's Conceptions of Self and Morality," she began investigating the differences in how women and men make moral decisions. As a result of her research and that of the many others who followed, we have learned that girls are more relational than boys. That is a critical construct that teachers need to understand and keep present in their thinking. Therefore, praise that "orients students toward comparing themselves with others and thinking about competing" is likely to have a negative impact on girls. "My best friend is so bad at this," Lilly thinks. "I will let her answer so she will feel better." Perhaps no male student would react this way, but girls often make decisions in light of their relationships, even if it means hurting themselves. For that reason, teachers must be cognizant of the negative effects thoughtless, ineffective praise can have on girls.

Since all students who do not suffer from cognitive disorders can learn, when a teacher attributes success only to a student's ability and not to the student's willingness to persist in the face of challenging material, and the girl believes she has no natural mathematical ability, where is she to go to get some? Do they sell math ability where you live?

Summary

In this chapter, we have explored the unique perspective of what *not* to do when managing children. We have approached this discussion from two viewpoints. Our first outlook recognizes that everyone makes honest mistakes. These are an inevitable part of life. Actually, they provide "teachable moments," as they allow us the opportunity to share with our students what to do when you get it wrong. Teachers are strongly urged to accept responsibility for their error, fix it, and keep moving. Students do not lose respect for teachers who demonstrate integrity; students normally comply with those teachers' directions because they recognize that they are being taught by someone who is honest.

On the other hand, there are mistakes that are neither honorable nor fixable. Most children survive both the error and the teacher who made it, but not without some scars. Such teachers are notorious for their narcissistic behavior, their lack of empathy, and their disinterest in the welfare of their students. They may fool themselves into believing that they are helping students; however, those of us who have been their victims know better. Perhaps in other occupations, these people would do a fine job; however, they should never have become teachers.

In contrast to the guidelines for effective praise, which help students attain and maintain success, Brophy (1981) provides a list of guidelines for ineffective praise, which has equal utility in showing us what *not* to say to children. Ineffective praise actually keeps children from knowing what they did or can do to achieve success; it is distracting, meaningless, and at times even detrimental to a child's chance of achieving mastery.

Theodore Roosevelt, in his speech at the Sorbonne, on April 23, 1910, captured the critical difference between the teacher who does not care enough to try and the teacher who tries hard, makes mistakes, and tries again:

The credit belongs to the man who is actually in the arena . . . who strives valiantly, who errs and comes up short again and again, because there is no effort without error or shortcoming, but who knows the great enthusiasms, the great devotions, who spends himself for a worthy cause; who, at the best, knows, in the end, the triumph of high achievement, and who, at the worst, if he fails, at least he fails while daring greatly, so that his place shall never be with those cold and timid souls who knew neither victory nor defeat (The Man in the Arena—April 23, 1910—Theodore Roosevelt Speeches-Roosevelt Almanac).

8

Practices of Reflective Managers

Nothing will work unless you do

Maya Angelou

Nothing we do is as personal, private, and rather intimate and yet simultaneously as open to public scrutiny as teaching. When you have made a meaningful and genuine connection with your students, the climate in your classroom is rich with caring undertones. There is a tacit understanding between you and your students that something rare and wonderful is happening. Many teachers could tell you about their moments like this, but the ones that count will be your own. When they happen, and they will, record them in your journal.

Just as I am sure that you will have these precious moments, I know you will have times when you wonder why you decided to become a teacher. Usually, those moments come after you lost control and some child or children took over the class. This happens to everyone, and it is always an unnerving experience. Again, when this happens, you need to record what you think happened. However, interesting new research (Janssen, de Hullu, & Tigelaar, 2008) indicates that student teachers who reflected on positive experiences have more optimistic feelings, create more innovative solutions to their challenges, and are more highly motivated to implement their ideas than those who reflect only after problematic experiences.

We have discussed the importance of keeping a reflection journal to help improve your teaching skills. We believe that reflection helps teachers to maintain success and diminish errors. However, in a study of the literature on reflective practices, researchers Marcos, Sanchez, and Telema (2011) found that there is a lack of agreement about how teachers should conduct reflection and about the usefulness of the wide variety of types of reflection. Many proposals lack empirical and theoretical support. Perhaps that is why there is so much anecdotal and descriptive information offered without empirical justification for the advice. Nevertheless, for more than two decades researchers have explored the role of reflection in teacher training (e.g., Calderhead, 1989; Hatton & Smith, 1995; Zeichner et al., 1987, as cited in Kreber, 2006). In addition, veteran teachers are reminded frequently of the importance of reflecting on their teaching practices (e.g., Brookfield, 1991, 1995; Cranton, 1998; Ramsden, 1992; Schön, 1995, as cited in Kreber, 2006). Although, as has been noted, the process of reflection itself remains poorly understood, reflection is still considered a key ingredient to success in the teaching and learning process.

In Chapter 4, the first chapter on reflection, we learned how to become a reflective planner. In this chapter, we will be discussing how to become a reflective classroom manager. We will review the basic ingredients of effective classroom management: rules, routines, and boundaries. We will re-examine the benefits of appropriate teacher–student relationships. Next, we will consider the importance of your dressing and acting like a professional. We will review the essential relationship between Ginott's (1972) teachings and Brophy's (1981) guidelines for effective praise. We will review what we have discovered about how the brain learns, and we will examine "Harriet's Helpful Hints." After that, we will consider fixable versus egregious errors and the guidelines for ineffective praise. You will be asked to respond to several scenarios that are designed to help you think through difficult management decisions. Finally, you will be asked to respond to the Template for Reflection—Management.

LET'S REFLECT ON WHAT WE HAVE LEARNED

By nature, I am a very reflective person. I understood a lot about myself when I was very young. For example, I have never been tall—really. I thought I was tall, but in the fifth grade, when I looked at the rest of the kids in my class, I got the feeling that I am not a tall person. (I never said I was a bright child, just reflective.) You may not think this is a salient detail, but when you need to get the attention of a lot of tall people, you realize that tall has its advantages. Therefore, I had to learn a lot about managing people from a vertically challenged position.

I do not like to raise my voice; I knew that it was a sign of rage in my home, and I had my fill of enraged adults by the time I entered kindergarten. I knew I would not use volume to manage students when I became a teacher, and I always wanted to be a teacher. Finally, I suspected that my talents as a storyteller and my sense of humor might be my strongest assets as a teacher. Therefore, I reasoned, I can't look down on my students from an intimidating height, and I refuse to yell; I will have to use my skills and assets to convince my future students that they will want to listen to me. As I grew older, I developed my deadly teacher "Did you do that and expect to live for long?" glare.

It has been my lifelong custom to look at life through the lens of, How will this (whatever this is) help or hurt me as a teacher? Now that you are ready to begin or are well along in your teaching career, we are going to examine what we have learned about effective management techniques so that these skills will help you to become the kind of teacher you want to be.

Rules, Routines, and Boundaries

This story simultaneously illustrates rules, routines, and boundaries. Use it to help you reflect on how they relate to each other. This event took place the day after Thanksgiving break when I was observed teaching the first cohort of the All Stars. I was quite convinced after we left school on the Wednesday before Thanksgiving that the children would come back to school after the holiday suffering from the contrast between how good they finally felt about school and the complete disappointment they would feel when they recognized that nothing about their home lives had changed. Unfortunately, I had underestimated the depths of their despair. The morning after the holiday was a disaster for which I had not adequately prepared. My supervisor sat in the middle of the room as I valiantly tried to get the students to work as hard as they had before the break.

After a few minutes of frustration and exhaustion, one of the most talented young women I have ever taught stood up and said, "I am going to F-cking Time-Out!" Time-Out was a space I had created where students could go to settle down or where either teacher could send them if we felt that they needed a few minutes to regroup. Clearly, the student had broken a rule by using profanity. However, she did follow our routine by self-selecting the use of Time-Out when she knew she could no longer cope with the demands of our class. She was trying to stay within our boundaries by respecting other students' safety, since she had an incredible temper, and by taking herself into Time-Out, she was displaying remarkable self-restraint.

You may not agree with how I responded to this child, but I knew that she had been abandoned by her mother, had been sent to live in various foster homes, and was currently living with a relative who was outspoken about wanting to send her back to the Department of Social Services. I went to speak to my student and said, "Jackie, I am so proud of you for taking yourself out of class and putting yourself into Time-Out. Tomorrow, could you just go to Time-Out and not to F-cking Time-Out?" She laughed and promised never to do that again (and she never did), and she got the bigger message that I was proud of her actions, but not her language. In this case, as in all others, the rules, routines, and boundaries were designed to protect each child and teach each one self-restraint. Normally, no one is allowed to use profanity in my class. However, everyone understood why Jackie did not get sent to the office that day. No student complained afterward that Jackie said a bad word and "got away with it." The students knew that no one had had much of a holiday, and hers was probably the worst of all. By Thanksgiving, we had become a caring community of learners who had added compassion and empathy to our English and geography skills.

As you prepare for your own students, you have to think about the management system you will use with your students. According to Freiberg and Lamb (2009), the lack of discipline in U.S. schools continues to be one of the public's top educational concerns. The traditional, top-down, teacher-directed rule by edict is clearly not working anymore. However, years of research indicate that a pro-social, person-centered form of management may provide alternatives that struggling learners can respond to successfully. In this model, there is an emphasis on social-emotional connections, school connectedness, positive school and classroom climate, and student self-discipline.

Even in this model, you must select a few rules you believe will be required to keep order in your classroom. Remember rules come with consequences. For the most part, a student who breaks a rule must experience a consequence. As a result of your students' maturity, you can include your students in determining how they can resolve the problems they have caused.

Next, every class needs daily routines to get through the everyday experiences of classroom life. Think through how you want your papers distributed, your books handed out, your students to enter and leave your room, and so on. Observe teachers who seem to have seamless control over their students, and try to replicate their routines.

Boundaries are less concrete, but they are very important. Children violate their teacher's and fellow students' boundaries when they go into their teacher's and others' belongings and when they make other children feel unsafe. When the teacher does not create safe and secure boundaries, children feel anxious and test the teacher's boundaries constantly. Everything must be explicit, transparent, and consistent for children to feel safe and secure. This is especially true for struggling learners, who may have no other safe haven than the one you provide.

Room Arrangement

An orderly classroom has a positive impact on students because it represents the teacher's high expectations and endorses the importance of pride in work well done (Linsin, 2011). Once your students have arrived and have started to create their own work, the room décor should feature their creations, not yours. However, when we talk about room arrangement and classroom management, we are really discussing your ability to see and get close to every student in your class. You never want to be in a position where you are so physically removed that you cannot intervene on behalf of a student who needs your help.

As children grow older, their need for personal space increases. As much as possible, you need to be sensitive about giving each child personal space for thinking and working. A four-student team arrangement works well because there is only one person next to any student, and even when two children face each other, there are two desks between them. The trick is to arrange the teams so that there is adequate space between all the teams. You cannot stretch your room or build a loft, but you can relocate your desk to the back of the room. You can always seek help from staff members who are more visual than you to help you rearrange your room to free up more space. Reflect about how to use the space you have, don't fuss about what you don't have, and you will get a lot more accomplished.

Positive Student–Teacher Relationships

Some students will be absolutely transparent to you. You will understand them intuitively because you have what is known as a temperamental fit. They are sufficiently like you and others you know that you don't have to work hard to predict what they need or what to do to help them succeed. Others, however, will be an enigma. They will remind you of people you have known who never made any sense to you, and you will feel awkward and unsure of how to operate around them. It is the second case that we need to concentrate on.

If the child to whom you do not relate well has a difficult temperament, she will need some extra time from you. You may be just as mysterious to the child as the child is to you. First, spend a few minutes talking to the child. Learn what interests the child; try to discover if you have any common hobbies or talents. In a recent longitudinal study of student–teacher relationships, children in grades 4, 5, and 6 were measured for difficult temperaments and risky behavior; the results suggested clearly that closer student–teacher relationships were associated with less risky behavior (Moritz-Rudasill, Reio, Stipanovic, & Taylor, 2010). It appears that present relationships with teachers can mediate students' future behaviors.

The important message for the child is to let her know that you are interested in her well-being and genuinely want to know what you can do to learn more about her interests, hobbies, likes, and dislikes. As long as there is no hidden agenda, your sincerity will provide you access to each child you teach. When you manage your students, your relationship is the underpinning of the trust between you. Keep in mind that struggling learners have been lied to and betrayed by many adults, and they will test you many times before they trust you. Think about how to be patient, transparent, and consistent, and you will do well.

Be a Professional

Teaching is both a vocation and a profession. It is a vocation in that it calls on us to use our aptitude, talent, and natural ability to help children learn. It is a profession because it requires years of education to earn our certification and additional course work in order to earn either a master's degree or a master's equivalency. As you reflect about your self-respect as a teacher, remember that it is demonstrated by the way you act, dress, and speak.

Ginott and Brophy

Using elegantly simple models, both Ginott (1972) and Brophy (1981) taught parents and teachers how to make positive connections with children. Ginott's (1972) brilliant analysis of what had been keeping children from processing some feedback led him to advise adults to "Describe the behavior, not the child." Brophy's (1981) guidelines for effective praise are similarly uncomplicated directives. These guidelines help teachers to make authentic comments based on students' performance, effort, and progress across time. Teachers need to use Brophy's guidelines for effective praise if they want their students to be able to recognize the connection between effort and success. Effective praise helps children understand specifically what they have done to attain their success. Effective praise helps children accept their accomplishments in light of past efforts and/or recognize current success in terms of the difficulty, for the child, of the current task. When you reflect on your management skills with children, you must consider your ability to provide positive, effective feedback that describes only the child's behavior. This is very difficult, and it requires all teachers to think carefully before they speak.

Brain Research

The field of neuroscience is growing rapidly, and teachers are the fortunate recipients of the work of researchers in this discipline. Not only do these new findings inform our instructional decisions, but also they help us to manage our students' behaviors and to see why, at key developmental stages, different management strategies are particularly significant. When you reflect on your management skills, it is important to review the data regarding your children's ages and expected brain developmental stage.

Current brain research tells us that students retain what they have learned when the learning is associated with strong, positive feelings (Willis, 2007). Therefore, it seems counterproductive to create a classroom environment that leaves students feeling anxious and tense. Neuroimaging shows us exactly what happens in such circumstances. Using positron emission tomography and magnetic resonance imaging, neuroscientists have been able to demonstrate that "when stress activates the brain's affective filters, information flow to the higher cognitive networks is limited and the learning process grinds to a halt" (Willis, 2007, p. 1).

When we prepare lessons and classroom management strategies, neuroscience has some practical guidelines to offer. Students learn best when the information is perceived to be relevant, when it is presented through novel and stimulating activities, and when the classroom is perceived to be safe and enjoyable (Willis, 2007).

Harriet's Helpful Hints

I learned each of "Harriet's Helpful Hints" through real-life experience. For example, I had only been teaching for two and a half years when I started working at Aberdeen Middle School, and I was anxious to improve my skills. Most of the seventh-grade teachers were grouped in an experimental team that year; it was considered an honor to be a member of the team. The other new seventh-grade teacher and I taught the rest of the seventh graders.

As you read my story, think about the people who are helping you now. What are you learning from them? In my case, at team meetings, when plans were made for the next phase of the curriculum, I listened very carefully. I paid careful attention to how the teachers I admired on the team made instructional decisions, and during that process, I realized that it was their attention to detail that helped me to see both the big and the little pictures concurrently.

I don't remember the name of the game we were going to teach the children to play, but it was designed to help the students understand the connection between goods and services, production and distribution, and supply and demand. Normally, that could have been a very dreary unit, but the game made the concepts very clear and interesting. The students understood the connections in a very sophisticated manner after they went through several cycles of the game.

It was the team's planning and management decisions that helped this event and me to be successful. The veteran teachers left nothing to chance. Every child was placed on a team based on the child's skills, attitudes, and work habits. Each routine needed for the game was discussed. In addition to those specific plans, the team helped the new teachers to understand the goal of the game, the strategies we would use, and the assessments that would follow. I may not remember the specifics of the game accurately, but I will never forget the training I received from those master teachers I will always honor.

Fixable Versus Egregious Errors

When we explored relevant issues regarding mistakes that teachers make, we found that there are two categories of errors: unintentional mistakes that can be fixed and misjudgments that can put children's safety at risk. In the first case, no child is ever harmed. The teacher is normally well intentioned, but, as a result of a natural misstep, fails to see or account for a problem. The issue is handled with grace and honesty. The children using observational learning benefit from a model who demonstrates that when an adult makes a mistake, she takes full responsibility, corrects the problem, and continues on.

In the case of poor judgment, a person who is supposed to be responsible for the social, emotional, and physical welfare of the students makes a decision that is in her best interests despite what might happen to the children. Such choices demonstrate imprudent thinking and a lack of maturity. We know of only a fraction of the problems caused by such individuals; unfortunately, children under their care could tell us about many more such incidents.

When you reflect after a difficult day with your students, be honest with yourself. Did you do anything that might have put the children at risk? Did you do anything that might have betrayed the children's trust in you? Only honest reflection will help you to remedy the problem and to understand the change in dynamics that occurred between you and your students.

Struggling Learners and the Effects of Teacher Quality

Children's emotional risk at the hands of a poor teacher is one of the least studied variables among the many that are considered when researchers evaluate teachers' performance. This is especially important in an age of high-stakes testing, which has made teacher performance a topic of intense scrutiny. Several important research teams in this hotly contested field are trying to determine the most important factor influencing student performance. King-Rice (2003) examined findings from such eminent researchers in the field as Rivkin, Hanushke, and Kain (1998) and determined: "Teacher quality is the most important school-related factor influencing student achievement. They conclude from their analysis of 400,000 students in 3,000 schools that while school quality is an important determinant of student achievement, the most important predictor is teacher quality" (p. 5).

Although such issues as teacher experience, preparation, and certification are fairly easily examined, teachers' ability to cope with their personal problems, emotional maturity, and ability to control their anger are not as easily subject to research analysis. Anyone who has lived through a year with a teacher who uses bullying techniques knows that the negative effects of those practices can last a very long time.

Let us put this discussion of teacher quality into the context of our book. We have been concentrating on the needs of struggling learners. Since there are so few rewards for good teaching, some administrators have used attractive schedules with highly motivated students as one form of compensation for those teachers who have earned their respect. However, this practice burdens those students who need the best teachers: struggling learners (Silva, 2009). Unfortunately, this "reward" system is viewed by some as a rite of passage that requires newcomers and novices to endure being placed with struggling learners until they have earned the right to work with more academically oriented students. This unwritten policy is not lost on the struggling learners or their parents, who already view schools with mistrust (Sagor, 1993). Since classroom management requires mutual trust among students, parents, and teachers, using the "good teachers get good students" system only reinforces the alienation that already exists among these key players.

Guidelines for Ineffective Praise

You have just been observed by your mentor teacher. The following is her feedback to you: "You did a nice job. Your plan was nice. The children were good, and you never yelled at anyone. I liked the way you wore your hair today. Nice job!" What did you learn about the quality of your lesson? Did you teach the children anything? How do you know? Were the children on task? How do you know? Were your strategies effective? Did your assessments measure your goal? What does "nice" mean? When you reflect on this feedback, what have you been told that will help you to improve? That's right, absolutely nothing. Ineffective praise does not give any information; that's why it's ineffective.

When You Reflect

Everyone makes mistakes. Honest errors do not affect the quality of your work or indicate a weakness of your will. You can take the mistake and turn it into a learning experience just by modeling how an adult takes responsibility for her actions. On the other hand, if you routinely find yourself angry at one child, in every class, every year that you teach, the problem may not rest with the children. If you really want to be a good teacher, please think about all the children you have singled out, and never do that again. Instead, do what you need to do to help yourself resolve your problem. If you teach only to get a paycheck, please consider other forms of employment.

YOUR TURN

SCENARIO 1 SUZY SYMPATHY   Many young people become elementary school teachers because they truly love children. However, as we have learned, love is only part of what anyone needs in order to become an effective teacher. In this case, Suzy Sympathy was assigned to do her student teaching in a school serving a low socioeconomic community. She did not like to reprimand the children because she felt sorry for them. Read what happened and help her to improve her management skills.

Ms. Sympathy's second formal observation went very poorly. Her supervisor was appalled by the children's lack of respect for Ms. Sympathy. They behaved only when her mentor intervened. At that point, the children settled down immediately. When Ms. Sympathy resumed control of the class, the children resorted to talking when she was teaching, playing with the items on their desks, and getting out of their seats at will. The problem got even worse when Ms. Sympathy brought all the children to the carpet for large-group instruction. Children crawled around to get to each other, fights broke out, and no child learned what Ms. Sympathy had so carefully planned to teach. At one point during the lesson, Ms. Sympathy told two children who were arguing to stop fussing. However, when they did not stop, she did not do anything else to intervene.

Her supervisor asked her during debriefing what else she could have done to stop the children's constant arguing. Ms. Sympathy replied that she hated to fuss at the children because they have so little. She believed her mentor teacher kept the children under such tight control that Ms. Sympathy thought they needed to experience freedom. The supervisor from the college gave Ms. Sympathy fair warning that, unless her classroom management skills improved, she would not receive a successful grade for her student teaching experience. She has come to you for help.

Discuss the following with her:

1. Is Ms. Sympathy being fair to the children? Why? Explain this to her.
2. How will Ms. Sympathy's current performance affect her students' ability to master content?

3. Specifically, what is missing in her management skills?
4. Where should she begin to remedy her problems?
5. Do you think that Ms. Sympathy has the capacity to become a good teacher? Explain.

SCENARIO 2 STAN SARCASM   Mr. Sarcasm wants to teach middle school math. He has a wonderful middle school demeanor. He is funny, he laughs a lot, and he is generally easygoing. However, he expects all his students to understand math concepts, and when they don't, he uses sarcasm. No matter how many times he has been told that children rarely interpret sarcasm accurately, he is convinced that in his class "It's my way or no way." His supervisor is not convinced he should be given a class of his own, but there is always a shortage of certified math teachers who want to teach middle school, so in some schools, he might be given more chances than he deserves.

During his last observation, he pointed at one child and said, "Everybody else gets it. Why don't you?" Later in the class, he called out the names of three male students who were not working quietly and asked each one to stand up and explain the new math problem to the class. When the students could not explain the problem, he said, "Next time, keep quiet, and maybe you'll learn something."

During the debriefing session, the mentor teacher and the college supervisor praised Mr. Sarcasm for the many excellent features of the lesson, but they both spoke out strongly against some of his negative classroom management techniques. Mr. Sarcasm was furious at what the two professionals said to him, and he stormed out of the meeting.

You are Mr. Sarcasm's roommate; he has just told you what happened. Help him understand the following:

1. What is wrong with using sarcasm as feedback to a child?
2. What is wrong with having a child stand up and explain something to the class that he clearly does not understand?
3. How does his "It's my way or no way" attitude make it difficult to help him?
4. What does he need to work on to improve his work with children?
5. What does he need to work on to improve his work with adults?
6. What should he do the following day?

SCENARIO 3 PEGGY POOP   When I began thinking about writing this book, I thought back on all the student teachers I have mentored, supervised, and advised. I have lost count of the many wonderful men and women it has been my privilege and honor to know in that capacity. However, one student teacher will always be with me. After you read her story, tell me what you would have done in my place.

The school was Joppatowne High School. Our principal was Doris Williams. I was teaching a class of Certificate of Merit (CM) ninth-grade students. I don't think that category is still in use, but students who elected or who were nominated to take CM courses were given more arduous course work during ninth and tenth grades in preparation for Advanced Placement courses offered in eleventh and twelfth grades. This class was made up of exceptionally hard-working students, and they were a delight to teach. We followed the ninth-grade curriculum, but they also had vocabulary exercises, additional reading requirements, and more-sophisticated writing assignments to enrich their age-appropriate curriculum.

My student teacher was teaching *The Odyssey* to the class. She had progressed to the point where I sat outside the room so that the students were under her control. I did not completely trust her judgment, so I always sat close to my room in order to intervene in case there was a problem. One day the class was reading about the time when Odysseus and his crew were in the land of the Laestrygonians. As you may remember, the Laestrygonians were cannibals who devoured Odysseus' crew. Only Odysseus was spared, and he sailed on to the island of Aeaea, where the goddess Circe lived.

The students were following the plot line and enjoying how the fates were treating Odysseus. I do not now understand the reason, nor will I ever, but my student teacher thought she needed to add spontaneity to her plan. She said to a multicultural class of very bright students, "Do you think the Black sailors tasted the same as the White sailors?"

In an instant, I heard screams coming from my classroom. The bell rang, and my students, who were always so pleasant, came storming out of the room. Immediately, I asked the student teacher what had happened. She looked a little upset and said, "I might have said something wrong." I asked, "What did you say?" She repeated her dreadful question to me. I was horrified. I immediately took several steps to remedy the situation.

Before you respond to me, I want you to think about why I included this example in the section on management. Then I want you to write me a letter outlining all the steps you would have taken in my place.

1. Start with the students. What should I have done to resolve the issue with them?
2. Do I need to inform the principal? Why?
3. Do I need to inform the college? Why?
4. What should I say to the student teacher?
5. What kind of grade should I give to the student teacher?
6. What kind of reference should I give to the student teacher? (Your mentor will be asked for a reference every time you apply for a job.)

Template 8.1 provides a framework that you can use to reflect on classroom management. When you have completed filling it out, paying close attention to those items that resonate the most with you, return to Template 4.3 in Chapter 4 to see what you can add now to make your first try more meaningful. I suggest that you continue this process when you complete the reflections listed in Chapters 11 and 14.

Template 8.1

Reflection—Management

1. What are the essential differences among rules, routines, and boundaries?
2. Why do you need each?
3. How do you teach rules? Routines? Boundaries?
4. When do you teach rules? Routines? Boundaries?
5. What are some of the fundamental questions you need to ask yourself after you have set up your room?
6. What is the fundamental difference between effective and ineffective praise?
7. Are you using effective praise to help your struggling learners recognize the connection between effort and success? How do you know?
8. Are you using effective praise to make sure that your students understand their progress over time? In light of the difficulty of the task? How do you know?
9. Why is it important to have an appropriate teacher–student relationship with your students?
10. How do you define classroom climate? How does it affect classroom management?
11. How can you tell when the climate has changed in your room? What should you do?
12. What message do you give your students when you dress like a professional? Why is that important?
13. What is the significance of describing the behavior and not the child?
14. Are you listening to yourself carefully to be sure you are describing the behavior and not the child?
15. What do you do when you make a mistake in front of the class? Why?
16. When you make decisions, whose interests come first? How do you know?
17. Are you comfortable with the quality of your teaching? Explain.
18. What are you willing to do to improve?
19. What does current brain research tell you about the types of management goals you should be using with your students?
20. Does your reflection journal indicate that you are becoming more aware of the intricacies of teaching and learning?

Summary

Classroom management has very little to do with controlling children so that they never misbehave. That is neither realistic nor healthy. Classroom management is the art and science of creating a classroom environment that is conducive to learning. Designed to respect the needs, rights, and welfare of all children, good management strategies are healthy procedures that support students' growth and academic achievement. Good management techniques help students to learn self-restraint so that they can then manage their behavior in order to reach their goals.

Leaders in the field of classroom management agree that when teachers treat children with respect, children learn how to become respectful. Using Brophy's (1981) guidelines for effective praise and Ginott's (1972) seminal work, we have learned that giving children specific information regarding their behavior, not the content of their character, can help them to duplicate success and decrease errors. I know from research and over 40 years of experience that even struggling learners can learn to trust adults who are transparent, honest, and consistent. Teachers who take responsibility for their mistakes, share a good laugh with their students, and take a genuine interest in their students' well-being become trusted adults.

On the other hand, some people enter the field for reasons of their own. Believing that teaching is an easy job that provides a comfortable lifestyle with an effortless schedule, many find themselves in a world that requires more from them than they are prepared to give. Children suffer the most from this situation.

We are fortunate to be teaching during a time when more is being discovered about how the brain learns. We can target our routines and boundaries to be congruent with the developmental path our students are experiencing. In addition, we can be more effective in supporting our struggling learners because our interventions are appropriate and well planned.

Test results in urban schools indicate that the convergence of multiple factors such as poor teachers, inadequate resources, and insufficient parental support keep some children from having much hope for success. Nevertheless, highly effective teachers can have a powerful influence on any child in almost any setting. We know that highly effective teachers believe that, since they can teach, their children can learn. Their routines are evident; their rules exist, but not in great numbers; and their boundaries, which are designed to protect the physical and emotional needs of children, are in place and will not move. Those teachers are my heroes. Building on what Christa McAuliffe said in 1985, they "touch the future; [they] teach" ("Brain Quote," n.d.).

Part Three

Instruction

Chapter 9   Guidelines for Effective Instruction

Chapter 10 Discovery Learning

Chapter 11 Practices of Reflective Teachers

Guidelines for Effective Instruction

Teachers are expected to reach unattainable goals with inadequate tools.
The miracle is that at times they accomplish this impossible task.

HAIM GINOTT

We have created careful plans for the first week of school. We have prepared our classrooms so they are inviting and well organized, and we are reasonably sure every student will be within easy reach. We have studied the basic principles of effective management strategies, and we believe that we are finally ready to teach our students.

Now that we are ready to begin our instruction, we will review several lesson plans. We will look at a plan that meets all of our criteria for excellence. We will also review a plan written by a novice to see how it can be improved. Each is filled with important examples of what makes teaching the rewarding experience that keeps us young at heart and lifelong learners.

Next, we will review a lesson plan for conducting a worthwhile classroom discussion. Although on the surface they appear simple, productive discussions require careful planning, effective strategies, and the teacher's good judgment. Finally, we will examine a reading lesson created for struggling learners in a primary class. We will unpack the lesson together to be sure that the plan has accounted for the instructional triangle, the Dimensions of Learning (DOLs), and what we now know about how the brain learns when children are 6 to 10 years of age.

A VETERAN'S PLAN

One of the best lessons I ever taught took place years ago when I was teaching Harper Lee's (1960) *To Kill a Mockingbird* (*TKAM*). Currently, the novel is taught in the ninth grade, but years ago, before our statewide curriculum was put in place, teachers had much more flexibility and discretion about which novels would be taught in each grade. I chose to teach the novel to a group of seniors. This class had been with me since they were in ninth grade. They had moved together from middle school to Joppatowne High School (JHS) because they had a history of being struggling readers. As the JHS reading specialist, I had a lot of options regarding their reading selections. By the time they were seniors, their reading skills and their general maturity had improved dramatically. However, many of these students were still having difficulty analyzing ideas from a different perspective.

As the hero of the novel, Atticus Finch revealed one of its themes: "You never really understand a person until you consider things from his point of view—until you climb into his skin and walk around in it" (p. 30). I believed that for their last experience with formal education, it was important for me to try to teach my students empathy, the importance of understanding someone else's perspective, and the critical role of acceptance of people's differences in order to live in a world of tolerance and peace. Table 9.1 is the lesson plan I used.

When each student came in the room, I handed him/her a folded piece of paper. After all the students had read the drill, they unfolded their papers and began answering their drill questions (see Table 9.1). Since the majority of the students were African-American, it was inevitable that one or two of the students would have to answer as either Mayella or Bob Ewell. One of the factors that made this lesson so memorable was the young man who had to take the role of Mayella Ewell. I could not have chosen a better scenario.

My student Earl was the most resistant of all the males in the class at trying to see anything from a female's point of view. He said he didn't have any White friends, and he befriended me only because I had been his English teacher for 4 years. Naturally, his team chose him to answer the drill question in character.

I don't remember who the #3 person was on his team, but after Earl answered, "What kind of man is Atticus?" in a falsetto voice and said that her daddy told her that Atticus is a bad man who hangs out with no-goods like other lawyers, judges, and other people who can read, the class was on the floor with laughter. He really helped me to set the stage for what was to follow. The other teams' choices were just as willing to answer in character and start thinking from a different person's perspective.

I drew Scout's name. The class knew who I was almost immediately. First, I answered the drill questions in character. Next, I used the interview questions in Table 9.2 with a student I had preselected. Again answering in character, I tried to build a framework for the rubric that I knew we were going to create.

As we created the rubric, which was to be the scoring guide we would use to evaluate the students' answers, it was clear to me that the students understood the importance of using the text to support their answers, avoiding their own feelings when answering in character, and checking for accuracy in terms of how the character would have answered the question.

TABLE 9.1	**Lesson Plan**

Lesson Title: Analyzing Perspectives
Lesson Unit: *To Kill a Mockingbird (TKAM)*

GOAL	Use literature to understand human interactions—DOL 1 Seek accuracy, be open-minded, persist—DOL 5
Lesson Objective	As a result of today's lesson, students will be able to analyze the perspective of the characters in *TKAM*.
Materials Needed	Text Names of characters folded up Placemat Interview question
Warm-Up Time:	When each student walks in the room, s/he will be given a name of one of the major characters in the novel. As that character, answer the warm-up 1. What really happened to Mayella? 2. What kind of man is Tom Robinson? 3. What kind of man is Atticus? 4. Who is Boo? What is he like?
Motivation Time:	Each team must pick the most interesting member to answer the warm-up question in character. Team member #3 has to explain why the person was chosen.
Guided Practice Time:	Mrs. Porton will select a folded paper and will answer the drill questions in character. Each team has to decide the following: 1. Who is Mrs. P.? How do you know? 2. Did Mrs. P. answer the questions accurately in character? How do you know? 3. Does Mrs. P. represent this character's attitude toward the other characters in the story accurately? How do you know? Next, Mrs. P. will answer a few of the interview questions in character with a preselected partner. Using the guided practice as our model, we will create a rubric for accuracy. The rubric will emphasize use of the text, each student's ability to answer questions from the character's perspective, and each student's willingness to forego his/her own perceptions in favor of those of the character s/he is representing.
Independent Practice Time:	Working with a teammate, each student will be interviewed in character. The partners will switch on a signal from Mrs. P. When both partners have answered all the questions, each team will select the person who did the best job using the rubric the class has just created. The entire class will watch and use the rubric to grade the four students who have been chosen to perform.
Assessment Time:	Each student will hand in this question in character for the day's assessment: Should Mayella be brought to trial for perjury?
Closure Time:	Answer in character: Who is the worst person in the novel?
Homework	Write 5 questions in character.

TABLE 9.2 Interview Questions

Directions: You will select one person on your team to be your partner. You must answer your interview questions in character, just as Mrs. Porton did. Remember everybody in Maycomb knows everyone! You will be given a few minutes to create three questions for your partner before you are told to begin. Mrs. Porton will stop by each pair to observe and evaluate each team for accuracy. Being open-minded, seeking accuracy, and persisting are part of your classroom points for today.

1. Who is Dill and why is he in Maycomb?
2. Why aren't women allowed to serve on the jury?
3. What qualities of being a lady does Scout lack?
4. Evaluate each person's job performance: Judge Taylor, Sheriff Tate, Atticus.
5. Define courage.
6. When Jem and Scout visited Old Sarum, how were they treated?
7. Whatever happened to Boo Radley? Bob Ewell?
8. Create your own question.
9. Create your own question.
10. Create your own question.

I had created the interview questions for their independent practice based on situations that had taken place during the novel and those that could have taken place. In order to answer in character, students had to reason in character. By the end of independent practice, I had listened to every pair of students, and I was convinced that every student had developed the ability to suspend his/her own perspective, if only briefly, in order to see a situation from another person's point of view.

The results of the assessment question verified my anecdotal data. All of the Ewells believed that Mayella was innocent of perjury; the judge felt she could stand trial, but would be acquitted; the Robinson family felt the same; and so on. No matter what the student's race, when the student answered the question, the answer in character was accurate.

Does This Meet Our Standards for a Successful Lesson?

I am sure you recognize that my goal, strategies, and assessment were tightly aligned. In addition, the students were very caught up in the strategies of the lesson, and I did not have to redirect one student during the entire class. Sometimes I had to quiet active voices so that all the students could hear each other, but that's because there was so much enthusiasm in the students' voices that the volume had to be readjusted. The students accepted the premise that what we were learning was more than just a literary skill; it was a life skill. Their animation and enthusiasm served as a catalyst for an incredibly productive and enjoyable experience.

Why Did It Work?

One of the premises of using cooperative learning groups (see Chapter 3) is that students learn best from modeled behavior, especially if the model is similar to the observer and has admired status (Bandura, 1977). In our teams, the models are other students, and although the status characteristics may not always be immediately apparent to an outsider, the students have their own system for identifying and granting privilege.

According to Huitt (2004), the theory of observational learning requires teachers to be sure that all students are paying attention to the model and, specifically, what the model is doing according to the lesson plan. Earl was an important factor in the success of my plan because he had status in my class, he participated appropriately, and the other students paid close attention to what he did. As a result of his performance, they were willing to follow in his footsteps. Therefore, Earl set the stage for Bandura's first step in learning from the model. He was so interesting that the other students paid *attention* to him. Next, the students had to *retain* his performance by rehearsing in their minds how they would sound when it was their turn to speak in character. Each student was given the opportunity to *reproduce* what s/he had observed during the independent practice portion of the lesson. Ultimately, each member of the team under Earl's leadership was *motivated* and performed as expected (Huitt, 2004).

The team serves as both an encouraging unit and a filter. If the student is performing up to expectations, the team can reward the student by selecting him for the demonstration to the class. However, if the student's performance is substandard, the team can use negative reinforcements to change the student's effort/presentation/willingness to participate. The force that the team can render is far greater than any that the teacher has available. Assuming that teams have been trained well, students are never bullied, just encouraged to do their work appropriately.

What Can Teachers Do?

We know that struggling learners do not believe there is a connection between effort and success because they do not believe they can control what happens to them. Bandura (1989) found that, "among the mechanisms of personal agency none is more central or pervasive than people's beliefs about their capabilities to exercise control over events that affect their lives.... Self-efficacy beliefs affect thought patterns that may be self-aiding or self-hindering" (p. 1175). Therefore, as teachers of struggling learners, it is our job to help them develop positive beliefs about their own self-efficacy. Although they come to us believing in their own incompetence and entrenched in self-doubt, we can provide "cognitive simulations in which individuals visualize executing activities skillfully" in order to "enhance subsequent performance" (Bandura, 1989, p. 1176). Their own visualizations are normally negative. In their mind's eye, they see themselves failing. As a rule, they dwell on what will go wrong, rather than on how well they will succeed.

It is through cooperative learning groups that struggling learners can begin to reshape their belief about their capacity to succeed. The models of other students who are like them and are now doing well in school in what they perceive to be rigorous course work can help reframe any student's belief system. Struggling learners can learn that, if they pay attention to the task at hand, accept feedback, put forth sufficient effort, and persist, they can succeed at any task. Their new self-dialog can help to create a sense of resilience, which is needed to sustain effort in the face of real-life difficulties and setbacks.

To Kill a Mockingbird and Self-Efficacy

After Earl clearly demonstrated that it was possible to look at the world through Mayella Ewell's eyes and not lose his dignity, the rest of the students were willing to try to visualize themselves being successful in front of their peers at the same activity. Please review the plan. You will see that scaffolding, the incremental help effective teachers provide for their students, was provided prior to each new activity. According to Vygotsky (1978), "The scaffolds facilitate a learner's ability to build on prior knowledge and internalize new information" (as cited in Ozan & Kesim, 2011, p. 1). In addition, the warm-up and the interview questions included a mixture of simple declarative through higher-level thought questions. Students who were more sophisticated in their understanding of character development had the opportunity to answer more rigorous questions, and students who were less skilled could participate successfully, but at their own level.

Next, students' positive self-efficacy was encouraged when team members selected individuals to answer warm-up questions for the class and others to answer some of the interview questions for the class. The selected students had the same time, opportunity, and support as every other student, but their persistence, willingness to be open-minded, and creativity allowed them to be cited for excellence by their peers. Finally, the presence of a caring adult in a classroom that supported and respected each student helped to reduce the effects of the negative variables that had so adversely impacted the students in my class.

My senior class that year formed the nucleus of a program that I called "Porton's Partners." This program paired incoming at-risk ninth graders with seniors I thought would have a positive influence on vulnerable ninth graders. Almost all of the senior partners came from the class you have just read about. They sat with their ninth graders each week and helped them do their homework, organize their notebooks, and improve their study skills. The results were impressive. Almost every ninth grader who participated in the program was able to pass the ninth grade that year. Although the n was too small to generalize from the data, it was clear that JHS needed a bigger and more intense intervention program for our incoming at-risk ninth graders.

Of course, the ninth graders were not the only group that demonstrated gains as a result of this program. The senior tutors, from this class, reported feelings of improved self-esteem, their grades in at least two other classes (besides English) improved, and four of these six senior tutors listed being a member of Porton's Partners as one of their greatest accomplishments. This was the genesis of the All Stars.

What Did the Students Say?

At the end of the semester, I always ask my students to think back and describe their favorite class. Almost every student in class for that lesson commented that the day we learned how to see things from another person's point of view was their favorite class because they learned so much and because they could see how important and useful their new skill was in their daily lives.

A NOVICE'S LESSON PLAN

Recently, I had the opportunity to supervise a wonderful student teacher who was assigned to teach math to high school students with special needs. Although she did not have a strong academic background in mathematics as an undergraduate, she embraced her challenge with enthusiasm and dedication. She is completing the traditional student teacher method of certification. She is truly dedicated to her profession; however, her initial lesson plans needed some help.

My student teacher, whom we shall call Miss Click, is teaching in an inclusion setting. There are two mentor teachers in the room with her. Miss Click is seeking certification in secondary special education. Her mentor is the special educator; however, since this is an inclusion class, the general educator is always present. Normally, the general educator does most of the instruction, and the special educators make the necessary accommodations, provide support for any students who are struggling, and add extra clarification when the general educator has gone too fast and/or generally confused the students. Since I was coming to observe, Miss Click was given the responsibility to write and implement the bulk of the plan, which appears in Table 9.3. I had provided Miss Click with the instructional triangle, discussed its implementation, and visited her a few times prior to this observation.

Instructional Triangle

The first thing we need to do is examine this plan according to our instructional triangle. Do you see the goal? Students will be able to solve one- and two-step equations by the end of this lesson. Good! What strategies will be used to help the students reach the goal? A discussion of two-step equations and work with dice are the strategies provided. Do you think this is sufficient to help students with special needs, who are normally grouped with struggling learners, master or practice this content? Neither do I. Nor do I believe that telling is teaching. Even after many years of teaching, I include an explicit description of both guided practice and independent practice procedures in all my lesson plans. Assessment is a checkoff of class participation, teacher observations, and a simple one-step equation problem. Do you think the assessment measures how well each student was able to reach the day's goals? Right. Let's make a list of what is missing just from the assessment:

- Where is the teacher observation checklist?
- What is the teacher observing for?
- What does participation look like?
- How will these instruments measure today's goal?

TABLE 9.3	Miss Click's Plan

Lesson Topic: Two-Step Equations

Goal	• Students will demonstrate their understanding of adding, subtracting, multiplying, and dividing numbers to solve one- and two-step equations.
Objective	• Students will apply adding, subtracting, multiplying, and dividing numbers to solve two-step equations.
Materials Needed	• Promethean Whiteboard • Calculators
Warm-Up	• What is the volume of a cylinder that is 20 cm. high and the base has a radius of 10 cm? • What volume will a cylinder hold if the base has a diameter of 16 in. and it is 30 in. tall? • I have a 24-in. tall cylindrical vase that I want to fill half full of water. The base has a radius of 3 inches. How much water do I need?
Guided Practice	• Discuss two-step equations.
Independent Practice	• Students will work with dice to develop an understanding of two-step equations.
Assessment	• Participation • Teacher Observation • Closure
Closure	• $5x = 15$
Homework	•

Evaluating the Plan

As we examine the rest of the plan, we see other gaps that would certainly interfere with instruction (and they did). Look at the layout of the plan. Do you see some important sections of the plan that have been deleted or completed improperly?

- Where is the section on motivation?
- When and how will the teacher differentiate during this lesson?
- Where are the accommodations for students with Individualized Education Programs listed?
- Why is the assessment question listed under closure?
- Why is there no closure question?

Although there are many worthwhile strategies for teaching, Marzano's (1992) Dimensions of Learning has provided a well-researched, practitioner-friendly approach to teaching and learning that is widely used in school systems today. "The five dimensions of learning are loose metaphors for how the mind works during learning" (Marzano, 1992, p. 2). As we explore this student teacher's plan in particular, we will send it through the filter of each of the dimensions. Dimension One deals with students' attitudes and perceptions. Dimension Two involves understanding how students acquire and integrate knowledge. Dimension Three explores successful instruction that helps students to extend and refine their newly acquired knowledge. Dimension Four provides higher-order thinking assessments that will help students to use their knowledge meaningfully and allow teachers to assess how well their students understand the material. Finally, Dimension Five surrounds and supports the entire learning process by helping students to improve their metacognition skills and is entitled "Habits of the Mind."

Dimension One reminds teachers that a good lesson plan always provides for the safety and motivational needs of the students. As you review this plan, in the absence of any motivation, can you find any provision that allows students to access their prior knowledge, see connections to real-life experiences, and/or understand the usefulness of today's learning? If you answered no to these questions, the plan did not meet an important criterion—creating a meaningful learning environment.

Dimension Two deals with helping learners understand where they are in the process of acquiring information. It is not clear from the plan if the students have practiced the process well enough to show mastery because the warm-up indicates prior exposure, but the closure indicates little to weak mastery. The plan should clearly reflect the status of the majority of the learners at this stage of the learning process. When plans are vague, students do not receive the level of instruction needed to move ahead in a clearly focused manner.

This plan does not even approach Dimensions Three and Four, which deal with higher-order thinking skills, but it could. The plan and its implementation remain on the basic introductory level despite the fact that with some differentiation several students could have profited from some extending and refining knowledge activities. I did not expect Miss Click, as a student teacher, to have mastery of all five dimensions, but one sign of an outstanding lesson plan is the inclusion of a Dimension Five goal. If Miss Click had included being persistent as one of her goals, she would have included Dimension Five strategies that would have helped her students stay on task even when the work was challenging. Her assessments would have explicitly measured the students' on-task behaviors, and her Teacher Observation Notes, which would have been shared with her students, would have had a high point value. Therefore, in addition to the benefits that come from teaching students how to persevere, she would have made the connection between effort and success clear to her students.

The Plan in Action

We have discussed the problems with the written plan, and since I observed the class, I can share with you the results of the flaws in the plan. In the absence of any motivating activities, the teacher completed the drill and went directly to guided practice. However, since the students had no vested interest in what Miss Click was teaching, very few students paid attention to her. During her discussion of one- and two-step equations, she had to spend a great deal of time redirecting her students' attention to what she was doing. Her mentor teachers tried to keep some of the more troublesome students on task, but it was clear that using whole-group instruction with such a mixed ability group was not a successful strategy. Students were not given any time to process the information she was trying to share with them. On some occasions, she asked them to talk to a partner, but because they were so off task, the discussions were just continuations of their personal conversations. Miss Click had developed a positive rapport with most of the students, who enjoyed her enthusiasm and recognized her dedication to their well-being. As a result, she did not experience direct defiance, just a steady stream of noncompliance that comes from students who do know not what to do or why they are being asked to do it.

The independent practice was not successful because the students had trouble understanding the directions and doing the seat work that was designed to help them master the day's goals. However, several students showed mastery during the lesson and completed the work easily and early. Those students became bored and looked for other ways to "entertain" themselves. When the assessment/closure question was distributed, many students worked together to solve the equation. Miss Click overlooked what her students were doing; she might have used the results as a valid indicator of every student's degree of mastery of the day's goals. In our postobservation conference, I shared everything with her that I am sharing with you. I am pleased to say that her next observation was more successful.

When teachers begin their careers, it is easy to become confused about how much information they need to include in a lesson plan. In general, it is best to include everything you will need to do so that you do not skip any of the essential steps required for your students to succeed and learn.

Let's Review

When we look at a lesson plan, the first thing we expect to see is an intact instructional triangle. If that is present, we know that the plan is focused, the students will be given strategies that match the day's goals, and the assessment will measure the students' abilities to reach the day's goals. Next, we have chosen to use one of the many worthwhile teaching and learning methodologies, Marzano's (1992) Dimensions of Learning, as our filter for an excellent plan. An outstanding plan provides for a safe and orderly classroom. In the plan, the motivation section is particularly important because it provides access to prior knowledge, stimulates an interest in the topic, and indicates the importance of the topic in the students' lives. Classroom management provides for physical comfort and safety, but only well-designed and -executed plans can make learning important to students.

Once the teacher has the students' attention, Marzano (1992) suggests that learning can be divided into declarative and procedural knowledge. It is the teacher's job to create a plan that is focused and sufficiently well conceived that the students can master the rudiments of the knowledge and move on to the dimensions that teach higher-order thinking skills.

Dimension Three moves students into the next higher level of thinking: Thinking Involved in Extending and Refining Knowledge. In this dimension, students are helped to analyze perspectives, compare and contrast, do error analysis, and perform similar problem-solving tasks. The most sophisticated level is Dimension Four, Using Knowledge Meaningfully. This dimension provides teachers of every level of experience the tools needed to supply students instruction with the utmost rigor, imagination, and authentic task application. Surrounding all of the other dimensions is Dimension Five, Habits of Mind. These habits include being persistent, seeking accuracy, being sensitive to feedback, avoiding impulsivity, and so on. As you know, these are life skills that struggling learners need in order to become successful.

No lesson plan includes all five dimensions, but an excellent plan will include provisions for Dimension One through the motivation; provisions for Dimension Two in the guided practice; and provisions for Dimension Three or Four in the independent practice, especially in a well-developed, differentiated lesson plan. Novice teachers and those who are working with struggling learners are encouraged to write a separate management goal that comes from Dimension Five as part of their instructional triangle to be sure the students know what specific behavioral skill they are learning, practicing, and being assessed on each day.

EFFECTIVE CLASSROOM DISCUSSIONS

"Education seems to be in America the only commodity of which the customer tries to get as little as he can for his money" (Max Leon Forman, "Finest Quotes," n.d.). Nowhere is this more evident than in a classroom when a teacher is trying to conduct a class discussion with reluctant learners. Dead-end questions start with the teacher, are answered in simple phrases by the students, are responded to by the teacher, and so on—until finally the bell rings, and the teacher and the students are put out of their misery.

Effective classroom discussions provide students with an opportunity to think aloud about complex problems in a safe learning environment. Neither opinions nor personal history is discussed; students learn how to listen, think, and challenge ideas in a respectful manner. Students leave class still thinking and discussing the issue. Teachers who conduct productive discussions help their students to leave childish, absolutist thinking behind and begin to develop mature questioning and analytical reasoning.

Results Depend on Preparation and Effort

Too often new teachers do not understand that a classroom discussion is like a symphony orchestra; it requires enormous preparation, goal setting, and effort before it can begin to sound like anything worthwhile. The teacher is never the sage on the stage; the teacher is the conductor. In order for the students to be able to hear each other and respond to each other effectively, they need to learn and practice each step of the process.

Before you begin any class discussion, you must decide on your goals. What do you want your students to learn? Essentially, the purpose for the discussion will come from your objective. Next, how will you provide the skills and knowledge to help your students reach the goal? There is a great deal in the literature that can help you to design the strategies you need to conduct a worthwhile discussion in your discipline. In general, be aware of the following:

- Keep the focus on the issues, not on opinions. Unless you want to hear specious arguments based on no data, require students to keep their remarks focused on ideas (with support to back up their claims), rather than stereotypical opinions.
- Use quotations from various sources to stimulate discussions. Try starting a discussion by putting a relevant quote on the board and asking each team to discuss the relevance of the quote to the topic you have been studying. In that way, students can practice airing their views before you open a class discussion.
- Avoid binary issues, topics that only have two sides, as much as possible. Complex problems almost never have simple triggers or resolutions. Where religion, politics, and biology intersect, we are looking at nuanced issues that are not started simply or resolved by easy solutions. If you discuss difficult problems that are worthy of lengthy deliberations, many conflicting elements should come into play (Highberg, 2010).

Staying on Track

Even the most carefully planned discussion can be taken off track. There are several reasonable solutions to the problem. Depending on your students, you can ask them to write for a few minutes on the topic that seems to have derailed them. I have a "bin" in my room for good ideas that we need to discuss later. If the energy of the class seems to be directed to a different topic, I ask a student to write down the topic and put it in the bin for a later time. I always return to our bin before the end of class; sometimes it replaces the closure that I had planned. Other suggestions include telling the student who brought up the new topic to see you after class and asking the student to make the connection between his comment and the current topic at hand (Connor, 2011).

Assessing the Discussion

How do you know the discussion met your goal? What evidence will you accept that each student learned what you wanted him to learn from participating in the discussion? This type of assessment is difficult to create. If a student is quiet, but attentive, did he learn? How do you know? If a student volunteers a great deal, but his comments were off the topic, did he learn? How do you know?

Your job prior to teaching the lesson is to create a rubric for the discussion. Practice using the rubric with the students during a focus lesson on classroom discussions so that you and they will understand how the rubric works. You can adjust the rubric in case it fails to capture what you value. You should not be the only one utilizing the rubric during the discussion; each student should be evaluating at least three other students to give every student a balanced evaluation. Our premise has been that "classroom discussion functions best when students are talking to students" (Barton, Heilker, & Rutkowski, 1997, p. 2). Therefore, the students need to be talking and listening to each other. If your rubric is valid and reliable, you will have an assessment tool that provides the evidence you need to measure the students' skills and that helps each student listen to others with an objective and open mind.

Lesson Plan on Classroom Discussions

Before you begin using classroom discussions as part of your instructional program, a focus lesson on how to participate in a classroom discussion is an excellent tool for helping your students understand the process and become aware of your expectations. The plan in Template 9.1 is for a focus lesson that can be used with middle school and

Template 9.1

Focus Lesson Planning Template	

Lesson Title: Focus lesson for classroom discussions

Lesson Unit: Introduction to the novel

GOAL	DOL 1–Safe environment DOL 5–Seeking accuracy There is no state curriculum goal for this lesson.
Lesson Objective	As a result of today's lesson, students will be able to participate in a classroom discussion by making claims, listening, thinking, responding, and challenging conflicting ideas in a respectful manner.

Materials Needed	Quote – On the overhead and at each desk: "I am always ready to learn, but I do not always like to be taught"—Winston Churchill
	    Placemat
	    Learn by Myself Poster—left side of the room
	    Being Taught Poster—right side of the room

Warm-Up
Time: 10 min.
	Each student will read and respond to the quote on the placemat.
	  1. Why don't you like being taught some days?
	  2. Are you always ready to learn? Why?
	  3. Are you always ready to learn? Why not?
	  4. What is the difference between being taught and learning?
	After each team has discussed the questions on the placemat, the class will review the drill together.

Motivation Time: 5 min.	Think of a time when you were "taught a lesson". What does that expression mean to you? What is the difference between being taught and learning? Which one is more effective for you?

Guided Practice
Time: 25 min.
	1. Divide yourselves into the two groups indicated in the room:
	    a. learn by myself
	    b. being taught
	2. In each group, define your terms.
	3. Supply specific examples of the benefits for your preference.
	4. Supply specific problems with the other style.
	5. Explain how your side supports Churchill's quote.
	6. Create graphics and look up examples to help your first spokesperson.
	7. Be ready to contribute to the rubric we will use.
	8. The class creates a rubric that covers both DOL 1 and DOL 5 goals. We account for the first spokesperson for each team and for each person's effort both before and during the discussion.

Independent Practice Time: 20 min.	Your team will be given 20 minutes to prepare for the class discussion. Be sure your first spokesperson is well prepared with information and graphics. Use the rubric we created to check your work.
Assessment Time: 25 min.	The first spokesperson for each team will be evaluated using the rubric we created. Next, each student will be evaluated against the standards described in the rubric. Three students will evaluate each student so that no one student will be assessed by only one assessor. The students' scores will be combined with the teacher's scores (higher point value) to arrive at the total score for the day.
Closure Time: 5 min.	Why is preparation essential for a worthwhile classroom discussion?
Homework	Our first graded classroom discussion this year will be focused on the importance of the author's tone in literature. Define tone and provide an example from one of the books you have read in school.

high school students. Since everyone has experience as a student, no other prior knowledge is required. This lesson is not part of any curriculum and should be used prior to using classroom discussions that include content because through this lesson your students are practicing the specific skills of listening, thinking, and challenging conflicting ideas in a respectful manner.

As part of the lesson plan, the class is expected to create the rubric. Since there are two goals, there should be descriptors of attempts to seek accuracy as well as proficiency with creating, defending, and responding to alternate claims. In addition, the first spokesperson from each team has been chosen to explain the team's position relative to the issue, offer the major claims and evidence, and provide any graphics the team has created to illustrate its ideas. The other team members should be ready to contribute to the flow of the discussion with accurate information, counterarguments, and supporting details. Students who are reluctant to speak up during heated discussions can get credit by working hard during preparation, as evidenced by the points given by their assessors on the rubric. If the rubric is effective, it will capture all of the hard work students do during the preparation and all of the application of their work during the discussion. Since the students helped to prepare the rubric, they should be able to assess their efforts prior to their performance so that they can strengthen their chances for success. Using this transparent model, the connection between effort and success should be clear to all.

PRIMARY-LEVEL READING LESSON PLAN

On the primary level, it is equally important to make instruction rigorous, exciting and engaging. In the following lesson, I have decided to help youngsters understand that there are many ways to help kindness grow. In Mirra Ginsburg's (1978) retelling of the folktale *Mushroom in the Rain*, lots of little creatures hide under a growing mushroom to stay out of the rain. Their willingness to help one another makes it possible for others to stay safe from predators and the perils of nature. My objective is to have the children understand how kindness grows by accurately reading a story and answering declarative and higher-level-thinking questions. The strategies are aligned with the objective because the students practice the skill of understanding the perspective of each new creature introduced in the story, the children are asked to see the problem from each creature's perspective, and the children are asked to compare the other creatures' decisions to ones they would have made. The children are constantly being made aware of what is growing during the story. The assessment requires the students to answer questions that reinforce the concept that kindness grows from kindness.

This plan utilizes Dimension One in that the children need to feel safe and secure in order to believe that they have the skills needed to complete the tasks expected of them. Most of the questions are at the declarative level, but through my scaffolding, I am building on their understanding so that they can reach Dimension Three. The routines and boundaries will be in use at all times, so that the students will know what is expected of them, and they will be able to self-regulate their behavior to stay on task, which is a Dimension Five goal.

Neuroscientists have given us many insights into what we can do to help children learn at every stage of their development. During the early school years, children develop reading, writing, and math skills. They also learn and practice social and emotional skills for which they need appropriate models. As natural as it is for children to be curious and learn, struggling learners need exposure to a variety of experiences so that their branching dendrites will be stimulated to grow. Since all primary-age children are especially sensitive to music and physical activity (Wolfe, 2010), I have included both in this plan (Table 9.4). I think this ambitious plan can be completed in 2 days.

TABLE 9.4	Primary Comprehension Lesson Plan

Lesson Title: Kindness

Lesson Unit: Caring for Others

GOAL	(SC)
Lesson Objective	As a result of today's lesson, students will be able to accurately read and understand a fantasy about animals in order to learn how kindness grows. The students will demonstrate their understanding of the concept of kindness by answering declarative and higher-level-thinking questions.
Materials Needed	Placemat Lined paper *Mushroom in the Rain* by Mirra Ginsburg
Warm-Up Time:	1. What does kindness mean? 2. What is one way you showed kindness to someone? 3. How do you feel when someone is kind to you? 4. How do you feel when someone is *not* kind to you? When the warm-up is complete, we will have a list of words on the board that describe kindness to help the students with motivation.
Motivation Time:	Every team will create a song about kindness. See the model in Figure 9.1. Each song will represent a facet of kindness. The songs will be heard at the beginning of class. After we read the story *Mushroom in the Rain*, the children will discuss how their ideas about kindness have changed or stayed the same.
Guided Practice Time:	Use the story guide in Figure 9.1 to help the children follow the sequence of the story. Find all the words on the first page that describe size. What do we know about the ant? The mushroom? What does the ant need? Why? Do ants change their size in the rain? Who came next? What did the butterfly need? Why? What did the ant do? What would you do? Do ants or butterflies change their size in the rain? Who came next? What did the mouse need? Why? What was the problem for the ant and the butterfly? What was their solution? What would you have done? Do ants, butterflies, or mice change their size in the rain? Who came next? What did the sparrow need? Why? What did the other creatures say? What did they do? What would you have done? Do ants, butterflies, mice, or sparrows change their size in the rain? Who came next? How did the other creatures feel about the rabbit? Why? How did the other creatures feel about the fox? Why? When the sun came out, all the creatures realized that something had changed! What grew while it was raining?

(Continued)

TABLE 9.4 (*Continued*)	
Independent Practice Time:	With your team, answer this question: While the little creatures were under the mushroom and the mushroom spread from the rain, what else was growing under the mushroom? Each team will be given one scene to act out from the story to prove your point! (Differentiated by team's skills)
Assessment Time:	See Figure 9.2.
Closure Time:	Have your ideas about kindness changed since we started our lesson? Explain.
Homework Time:	Write 3 sentences about kindness.

What does the ant need? _____ Why? _____

Do ants change their size in the rain? _____

Who came next? _____

What did the butterfly need? _____ Why? _____

What did the ant do? _____

What would you do? _____

Do ants or butterflies change their size in the rain? _____

Who came next? _____

What did the mouse need? _____ Why? _____

What was the problem for the ant and the butterfly? _____

FIGURE 9.1 Story Guide (*Continued*)

What was their solution? _____

What would you have done? _____

Do ants, butterflies, or mice change their size in the rain? _____

Who came next? _____

What did the sparrow need? _____ Why? _____

What did the other creatures say? _____ What did they do? _____

What would you have done? _____

Do ants, butterflies, mice, or sparrows change their size in the rain? _____

Who came next? _____

How did the other creatures feel about the rabbit? _____ Why? _____

How did the other creatures feel about the fox? _____ Why? _____

When the sun came out, all the creatures realized that something had changed!

What grew while it was raining? _____

Song Model: Sharing

Tune: Happy Birthday to You!

I share my toys with you.
You share your toys with me.
We share our toys with others.
We're as kind as can be!

FIGURE 9.1   (*Concluded*)

Although the students are all struggling learners, the groups can be differentiated as follows: **Lilly** (top readers); **Rocky** (average readers); **Ruby** (low average readers); and **Lexus** (struggling readers).

Lilly's Assessment

1. What is the difference in the way the creatures treated the fox and the way the creatures treated everyone else? Why?
2. How do you think the fox felt?
3. Which animal received kindness? Which one did not? Why?

Rocky's Assessment

Pretend you were one of the creatures under the mushroom.

1. Who are you?
2. Who showed you kindness?
3. What was the best part of being there? What was the worst part?

Ruby's Assessment

Pretend you are the mouse.

1. Who showed you kindness? How?
2. Are you ever afraid of the other creatures under the mushroom with you?
3. Why? Why not?

FIGURE 9.2   Assessments (*Continued*)

Lexus' Assessments

1. How did the creatures show kindness to each other?
2. How do people show kindness to each other?

FIGURE 9.2   *(Concluded)*

A Few Reflections on the Lesson

After I had almost finished the lesson, a few children leaned close to me and whispered softly: "We don't sit still this long. We are ready for show and tell. Are you almost finished?" I appreciated their honesty and their kindness. By the end of the lesson, the room was filled with guests, and it was clear to me that the plan was too long for my wonderful students. This overambitious plan should have taken 3 days, not 2. The grouping was fine, but the song was too hard for the groups to generate; it could easily be replaced with something more reasonable to create. However, when I visited the same class 2 months later, the majority of the students remembered the story and its lesson.

Summary

In this chapter, I have shared several lesson plans with you. Using the lesson I taught for *To Kill a Mockingbird* as a model, we were able to examine how a carefully-planned and well-orchestrated lesson can help students become actively engaged in a lesson they found meaningful. The students understood the utility of the lesson, both from a practical and from an academic point of view. Because they were immediately engaged in the lesson's objectives, the students began the lesson by responding in character in order to learn how to analyze perspectives.

Each step of the lesson provided students the scaffolding they needed to succeed. Utilizing cooperative learning groups allowed each student to get the support and feedback required to move through each step of the plan without fear of failure or embarrassment. Their previously held belief of incompetence was not in evidence. Any observer would have assumed that this was a group of high-achieving students enjoying a stimulating activity.

Novices begin their teaching career with a lot of enthusiasm and dedication, but a lack of understanding of the consequences that can accrue when we forget essential ingredients of lesson planning. The instructional triangle must be intact for any plan to have focus, to include strategies that are likely to help the students reach the goals, and to create an assessment that measures students' ability to demonstrate mastery of the goals. Knowledge of any of the researched approaches to teaching and learning will provide teachers with a list of "must-haves" for excellence in teaching and learning. We saw that instructional practices become richer, and more challenging, and students' work is more carefully framed when using Marzano's (1992) versatile framework, the Dimensions of Learning. Excellence, when viewed through the Marzano (1992) model, requires all plans to provide for Dimension One, students' physical and emotional safety. Dimension Two provides students with the basic declarative and/ or procedural knowledge needed for the topic they are studying. Dimensions Three and Four cover skills described as higher-order-thinking skills and result in rigorous instruction, expanding simple ideas into more sophisticated and nuanced constructs. Finally, and very importantly for struggling learners, Dimension Five, Habits of Mind, teaches students how to stay on task, persist, seek accuracy, and in general demonstrate the attributes that resilient students display naturally.

The seniors who participated in the *To Kill a Mockingbird* lesson on analyzing perspectives were well prepared by all of our previous work to do a thorough analysis of 1940 Southern thinking, as portrayed in the novel. Knowing how to be a good teacher may be intuitive, but knowing the steps to lead your students through the process of learning is not intuitive. As a veteran teacher, I have found the Dimensions of Learning model to be the most accurate description of good teaching I have ever encountered. It provides the language for what good teachers do, and it organizes our procedures into a framework that makes our efforts replicable by other teachers, no matter how long or how well they have been teaching.

In this, as in all other matters related to teaching, classroom discussions require careful, reflective planning to succeed. Since the stakes are very high, the payoffs can be substantial. In a carefully executed discussion,

students can actually be taught to listen, think, and respond in a respectful and mature manner to another person's ideas.

The lesson plan for primary readers consolidates what we have learned about the Dimensions of Learning, the instructional triangle, and the developmental trajectory of young learners. If we have been careful and thoughtful, our plan should include age-appropriate, stimulating activities that will expose our young learners to the types of activities and experiences that will help them to succeed at their most important academic tasks: learning to read and write successfully.

As a teacher, you have taken on an enormous challenge and responsibility. However, if you have faith in yourself, believe in your students, and work very hard, there is no better calling. Einstein once said, "Strive not to be a success, but rather to be of value" ("Think Exist," n.d.). We may never be famous or wealthy, but our students recognize our value long after they leave us. This is a message I received recently from one of my former students. I was his ninth-grade English teacher; he is now in his thirties: "I just wanted to say that you are my greatest ethical mentor. I keep a copy of Frost's 'Nothing Gold Can Stay' in my portfolio with your name on it." I know that for me, these sentiments and others like them are the real evidence of my success.

Discovery Learning

A shared vision is not an idea ... it is rather, a force in people's hearts ... at its simplest level, a shared vision is the answer to the question "What do we want to create?"

PETER SENGE

In a constructivist/discovery learning–style classroom, the essential question to ask before every major undertaking is this: During this journey, what is it we want to learn? Create? Discover? During the process of discovery, students and their teacher will be able to find the answer to their overarching question, and a great deal more. Certainly, the teacher establishes the goal for what she must teach the children—that is, what they must learn or be able to do at the end of each class. Material can be presented to the students as if they were passive starfish waiting to be saved. Or learners can be allowed to construct knowledge for themselves in a controlled, social learning environment. The constructivist philosophy that supports the latter approach accepts the views of Dewey, Piaget, Vygotsky, and Bruner that knowledge is a personal and social construction of meaning (Hein, 1991).

We need to have a working knowledge of constructivist philosophy in order to be able to apply it to our instruction. (In this chapter, we are using the terms *constructivist* and *discovery learning* interchangeably.) Therefore, we will consider its proponents' core beliefs. Next, we will measure the instructional triangle and the lesson plan template against the discovery learning positions to be sure that our philosophies and practices are truly aligned. We will then examine two focus lessons on problem solving. Students need to be taught how to problem solve. Using a focus lesson helps them to understand the process from a personal point of view before they apply it to any content. Finally, we will examine some exciting new technology that fits especially well in the new high school science curricula. As you design your strategies, you will find that using a constructivist approach provides for an energized, engaged community of learners.

Sometimes the students find treasures that you would have never seen. I know that was my experience. Although the trips were often messy and bewildering, I would not have missed my journeys with the students for the world.

CONSTRUCTIVISM

As you know, the use of cooperative learning teams has been strongly encouraged throughout this book. One reason for the continued support for this practice is the constructivists' belief that learning is a social activity that is directly associated with our relationships with others. As Smith (2009) noted, learning involves our participating in a community that provides the proper context for us to acquire and process new knowledge. In every learning community, there are those who have mastery and those who are newcomers. A learner's goal is to become engaged in the process of learning so that she can become less like the newcomer and more like the master. For example, when siblings play at home, the older sibling might show the younger one how to play with a toy "correctly." Correct usage is not always a matter of the older child having read the directions; it can just be what the older child has determined to be acceptable. Nevertheless, the younger child must follow the directions given, and if she plays with the toy "correctly," she may be allowed access to the toy. If I paid a nickel, I could watch Susie play with our toys. Apparently, I could never get all the rules right.

Constructivists also believe that we learn by doing and participating in the process and by making sense out of the experience. Other core beliefs include the notion that people learn while they are learning. Learning is not linear. We connect in multiple directions as we go through the process of learning. For example, you know that at a certain time period all plays had five acts, but now you are learning what happens in each act, while you are simultaneously learning the basic elements of dramatic action:

Act one—Introduction

Act two—Rising action

Act three—Climax

Act four—Falling action

Act five—Resolution

The two happen simultaneously: You learn the name of each category for the five acts, and you learn how to categorize dramatic action. The information gleaned from neuroscience has special utility in this arena. "Gifted brains are remarkably intense and diffuse metabolizers. But the amazing insights do not stop there. The orchestration of activity is planned and complex, and it seems to require the coordination of diverse visual, spatial, verbal, and sensory areas of brain. Gifted thinkers are rarely one-mode thinkers. Rather, they are great organizers of diverse and multimodal information" (Eide & Eide, 2006, p. 1).

Next, constructivists believe learning is a mental activity that can be facilitated by physical activity. For kinesthetic learners, physical movement helps secure the mental construction of meaning. As we have learned, physical activity is highly correlated with stimulating the growth of new neurons (Jensen, 2008). Proponents of discovery learning also believe that learning involves language. Watch children talk to themselves as they practice new skills. According to Bruner (1996), a major contributor to the understanding of discovery learning, we all use multiple forms of language. He refers to iconic, which is largely models and pictures, and to symbolic, which is largely our ability to think abstractly. Bruner suggests that teachers use a combination of iconic and symbolic activities to help children learn.

Learning is contextual. If you were given some part of a formula and asked to apply it without any other information, would you know what to do? If you were shown one line of poetry, could you explicate it? No, we don't learn abstract and isolated facts that may have utility for us unless the information is put into a meaningful context. We learn new information in relation to our previous knowledge. How well we are able to process new information is a product of our past skills, talents, and beliefs about our own competence in that area. Even with a skilled mathematician by my side, I would struggle with a formula for solving any equation. However, in the context of a whole poem, I can explicate most poetry because I have prior knowledge and skills in that field. Because it isn't possible to process new knowledge without some earlier learning to build on, the teacher must provide the pathway between the prior and the new knowledge for learning to occur.

It takes time to learn. Some people process new information more quickly than others. Speed is only one indicator of intelligence. Some thinkers are very thorough and will not move on from a new idea quickly. Others are more intuitive, and when they believe they have achieved mastery, they move ahead. Although there are brilliant people who think quickly, some think slowly and deliberately. They are reflective. They may not comment first, but when they speak, it is worth the wait.

Finally, constructivists believe that motivation is essential to learning. Unless students know and understand why they are learning something, they are not likely to be involved in what they are doing (Hein, 1991). In addition, one of the real stumbling blocks that has compromised the implementation of constructivism has been the extent to which the models have explicitly integrated motivation (Palmer, 2005). If the motivation to become involved with the community of learners is not present and the master's knowledge is not deemed important or meaningful, then the newcomer will not be engaged and will remain on the periphery of the experience (Smith, 2009).

This is true not only of struggling learners, but of teachers as well. Let me remind you of the last professional meeting you attended. You were tired; the speaker was boring; you could not see any connection between the topic and what you are teaching. Did you (A) fall asleep, or (B) take notes? Be honest! Most of us would have taken a short snooze; we need to believe that what we are learning has some value, or we are unlikely to put forth any substantial effort to master the content.

REVIEWING THE INSTRUCTIONAL TRIANGLE AND LESSON PLAN TEMPLATE

Instructional Triangle and Constructivist Learning Theory

According to what we know about the discovery learning theory, does the instructional triangle match its core beliefs? The goal may have to stand apart from any teacher's philosophy or pedagogy, since most of us teach from a statewide curriculum guide the forthcoming Common Core State Standards. However, whenever it is possible to integrate discovery learning and the content goal, we should try to do that. In any case, it is up to us to design our strategies. We can create the strategies that we believe are best suited to help our students reach the goal. The strategies espoused by discovery/constructivist teachers allow for students to make meaning in a social context from the material presented. Cooperative learning is a perfect design for this belief system. The assessment you create should mimic the strategies the students practiced. Therefore, in a problem-solving model, the assessment should include a new problem to be solved. Review the instructional triangle in Figure 10.1.

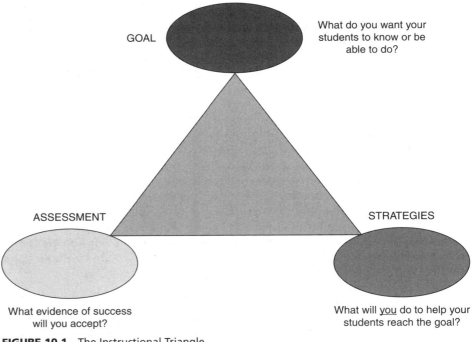

FIGURE 10.1 The Instructional Triangle

Lesson Plan Template and Discovery Learning

We are going to examine each specific section of the lesson plan template (Template 10.1) to be sure that our practices and policies are congruent.

I believe the originators of constructivism and discovery learning theory were influenced by their interpretation of John Dewey's thinking. I acknowledge there is some controversy about the claim that his positions laid the foundations for the theories that are in current favor (Professor Eli Velder, personal communication, 2011). It was Dewey who said, "We only think when we are confronted with a problem" ("Think Exist," n.d.). Perhaps that is why creating a problem-solving situation helps initiate thinking better than any other. It seems that we have made the case that both the instructional triangle and the lesson plan template conform to the philosophical principles of discovery learning, which has its basis in Dewey and is an outgrowth of the work of Piaget, Vygotsky, and Bruner.

IT'S NICE, BUT HOW DO YOU DO IT?

Understanding a discovery learning classroom in the abstract may be interesting, but seeing it in application should make it seem more plausible. You will be reading two lesson plans that I taught as focus lessons. The first is a focus lesson on how to be a reflective reader and responder. There is no right answer; each person reads the short piece and makes meaning for herself. It is in the personal construction of meaning that we learn who we are and how we are. Sharing our self-awareness makes our learning both meaningful and unique.

The second lesson is entirely teacher created. My students were very poor problem solvers. Their thinking was "fight or flight," and that had led to tragic outcomes in their lives. I needed to help my students learn how to solve problems by using more alternatives. Correspondingly, the problem-solving process I used for the game in the focus lesson is the one I used to teach my students how to analyze errors, categorize, and support positions. These are all Dimension Three skills we used when studying fiction and nonfiction. I created the game and the rubric. I never would have thought of some of their solutions.

Template 10.1

Lesson Plan Template—Constructivist

Lesson Title:

Lesson Unit:

GOAL		CCSS Goal based on grade level and CCSS standard
	SC State Curriculum *This comes from the state* *curriculum guide.*	
Lesson Objective	As a result of today's lesson, *students will be able to . . .* *This comes from* the state curriculum guide or the CCSS and refers to the goal for the day.	
Materials Needed	As the teacher, you need to have the materials needed for the day's journey.	
Warm-Up Time:	During the warm-up, your job is to access prior knowledge. Constructivists believe that learning is contextual and can be obtained only in relation to prior knowledge.	
Motivation Time:	According to those who believe in discovery learning, motivation is essential to learning. If learners do not understand why they are learning, they are unlikely to be active participants in the process.	
Guided Practice Time:	When discovery learning methods such as problem solving are employed, you must model the process to be used so that each team can follow the process carefully and correctly. No answers have been pre-established. Only the process and the path are clearly outlined.	
Independent Practice Time:	Learning is an active process: Knowledge is gained through a personal and social construction of meaning. During independent practice, students, working in teams, create meaning for themselves using the constructs you shared during guided practice. The findings are their own and should build on their prior knowledge of the topic under study.	
Assessment Time:	The assessment should mirror the strategies used during instruction. However, in order to determine each student's mastery of the goal, this work must be done independently.	
Closure Time:	Learning involves language. When you ask effective closure questions, you learn a lot about how the students feel about their experiences. This information is very useful in planning similar experiences for future classes.	
Homework	Learning takes time. Practice at new learning should be a daily feature of each student's routine. As long as the practice is useful, and not onerous, it provides the repetition needed for effective learning to take place.	

"My Name"

When Sandra Cisneros wrote *The House on Mango Street* (1984), I should think she never expected English teachers would be taught how to use her chapter entitled "My Name" to encourage reluctant writers. That was my first introduction to this compelling piece. I loved its cadence, its comedy, and its foreign sensibilities. My response was visceral and immediate. I knew that I never liked my first name, but in this exercise, I was given a chance to explore who I was and how I was in the context of my name. I used the exercise with my class exactly as it was taught to me. Since the demonstration was taught using a discovery method of instruction, it was a perfect match for my class (Table 10.1).

I would like to share what I wrote the day I participated in this lesson as a student:

I was named for my paternal grandfather, Harry. According to Jewish tradition, each child is named for a deceased relative in order to keep that person's memory alive. My father had very mixed feelings about his flamboyant, brilliant, but frequently bewildering parent, and I think he transferred those conflicted feelings on to me.

The irony is that I am not in the least bit like my dad's family. If it is possible to inherit 100% maternal genes and 0% paternal genes, then that is what is true of me. And so my dad placed on me a set of feelings and attitudes that colored our relationship all his life. He never saw past my name, and I never lived inside it.

TABLE 10.1	Lesson Plan—My Name

Lesson Title: My Name
Lesson Unit:

GOAL	(SC) This is a focus lesson that is designed to help students make meaning from a reading selection, write their response, and share their response with others. CCSS- 3-Write narratives to develop real or imagined experiences or events using effective techniques, well-chosen details, and well-structured event sequences.
Lesson Objective	*As a result of today's lesson, students will be* able to respond to a reading selection in writing in a personal and meaningful manner.
Materials Needed	A copy of "My Name" by Sandra Cisneros Placemat paper and writing utensils for everyone on the team
Warm-Up Time:	1. What are some of your favorite names? 2. How are people in your family named? 3. What name do you wish you had? Why? 4. What name do you really dislike? Why?
Motivation Time:	Read "My Name" to the class. Tell the class that they will be reading the piece to each other in their teams. Explain that we will be learning about ourselves by responding to Cisneros' story of her name and how she feels about her name. We will be writing about our names, how we got them, how we feel about them, and what they mean to us.
Guided Practice Time:	**Part I.** First, using one team as a model, I start reading "My Name"; when I stop, another person starts reading. After that, I explain that the group continues reading that way until the reading has been completed. **Part IV.** Last, I read my response to the class.
Independent Practice Time:	**Part II.** Second, the teams read the entire selection. **Part III.** Third, each student writes his/her own response. When all of the responses have been written, each student reads his/her response to the team. Finally, the team selects the one student who will read his/her response to the class. Each team has one person read to the class.
Assessment Time:	What does your name not say about you? Explain.
Closure Time:	What was the best part of today's lesson? Why?

Just by listening to my students tell their stories, I learned volumes about their histories, their hopes, and their heartbreaks. By reading and responding, they learned how to process information and make it their own. However, it was in the discourse among the members of the teams that I heard true kindness. A proverb tells us that "in teaching others, we teach ourselves," and that was certainly the case. In our journey of self-discovery, we all learned that when we are heard with compassion, no secret is too sad to tell. It's true that my students' writing skills improved that day, but even for an English teacher, that seemed small in comparison to their greater accomplishment.

The All Stars Problem-Solving Game

The year I started the All Stars, my son was studying at the University of California in San Diego. After I went to visit him, I had a lot of time to reflect on the long plane ride home. I began thinking about the problems some of my students faced on a daily basis. I knew that their previous solutions had led to some dreadful outcomes, and I wondered what I could do to help them become better problem solvers. This was the context of the creation of my problem-solving game.

When you create this game for your students, you will need to tailor it for their ages, life circumstances, and life challenges. The problems I designed came directly from my students' lives. I have updated the technology for problem 3, but the issue is the same. The students responded because they appreciated the authenticity of the situations. The game works only if the problems are real and if the students are forced to think about complex solutions to address complicated problems.

In a discovery learning classroom, the problem-solving game is not an end in itself. You are teaching your students how to engage in the problem-solving process. There is certainly a procedure that must be followed in your discipline for problem solving. When you use the focus lesson to help your students learn the procedure outside of the content, they will learn a new approach for coping with their own problems; when they later apply it to your content, they will see the value of that content.

Briefly, the game works like this. Each team is assigned one problem. When all the teams feel they have created the best possible solutions and have met the criteria for a successful solution according to the rubric created by the teacher, they regroup and listen to the teams' responses to each of the scenarios. The teams' responses are scored by students using the rubric, and then the class is allowed to discuss the scores with the scorers. Everyone in the class is expected to be involved in every phase of the class discussions.

DIRECTIONS   I introduced the game to the All Stars as follows:

Today we are going to practice how to solve problems together. There are no right or wrong answers. However, there is a rubric (Table 10.2) that your senior tutors will apply to each team's solutions. Each team will be given its own problem. Using the problem-solving system posted in our classroom (Figure 10.2), your team must examine and evaluate the problem from all sides. Together, you will look for the most promising outcomes for each of the parties described in the incident.

PROBLEM 1

Your best friend's life at home is terrible. He sleeps at your house a lot. His mother no longer lives at home. His father has been using drugs ever since she left. There is never enough food for your friend to eat, but he doesn't like to eat at your house all the time. He has become very sad and moody. He isn't interested in hanging out with your friends anymore. He doesn't sleep well. He has started giving his stuff away. When you try to make plans with him, he doesn't seem involved or interested. If you tell your mom about him, he will feel that you have betrayed his trust in you. You don't think his father cares about him. What should you do?

TABLE 10.2   Rubric

Directions: Score each team on its solutions. All scorers must agree on a team's score and explain the score to the team after announcing it.

4 = Excellent solution. All parties' needs are met. Response shows original thought and creative solutions to the problem.

3 = Good solution. Most parties' needs are met. Response shows adequate thinking to resolve the problem.

2 = Fair solution. Some parties' needs are met. Response shows thought, but parts of the problem are left unresolved.

1 = Poor solution. No party's needs are really met. Response shows immature thought, and the problem remains largely unsolved.

FIGURE 10.2   Problem-Solving System

PROBLEM 2

You live at home with your mother. She does not make enough money to pay the bills. She needs you to get a part-time job to help pay the bills. She is desperate and talks to you all the time about how much she needs money. Your boyfriend has a job. He is always complaining because you are never available to see him when he isn't working. You really miss being with him, but you need to help out at home, and you are looking for a job. What should you do?

PROBLEM 3

You hang out with a tough crowd. You like them, but you know they can be very mean. They are cyberbullying one boy in your class because they are sure he is gay. You don't really care if he is gay or not, but you don't want to say anything because you don't want to be their next victim. You saw the boy in school, and he looks terrible. One of the kids in your class said that she heard that the boy isn't gay, but he's really miserable because of all the cyberbullying he is getting. Your sister told you about a boy in another school who killed himself because he was the target of cyberbullying. You believe her. What should you do?

PROBLEM 4

Your friends have "borrowed" a car that belongs to a neighbor down the street. Your little "brother" just called to say that your friends are outside waiting for you. You know they don't own a car; you look out your window and recognize the car they are driving. Last month you were released from the local juvenile detention facility. Your foster family said that, if you get arrested again, they are sending you back to the Department of Social Services. You don't want to punk out. What should you do?

For guided practice, I walked through the problem-solving system in Figure 10.2, using a different problem. At **Stop**, I explained that first the students have to stop and listen to the problem from everyone's perspective. Each person on the team must explain the problem from one of the character's points of view. Next, at **Think**, they need to think about all the dimensions of the problem and array the problem so that everyone can see all of its implications. **Make your choice** requires the students to select an action plan for the problem as it has been arrayed, being sure that each facet of the problem has been addressed. When they get to **Do**, they learn that it is not enough to say what they would do; they have to follow through. Finally, **Evaluate** is a critical last step that many struggling learners never consider. Reflection regarding the success or failure of a plan can make a huge difference in whether students attempt to solve problems thoughtfully or rashly.

Independent practice occurred when the students worked as teams to determine the answers for their own scenarios. The senior tutors' responses were outstanding. They were close in age and highly regarded peers, so the ninth graders accepted their feedback and learned from it.

For the assessment, each student had to follow the same steps and give advice on this scenario:

A friend of yours lives in a foster home he really likes. He has told everyone that he expects this foster family to adopt him. You know the son of the family, and he has confided in you that, since his dad lost his job, the family's plans have changed. They will not be adopting your friend. Your friend finally seems happy. You hate to be the one to spoil his happiness. What should you do?

DID IT WORK?   As an aside, later that year one of my All Stars was taken to a drug rehabilitation center by his/her parent. After the two of them walked around the facility, the parent said to the child, "What do you want to do?" The youngster said, "Mrs. Porton taught us a way to figure things out. First I have to stop, and then I have to think about what is best for me. When I know the answer, I will make my choice, and then I will do what I need to do." The student's parent called me at home that evening to share the conversation with me. We both cried as the conversation was repeated, and we prayed that the rehab center would be able to help "our" child, who was finally able to make a decision using a system, not an impulse.

TECHNOLOGY, SCIENCE AND DISCOVERY LEARNING

I have had to do a lot of reading, talking, and learning recently to be able to address this topic. Although I am comfortable in the world of discovery learning, I am out of my element in a discussion of the use of technology in science. For the most part, technology has enriched the social sciences in the form of computers, the Internet, intranets, and Smart Boards. However, the vast majority of technology spending has gone, and rightly so, to the math and science departments, where it has revolutionized instruction. Where I speak from authority about struggling learners, I will have to rely on experts in the field when I discuss anything that deals with science instruction. I know what I know, and I know what I don't know. I also wish to acknowledge the help of my older brother Bob, who once again has been called upon to help his younger sister.

We have noted in this chapter that each field of instruction has its own protocol for investigation. Scientific inquiry may be the most highly regarded of all; therefore, we will examine the relationships among technology, curricula, and inquiry by looking through the lens of a geoscience experiment. In addition, science education has an extremely important role in everyone's life. The modern world has damaged the environment to such an extent that it is possible human life may not be sustainable unless new science and technology can effectively respond to the challenges we have created. We need a method of teaching science that engages every student because all of us will make decisions that can have a significant impact on our collective future (Taber, 2009).

High School Science and Discovery Learning

According to the National Science Education Standards, "Students at all grade levels and in every domain of science should have the opportunity to use scientific inquiry and develop the ability to think and act in ways associated with inquiry" (as quoted in Edelson, Gordin, & Pea, 1999, p. 3). Recently, science educators under the auspices of the National Research Council have moved away from the traditional passive form of science instruction and toward a more active, question-driven, open-ended process. Educators believe that students must have more personal experiences with scientific inquiry in order to understand that it is a fundamental aspect of science. Concurrently, computer technologies are receiving more attention from the education community because of their ability to support the inquiry method of discovery. A whole body of educational research has sprung up to explore "the use of computers and networks to collect, exchange, and analyze scientific data" (Edelson et al., 1999, p. 3).

In addition, recent data indicate that on their own, students from less-affluent backgrounds have a tendency to choose less challenging online material than their more prosperous peers—even when access to technology has been accounted for (Quillen, 2011). Only in an educational setting where materials have been selected for them can we be sure that all students are exposed to the rigorous and exciting information available through today's technology.

Technology can be used to stimulate students' interest, improve their performance, and increase their collaboration in every content area. In many classes, students can be given the opportunity to respond to questions individually and to edit their written responses through the use of the interactive whiteboard. When teachers use this new technology as more than an expensive overhead projector, they can assess how every student is progressing in her understanding of the reading; for example, teachers who use the student response system get the tally of students' answers in real time on the screen. In addition, the interactive whiteboard allows teachers to walk around the room and interact more with their students while introducing new information. It also provides access to more students-as-teacher opportunities as teams find new information that can help other teams conduct their inquiries (O'Connor, 2011).

There is no difference between my approach to discovery learning in my high school English classes and that of my friends who teach high school science; we both believe that inquiry learning should be based on the idea that the authentic protocol of each discipline should be taught and then expected from every student. Berube (as cited in Taber, 2009) believes that when students learn science, they should be taught to think for themselves, question, and create their own learning. Authentic practices give students the motivation to acquire new knowledge by explaining why students are learning the new information and by attaching the new information to prior knowledge. The students must have a genuine opportunity to apply their new knowledge and to construct meaning in a social context based on their active participation. These constructs are true whether you teach chemistry or English 9. Each field has its own protocol for acquiring, analyzing, and accepting the legitimacy of claims based on the data.

In a science classroom, scientists' knowledge of scientific concepts, inquiry skills, and understanding of scientific tools are bound together. Students must be able to employ all three simultaneously in a way that is not manifested in other disciplines. The demands on science teachers are unique and noteworthy. Edelson et al. (1999) point out that each field of science requires a different method of investigation and distinct standards of evidence.

Assuming that you have been assigned to teach in your own field, knowing the rules and procedures for your domain is not your challenge. However, sharing all of these intricacies with your students can be daunting. In addition, if there is a long delay between the time you motivate your students and the time they can begin to investigate, many of your struggling learners will lose interest.

It is at this point that technology can become the most dramatic support to discovery learning. The new technologies offer easy access to information and help in structuring the inquiry process (Edelson et al., 1999). If you had to provide all of the background knowledge that these students were missing, you would never get to inquiry. Suggestions for how to provide missing but necessary background knowledge will be forthcoming.

Climatology

The experiment under investigation for our purposes involved teaching students about climatology because, "like the other geosciences, it integrates the sciences of physics, chemistry, biology, and geography" (Edelson et al., 1999, p. 4). The researchers in this study used *scientific visualization*, which is a class of techniques that uses the computer's powerful abilities to change complex analytical data into imagery, which is easier for people to see and understand. In addition, the researchers, working in the field with actual teachers and students, went through a variety of computer programs and teaching and learning models while they faced and overcame real-world challenges (Edelson et al., 1999).

The researchers' objectives for the classroom application of the technology, which they were blending into the curriculum, came from the required statewide curriculum guide. Ultimately, they were able to integrate their learning goals with both inquiry and science content. However, they found in the process that the following core beliefs of discovery learning create both the burdens and the benefits of applying the scientific method to a high school science curriculum.

1. Motivation. "When students are not sufficiently motivated...they either fail to participate in inquiry activities, or they participate in them in a disengaged manner that does not support learning" (Edelson et al., 1999, p. 7).
2. Accessibility. Students must be able to understand the goals, perform the tasks, and interpret the results (Edelson et al., 1999). Unfortunately, that assumes an enormous array of skills that many learners, especially struggling learners, do not possess.
3. Background knowledge. As we noted earlier, the absence of necessary background knowledge makes even the best-planned inquiry lesson ineffective because the students do not know how to pose a research question, develop a plan, collect the data, or interpret the data. Unless the students are provided with missing information at each key point, anything they learn is apt to be meaningless, and they will know that.
4. Management of extended activities. Lack of organization, poor management of paperwork, and poor management of extended processes are cited by the researchers as frequent problems, but there are others. Absenteeism is a huge problem among struggling learners. In addition, in a high school science classroom, storage of materials can be a challenge that is difficult to overcome.
5. Time constraints. Some high schools use a 45- or 50-minute period. Classes hardly have enough time to set up before it is time to close down. In high schools that work on a four-period day, the resulting 90-minute class period is more conducive to inquiry learning. However, the method must be managed within the time constraints of the school where it is being used.

As the researchers went through the challenges and victories of their work, they arrived at some intentional conclusions and some surprises as well. From one of their earliest design flaws, they learned that they had to create data sets that would interest high school students. For example, in their early scientific visualization programs, they expected students to be able to pose their own questions for inquiry. The students asked the computer to show them what the weather was like on the day they were born. After the computer did that, the students had no further questions. A few students asked about global warming, but the programmers did not expect any interest in that topic, so the computer could not respond. The absence of a program that would be responsive to current issues and that would create initial engagement and then motivate and extend to the creation of open-ended investigations taught the researchers a valuable lesson.

Edelson et al. (1999) concluded that in order to address the five research challenges they had encountered, they needed a more sophisticated and nuanced computer system. Ultimately, they chose WorldWatcher. They believe this technology has all the resources needed to meet the demands of instruction that the earlier technologies did not possess. Since technology advances so quickly, I will leave it to the scientists among you to determine its current utility.

As for the five challenges that Edelson et al. (1999) encountered, they helped me to frame my advice for any science teacher working with struggling learners.

1. Motivation

The topic must be authentic and of high interest. It should be introduced in a manner that will give struggling learners a sense of competence before they begin.

Use a clip from the Tappet Brothers' "Car Talk" radio show that is relevant to your lesson for the day. This show is broadcast on National Public Radio and can be accessed by going to www.npr.org. The Tappet Brothers, who are graduates of the Massachusetts Institute of Technology (M.I.T.), have a wonderful sense of humor. They take calls from people who are experiencing unique problems with their cars and who are willing to be harassed before either one of the brothers begins to diagnose and provide practical solutions to the caller's problem. My suggestion is this: Before either of the brothers starts to reply seriously to the caller, stop the clip and ask the teams to think about how they would try to solve the problem. After all the teams respond, play the rest of the clip.

In addition, "Car Talk" includes brain teasers created by listeners that the brothers try to solve. The two men are especially gifted at explaining how they solve the problems they are sent. Again, let the students hear the problem, work with their teams to either answer the problem or develop the solution, and then listen to one of the Tappet Brothers explain in detail how the solution was found. This is engaging, high-interest material that is sure to interest your students, who will be taught sophisticated problem-solving skills while they are laughing.

Use this quote from Einstein before a particularly difficult lesson: "I have no special talent. I am only passionately curious" ("Einstein Quotes," n.d.). Or this quote: "Do not worry about your difficulties in Mathematics, I can assure you mine are still greater" ("Einstein Quotes," n.d.). Take time to discuss your students' feelings and remind them that even the best scientists are humble people looking at a vast universe and trying to understand how things work.

2. Accessibility

In order to be able to understand the goals, the teacher must explain them to the class. The announcement sign in Figure 10.3 is a technique I introduced in Chapter 1. Since I "liberated" the idea from a science teacher, I know it can be useful in any class.

In order to teach struggling learners how to perform the task, it is essential to teach each step of the inquiry process for your discipline as you would any routine. Teach one step at a time, have a male and a female explain the step in his/her own words, and follow the same procedure when you explain how each step fits in the process. Do this as a focus lesson with a topic that is *not* scientific in nature. A problem that is based on students' experiences will serve as the best method for helping them to master the

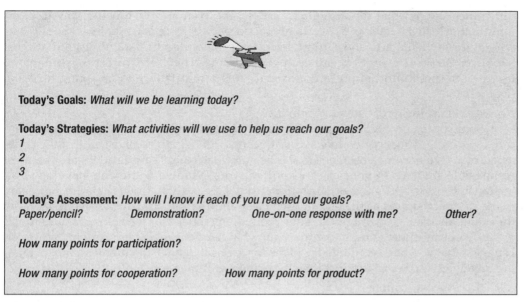

Today's Goals: *What will we be learning today?*

Today's Strategies: *What activities will we use to help us reach our goals?*
1
2
3

Today's Assessment: *How will I know if each of you reached our goals?*
Paper/pencil?   Demonstration?   One-on-one response with me?   Other?

How many points for participation?

How many points for cooperation?   How many points for product?

FIGURE 10.3   Today's Schedule

scientific inquiry process without having to worry about the content. Scientists in the field have provided a list of excellent suggestions that will work as focus lessons in either physics or chemistry:

a. Sports
b. Music
c. Car repair
d. Cooking
e. Household cleaning products

Finally, during a focus lesson on how to evaluate data, you can utilize a variety of data to teach the type of evaluation you want your students to learn. Please note that once again, only through careful planning will your implementation succeed.

Sir Isaac Newton (1729) said, "If I have ever made any valuable discoveries, it has been due more to patient attention, than to any other talent" ("Think Exist," n.d.). If your students are to learn how to pay close attention to detail, you must model and discuss what paying attention looks like in every phase of the experience.

This time to get help I went to my resident M.I.T. graduate, my husband. He told me the story of how his high school advanced chemistry class was taught to be observant. His teacher asked the class to read about an experiment in their text. Next, using materials that resembled those described in the text, but not named, the teacher asked the students to conduct an experiment and record what they observed. Most of the students recorded the results exactly as they had been described in the book. Expecting their usual excellent grades, the next day most of the students were disappointed when they received poor grades on their observation notes. The teacher commented, "I am somewhat amazed at the number of you who recorded seeing chemicals react to each other that were not used in your experiment yesterday. Never record what you expect to see. Only record what is there." In the 1950s, a wise teacher knew that, if he wanted his students to be able to observe correctly, he had to teach them how to do it.

3. Background knowledge

If you plan carefully, you can determine points in the inquiry process where missing background knowledge is vital and must be provided. At each point, you can direct your students to Internet sources that will give them the information they need to know.

At-risk students, even those who are struggling readers, will push through text if it is on a screen. According to an article in *The New York Times*, "Experts on reading difficulties suggest that for struggling readers, the Web may be a better way to glean information" (Rich, 2008, p. 5). Certainly, good pedagogy tells us that we should start where our students are, and our students are online. Recent data indicate that most adolescents spend over 40 hours each week online. Therefore, directing students to use the Internet to find important information is comfortable and engaging for them (Hartjes, 2009).

4. Management of extended activities

Some of the problems inherent in the issue of management are beyond your control. However, using cooperative learning teams will help to resolve some of the problems related to chronic absenteeism. Make sure that your Team Leaders are the most responsible students in your classes and that your Number 2 students have good attendance records and good organizational skills. Be sure that materials are put away in the designated area at the end of each class and that no students can gain access to the materials when you are not in your room. Remember that the rules in your empire are the same as mine; you can control only what happens inside the empire. However, I suggest that you have contingency plans for teams that have too many members missing on any given day to conduct their experiments as planned.

5. Time constraints

Plan your lessons so that every day your students get adequate time to work on the computer or use whatever technology is available; otherwise, they will not feel their time was well spent in your class. This point brings us back to motivation. Technology is both the catalyst for posing the appropriate research question and the source for sustaining your students' interest in finding the answer.

In addition, due to current state mandates, some science teachers are under severe time constraints to move through the curriculum in order to get their students ready for the statewide assessments. Student inquiry often gets shortchanged in order for large amounts of content to be covered, but not necessarily taught. This is especially counterproductive for struggling learners. Teachers must explain the reasons for their choices and do their best to turn as many lessons as possible into discovery lessons simply by allowing students to find answers for themselves, whether through the Internet or the text or their labs. Every attempt made to allow students to do inquiry learning helps all students learn science by doing science.

Summary

Mark van Doren said, "The art of teaching is the art of assisting discovery" ("Think Exist" n.d.). If we all knew how to do that without any further assistance, this book would consist of one sentence. However, knowing how to assist discovery requires thoughtful, reflective planning. When we reviewed planning for a discovery lesson, we found alignment among the instructional triangle, the lesson plan template, and the constructivists' core beliefs. We know that in order to conduct any active, engaged lesson, each teacher must create a safe climate for the students. Learners must be treated respectfully in order to learn how to treat others with respect. Errors are not punishable by humiliation or scorn; they are opportunities for learning and growth. Effective praise is used to stimulate further growth; even when the product does not meet expectations, the process can exceed students' expected potential.

At every level of instruction and in every field, discovery learning is appropriate. However, due to the pressure to cover the content in time for statewide assessments, teachers must be instructional decision makers who select from a wide array of methodologies those strategies that best fit the multiple and conflicting demands made on them. If you believe in active participation as your centerpiece for learning, you will want to give your students multiple opportunities to construct knowledge in a controlled, social learning environment. To support your efforts in this direction, I have included in the Appendix a template for creating a constructivist lesson plan.

Using this plan, students' prior knowledge is accessed during the warm-up, and the reasons for the day's exploration are discussed during the motivational activities. Focus lessons should be provided as needed so that when a new procedure or technique needs to be taught, the students can develop competence with the process without trying to master content and skills simultaneously. Finally, if you believe that you and your students are a competent community of learners, using the discovery/constructivist/inquiry method of instruction helps your students learn what you have to teach them and a great deal more.

Practices of Reflective Teachers

You learn something every day if you pay attention.

Ray LeBlond

At the end of every part of this text, there is a chapter devoted to helping teachers develop reflection skills relevant to the topic we have been exploring. Nowhere is this more important than in this section on instruction. After your mentors and supervisors are no longer with you and you get observed only once a year, or less, you are really dependent on your own ability to reflect daily to help you diagnose and treat your instructional strengths and weaknesses. This chapter is constructed differently than the two prior chapters on reflection. Now you will be asked to do your own problem solving. You will be given scenarios with sufficient information, but it will be your job to participate in the process and make sense out of the experience. Use your classmates, or peers, or mentors to help you through this step of the journey. There are no right answers in the back of this book.

Although assessments, formal and informal, can measure how much your students have learned, you need to know much more than that. Only through careful reflection can you learn what the data cannot tell you: How did the students feel about what they were learning? How many children were engaged during the lesson? How well motivated were the children? Did they understand what they were learning and why? As the instructional leader in your classroom, how much passion, enthusiasm, and energy did you bring to school today?

LOOKING BACK

In 1952, when I was 8 years old, a small group of Holocaust survivors moved into our neighborhood. I was immediately intrigued by the children; they were my age and had such vacant stares that I can still see them in my mind's eye today. Even though their parents did not speak any English, many of the children learned to speak English very quickly, and after a while, some of the children became my playmates.

For Halloween in 1952, my mom allowed me to have a small party and invite some of my new friends to join us. After the party, we were going to a circus, but there would not be enough room in the car for all the children. My parents decided that it would be better to only take the children whose parents could speak English and would understand where we were going. I remember this very vividly. A few weeks before the party, my mom came into the room I shared with Susie and asked why I was so upset. (I guess Susie told her that I was unhappy, or my mom's intuitive nature brought her to me.) I told her that I kept thinking about the faces of the children who would be standing on the sidewalk as our car pulled away. I didn't want to go if it meant leaving sad children behind. My mom said, "You have a big heart." It didn't sound like a good thing, but I have always remembered it.

I know why I teach, and I know why I teach struggling learners. I still don't want to be in the car that pulls away and leaves children behind.

Your Turn

Before we return to the reflection process relevant to instruction, I want you to stop, think, and write about why you became a teacher. What is it about you that keeps your passion alive, that drives you most days to do your best for children, and that gives you a sense of personal satisfaction when children learn? Keep this writing someplace very safe. When you need to remind yourself about why you became a teacher, it will be invaluable.

BACK TO BANDURA

I am frequently asked to support veteran teachers who are learning how to work with struggling learners. Before I observe the teachers, normally I have heard them with their students. Their frustration precedes their administrators' requests for me to help them. Their comments to their children have included the following: "I have taken everything away from you, and you still don't listen.... I don't care about you if you don't care about yourselves.... I would call your mother, but she is never there." This brief collection comes from elementary and middle school teachers.

In their classrooms, I have observed children sitting isolated from their classmates and sitting turned away from instruction. If we apply what we have learned from Bandura (1977), we know by observation alone that the students who have learned errors are punished by physical and emotional distance. We also know that self-efficacy beliefs are critical to determining everyone's willingness to persist. Henry Ford said it best: "Whether you think you can, or you think you can't, you're right!" ("Think Exist," n.d.) We can hear how some children, often at a very early age, are being taught whether to think they can or think they can't.

Your Turn

Based on your own teaching experiences and your knowledge of Bandura (1977), respond to what I have just described.

1. What messages are the children hearing?
2. How do you think the children will respond to these comments?
3. Why is isolation a violation of what Bandura tells us about the needs of struggling learners?
4. Why is it counterproductive to punish children with physical and emotional distance?
5. What self-efficacy beliefs do these teachers promote among the children?

For this exercise, find a partner and discuss your answers to these questions. It is important that you never duplicate what has just been described. However, unless you understand what has gone wrong, you can easily fall into these patterns.

MEET MARZANO

According to the Dimensions of Learning model first introduced by Marzano (1992), the classrooms I have described above fail to meet the primary goal of Dimension One. The teachers have not created a safe learning environment. In addition, the students are not being provided with the type of climate that promotes their self-efficacy.

Let's move on to the next phase of my intervention. Once I have been invited into the classroom, I frequently do a demonstration lesson. Perhaps for the first time in a very long time, the teacher has an opportunity to see his students actively engaged in the instruction. When I teach, the students always work in cooperative learning teams, and there is always a team leader assigned to each group.

Recently, I had the privilege of doing an impromptu demonstration lesson, ironically with the same group to which I had taught a demonstration lesson the year before. At the time of my second lesson, the students had a dynamic, veteran fifth-grade teacher, Ms. Great, who was working very hard to regain some of the losses the children experienced the year before. Ms. Great was so dedicated to their well-being that she asked me to visit, observe, and offer suggestions that would help her to improve her efforts to bring about positive changes in her students. I am always impressed when a successful, veteran teacher seeks help. Nevertheless, cooperative learning and some of my other strategies were new to her, so we decided to team teach for a while. Ms. Great taught the lesson, and I joined in just to "take the temperature" of the climate among the students. After I describe the mini-lesson that I taught, I want you to reflect about what I did and why.

Ms. Great started the lesson by dividing the class into four groups. Each group was assigned a section from a health magazine to read. The article that the students were reading described the major function of each part of the brain. The students were told to read silently and then answer Ms. Great's questions regarding the part of the brain they had been assigned to read about. Prior to the reading, there was no purpose for reading established. The group assignments seemed arbitrary to me, and the children didn't seem to recognize the other team members based on any previous work history. The children chatted during the reading and the discussion. I recognized those behavior patterns as being typical of what they had done with their fourth-grade teacher. From our preobservation conference, I knew that Ms. Great was concerned by the students' lack of engagement, poor behaviors, and difficulty getting along with each other. When the discussion about the various parts of the brain was over, I asked permission to tell the children what I know about how the brain learns.

The first thing I did was to use what I had been observing to create four student teams. It was clear to me that there were at least six student leaders in the class. I announced that, while I was watching the students learn, I had been watching to see how they learned. I had determined that there were many excellent leaders in the class. I appointed four student team leaders. After that I put the rest of the children in teams.

I explained the job of the team leader, but I didn't go into the other jobs due to time constraints. Every child except one paid attention to me during the course of the lesson. There was no chatter unless the teams were working on an assigned problem. I drew the picture of a brain cell and explained each part. I told the class that neuroscientists define learning as two neurons communicating with each other. I also told the children about some of the findings at Albert Einstein's autopsy.

These students had been treated for over a year as if they were deficient because they had been taught by someone who had given up on herself, and, after she left, by a series of substitutes. For fifth grade, they had a wonderful teacher who had found she needed to go back to the fourth-grade curriculum, especially in math, because they did not get the basic building blocks they needed to do fifth-grade math. However, these children processed sophisticated information about how the brain learns very well.

Your Turn

Based on what you know about Dimensions of Learning and Marzano, why did I make some of my instructional decisions?

1. What did I see and hear that encouraged me to form cooperative learning groups?
2. Why did I choose to teach a lesson on how the brain learns?
3. What did I expect the children to do when faced with sophisticated information?
4. Why did I announce the reason for my selection of team leaders?
5. What would you have done with the one child who did not participate in the lesson?

Again, find a partner and discuss your answers. Or if you are reading this text by yourself, write your answers. When you finish reading this chapter, go back to see if you are comfortable with your responses.

HAVE YOU HAD ANY GOOD CLASS DISCUSSIONS LATELY?

Whether you are a new or a veteran teacher, classroom discussions can be very difficult. I suggest you do a focus lesson before you start any content-driven class discussions. Tom Bodett said, "The difference between school and life? In school, you're taught a lesson and then given a test. In life, you're given a test that teaches you a lesson" ("Think Exist," n.d.). Since everyone in your class has experience with this topic, you can use this quote. Let's create a lesson plan (Figure 11.1 and Table 11.1), using this quote to begin our discussion.

Your Turn

It would be nice if we could get someone to use a rubric on our performance during a class discussion to see whether we encouraged higher-level thinking or whether we asked only declarative-level questions. Since that is not possible, I will pose some questions that you might want to ask yourself after your next class discussion. If you are serious about developing your skills as a reflective teacher and as a skilled leader of class discussions, you will want to think about how you handled these issues after your next discussion.

1. What kinds of questions did you ask your students? How do you know?
2. Did you call on boys or girls more often? How do you know?
3. Were your questions provocative, or did they usually result in yes or no answers?
4. Did you ask other students to respond to students' replies?
5. Was there any evidence that some children changed their minds as a result of the discussion? How do you know?
6. Were the children actively engaged in the discussion? How do you know?
7. Were the children challenging each other for proof, or did they accept each other's responses?
8. Did anyone bring up a topic that was completely off track? What did you do?
9. Did you see evidence of more mature thinking from your students?
10. When the children left your classroom, were they still talking about the topic?

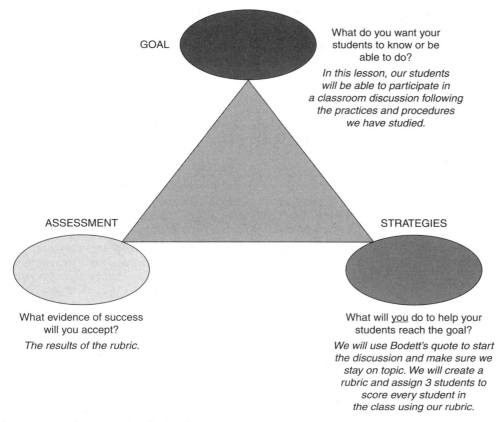

FIGURE 11.1 The Instructional Triangle

TABLE 11.1	Focus Lesson Plan

Lesson Title: Why do we come to school?

Lesson Unit: Speaking and listening effectively

GOAL	(SC) CCSS
Lesson Objective	As a result of today's lesson, students will be able to participate in a class discussion using support to back up claims, effective listening skills, and the ability to stay on track during the discussion. CCSS Speaking and listening -1. Prepare for and participate effectively in a range of conversations and collaborations with diverse partners, building on others' ideas and expressing their own clearly and persuasively.
Materials Needed	Each team will be given a copy of this quote: *"The difference between school and life? In school, you're taught a lesson and then given a test. In life, you're given a test that teaches you a lesson."* Placemat Computer access Paper for rubric
Warm-Up Time:	On your placemat, answer the following questions: 1. What is the difference between real life and school? 2. What kinds of tests do you take in school? 3. Do school tests really matter? 4. What lessons do you learn from life?

TABLE 11.1 (*Continued*)	
Motivation Time:	You are not the first people who wondered why you have to come to school and what you really learn here. With your team, you will be discussing the quote you have been given. Explain the importance of learning how to participate in a meaningful discussion. Put the requirements for a good discussion on the rubric. These are not negotiable. Ask students for their suggestions. Create a rubric with the class. Keep the rubric posted during class so the students can rate each other. Assign three students to rate every member of the class.
Guided Practice Time:	How many of you have made the same mistakes again and again? Why? What seems to happen the next time you make the same mistake? What seems to help you finally understand the nature of your mistake and why you keep making it?
Independent Practice Time:	With your team, determine what the author of the quote means. Talk about the similarities between school and life. Discuss their differences. Be specific. What do you think are the most important differences between real life and school? Do you think you could manage real life's challenges if you did not have an education? Be prepared to support your claims with information, not just opinion.
Assessment Time:	Using the rubric that the class has developed, each student's score will be determined by averaging the scores of the three students who were assigned to use the rubric for that student.
Closure Time:	Why is it important to understand the requirements of an effective class discussion? How would you score your participation today? Why?
Homework	Our first graded class discussion will cover the topic of the United States' involvement in foreign wars. Look through your text to find the reasons given for our involvement in the wars in Vietnam and Korea.

A classroom discussion is an instructional tool. You should evaluate your effectiveness at using it as you would any other. You are a work in progress; you are working toward constant growth. Keep your eye on the issues where you are unhappy with your answers, and continue to develop your skills in the areas where you recognize your strengths.

PRIMARY READING LESSON

It has been too long since I taught primary grades for me to feel comfortable writing, before trying to implement, a primary reading lesson plan. Therefore, after I created the lesson plan on *Mushroom in the Rain* included in Chapter 9, I showed it to a primary reading specialist, an instructional support teacher, and a very excellent primary teacher at an urban elementary school. After receiving very helpful upgrades from all of them, I implemented the lesson. In this section, I will share with you the results of the lesson, and we can reflect together.

Step One: Were my goal, strategies, and assessment aligned?

> *Goal:* I focused on helping the children to recognize that by sharing the space under the mushroom, the creatures' kindness grew.
>
> *Strategies:* The strategies included making up a song about kindness, using the story guide to help keep the children focused on the plot and the importance of showing kindness, and acting out each of the major scenes where the creatures demonstrated kindness.
>
> *Assessments:* The differentiated assessments helped each student to demonstrate his understanding that by sharing space under the mushroom, the creatures' kindness grew.

Step Two: What caused my management issues?

> The management problems that surfaced during implementation were a function of the plan's being too long. The plan should take at least 3 days. The children got very fidgety, but I had to continue, since I had only one opportunity to work with them. If I were to do this lesson again, I would change the song to a poem on day one, since creating the song appeared to be onerous for both the children and the teachers who were helping them. On day two, we would recite the first stanza of the poem as part of our drill and only get through guided practice. Day three would be devoted to independent practice and the assessment. Although I stopped several times to give the children a chance to stretch and move, I knew that they had reached their saturation point long before I ended the lesson the way it was written.

Step Three: Was I satisfied with my instruction?

> Since I had two other teachers in the room with me, I could divide the class as planned throughout my lesson. However, that is very unusual. If I were alone with my students, I would have created a short poem about kindness and worked with each team to create either another stanza or a few lines to finish the poem. The children were able to follow the plot and the characters by answering the story guide questions. They enjoyed talking about the story, and they loved shouting out the answer "NO!" to "Do ants, mice, etc. grow bigger in the rain?" At the end of the story, I asked them to think like adults and tell us what else (we already knew that the mushroom grew in the rain) grew larger during the story. One little girl said, "Kindness." I asked her to stand up, and all the children applauded her grown-up thinking skills. She was not the only child who understood the concept, but she was a member of the group that struggled the most, and I was happy to give her an opportunity to shine.

Your Turn

Now that you have read over the plan and my reflections, think of at least five changes you would make to the plan so it would be stronger. Describe exactly what you would change and how the lesson would work as a result of your idea. How does your change support the goal, strategies, or assessment? How does brain research or any other research support your change?

DISCOVERY LEARNING

Proponents of discovery learning recognize that learning is a social activity in which individuals learn by doing and by making sense out of the experience together. Each person's contribution is valued, and the total product is far better than any one person could have achieved.

> During my last semester of my senior year in college, I took a class in the History of the English Language. One of my best friends, Joe X, a history major, took the course with me because he needed the credits and he saw "History" in the course title. Our instructor taught the course through a lecture/test/lecture format. Most of us never discovered any meaning or purpose in our course work, especially during the long hours we spent hearing about the Great Grimm Vowel Shift.

> Although I didn't know it at the time, using a discovery method of instruction would have made this topic meaningful and memorable for all of us. As a historian, Joe could have helped his teammates become aware of issues that we English majors overlooked; whereas we understood language as a discrete entity, Joe recognized the connections between language and culture, language and privilege, and so on. Joe's perspectives would have broadened our approach, and our knowledge would have helped him to understand what the Grimm vowel shift means. Instead, Joe's last course in college was a dismal learning experience, and ours wasn't much better.

Your Turn

We have looked at discovery learning through our prior perspective as learners. Now I want you to think about using discovery learning in your classroom. How many absolute answers to your questions actually exist? Discovery learning is a viable teaching strategy when the answers cannot be found in the back of the book or when it's how the children arrive at the answers that matters. Ask yourself some of these questions before your next decision regarding the use of discovery learning, and review the others after you have taught your lesson.

1. After I establish my goal for the lesson, what is more important, the answer or what the children learn as they work toward finding the answer?
2. Will cooperative learning teams help my students during this lesson? Why? How?
3. Do my children need to access their prior knowledge in order to be successful?
4. Do my children need to know why they are participating in this lesson in order to be motivated?
5. Do my students work at different rates of speed? Do I have a system for allowing students to finish at different rates?
6. Are my students learning this content by following the protocol inherent in this discipline or by hearing about it? Which is more effective?
7. Why did I choose the strategies I used for this lesson?
8. Were my students involved during the entire lesson? How do I know?
9. What do my assessment results reveal about my students' mastery of today's goals and objectives?
10. Would I use the same strategies again for this lesson? Why?

From the comments I have heard from science teachers and science supervisors, the only way to learn science is by doing it. After more than 40 years of teaching, I can promise you that the only way to improve reading skills is by reading. There is very little that can be taught in splendid isolation. It was 1965 when I took the course in History of the English Language. The only things I remember from the class are the name of the Grimm vowel shift and the fact that *butterfly* was originally *flutterby*. I know that I remember much more from the courses where I had to discover meaning for myself. My other literature and writing courses, all of my psychology courses, and some of my junior and senior history courses come to mind. The first page of this book begins with a Native American proverb that bears repeating again:

Tell me, and I will forget
Show me, and I may not remember
Involve me, and I will understand.

ALIGNMENT AND ALLIANCES

From the first page of Chapter 1 until the last page of Chapter 14, I will be urging and reminding you to keep your lesson plans aligned with the instructional triangle. If your goals, strategies, and assessments don't match, your plan will fail. You and your students may have had an enjoyable time together, but that is only a part of what you are being paid to do. First, teachers, make sure your students learn what you said you were going to teach them.

The following is a true example, and I will let the details speak for themselves. In one large metropolitan school system that was trying to improve the students' math scores, the leadership created a curriculum guide that every teacher had to follow exactly as written. However, the homework that teachers were required to assign rarely reflected practice on any part of the day's instruction.

Your Turn

Stop and think! When there is a separation between what students learned and practiced in school and their homework assignment, brainstorm all the problems that were created. With a partner, discuss the following: How did that practice erode teacher–parent–student relationships over time?

GETTING TO KNOW YOU

In order to build healthy relationships and alliances between you and your students, I strongly recommend a "getting to know each other" strategy whenever you are working with new students. I love "My Name" by Sandra Cisneros (1984), but there are many other short readings that will lead to similar levels of self-discovery between you and your students. Researchers (Morse, Allsopp, & McHatton, 2009; Murray & Pianta, 2007) reinforce what we have been saying throughout this text: The presence of supportive relationships between students and their teachers can improve positive outcomes for children with emotional, social, and cognitive challenges.

Again, using a discovery learning format, I recommend that you choose an age-appropriate reading selection that will allow your students to use their prior knowledge, their team members' support, and their motivation to talk about themselves and learn about you. If your students are very young, create a short but true story about yourself, and illustrate it (see Figure 11.2). Then allow your students to create their own. If your goal is to let the children in on who you are and how you are, this can be a very entertaining, nonthreatening, and effective device.

FIGURE 11.2 Mrs. Porton's Book

This incredibly simple book took only a few minutes to create. If I were doing a lesson with a primary class, I would make a copy for each of the children and have them follow along as I read the story to them. It would not be difficult to stimulate a brief discussion about my siblings and what they were like and then, of course, move on to the children's life experiences. Using the model of the little book the children would have in front of them, each child could create his own book about himself.

A simple procedure such as a "getting to know you assignment" can begin to develop the trust needed among the three major participants in your students' success: the students, their parents/guardians, and *you*. If you need to explain a situation that is beyond your control to your students' parents, you will have a history of trust and respect that you have forged and that you can depend on when you need their understanding. However, you can never be dishonest and expect the students and/or their parents to trust you.

Your Turn

Struggling learners are hypersensitive to those who perceive them to be dangerous, damaged, stupid, and/or any other negative descriptor. They will not learn from someone who does not like them, and their expectation is that teachers will not like them. James Baldwin said, "A child cannot be taught by anyone who despises him" ("Brainy Quote," n.d.). This is especially true of struggling learners.

Some researchers (Hall, 2009; Moje & Dillon, 2006; Tatum, 2006) have suggested that the ways students identify themselves in the classroom have less to do with their skills and more to do with the way they want others to perceive them. Teachers may not recognize the dismissive behavior of struggling learners for what it is, their "need to do [what is necessary] in order to hide, maintain, or promote a specific identity amongst their peers, teachers, or family members . . . . On the surface, it may appear that teachers' and students' actions are about cognitive difficulties and motivation, while a closer look is likely to suggest that they are about the identities that are prioritized and marginalized within classrooms" (Hall, 2009, p. 287). Therefore, in order to have the kind of effective lessons we have been discussing, teachers need to develop a positive classroom environment that devalues the prestige of disengagement and replaces it with respect for the team and valued relationships between students and their teacher. Every student, no matter what his skill level, must be considered an esteemed member of the community of learners. When you go through the following reflective questions, you must be honest with yourself.

1. Do you treat every student in your class with respect, courtesy, and kindness?
2. Do you let your students know about you and your life outside of school?
3. Do you tell your students funny stories about yourself as a child?
4. Do you feel attached (appropriately) to any of your classes?
5. Do any of your students feel appropriately attached to you?

Even if you are not the type of teacher who is comfortable sharing yourself and your home life with your students, that does not mean that you cannot be successful with this population. It does mean, however, that you must look for other ways to let your students know that you like them and are interested in them. You can ask about their interests and their hobbies outside of school. You can discuss sports and local sports teams or other topics of mutual interest. You cannot be distant and cold; struggling learners perceive that posture as being directed at them, and they react negatively to it. If nothing else, always keep your sense of humor alive and available. Lily Tomlin once said, "I like a teacher who gives you something to take home to think about besides homework" ("Quote Garden," n.d.). I do, too!

CREATING AND IMPLEMENTING AN EFFECTIVE LESSON

B. B. King said, "The beautiful thing about learning is that no one can take it away from you" ("Think Exist," n.d.). As you evaluate the student teacher's lesson plan in Table 11.2, using a discovery learning model, think about the plans you are writing. Take your new skills as a peer editor with you when you edit and strengthen your own plans.

TABLE 11.2	Recognizing Geometric Forms

Lesson Title: Solid Geometric Figures

Lesson Unit: Foundations of Math

(Nongraded, self-contained high school math class)

GOAL	(SC) None provided CCSS Modeling with Geometry—Look for and make use of structure
Lesson Objective	As a result of today's lesson, students will be able to use appropriate geometric vocabulary to 1. Describe properties and attributes of two- and three-dimensional figures. 2. Examine, recognize, name, and explore the properties of geometric solids. 3. Identify geometric solids in the world around them.
Materials Needed	Whiteboards and markers Teacher-created PowerPoint Handouts with overheads Milky Ways, Tootsie Rolls, caramel cubes, Whoppers
Warm-Up Time:	Whiteboards—flat shapes
Motivation Time:	Check homework
Guided Practice Time:	Guided notes with PowerPoint. Three-Dimensional Figures Matching the worksheet—Identify the figures.
Independent Practice Time:	Candy activity Shape scavenger hunt
Assessment Time:	Taken from prepared materials.
Closure Time:	Summary Return to objective
Homework	Bring in solid geometric form from home.

Notes for accommodations: Color code for R.P./Counting shapes for R.T.

Your Turn

Evaluate the lesson plan, using these questions.

1. Is the instructional triangle intact? How do you know?
2. What strategies are used to aid in discovery learning? Should there be more?
3. Based on the strategies listed in the plan, do you see any signs of differentiation in the plan? Do you expect whole-group instruction?
4. Is there evidence of cooperative learning or are the students working alone?
5. Would you expect prepared assessments to measure these students' ability to meet the day's objectives? Explain.
6. If you can, make a few revisions to the plan so that it is more likely to be effective.

Summary

In order to be an effective teacher, you must be able to evaluate for yourself how well you have taught every day. You have to take the time to reflect on the results of the assessment data, the level of engagement that you saw among your students, and your own commitment to your students. The emergence of discovery learning and the technology available to support its use has revolutionized teaching. Discovery learning matches what we know to be true of developmental issues and of the problems facing struggling learners of all ages, and it focuses instruction where it belongs: on the ingenuity and creativity of the learner.

Based on what we know about Bandura's (1977) theories, teachers who use negative comments to control children are giving them the message that they have limited self-agency and are not likely to be successful. The earlier and more long-lasting these comments are, the more permanent their results. The consequences of a low sense of competence and low self-esteem have been thoroughly documented in this text, as well as in many other sources. Nevertheless, I must remind you again that "data suggests that an increasingly larger segment of today's youth [is] becoming involved in risk-taking behavior. However, what is even more serious is the fact that such activity begins at earlier and earlier ages" (Muuss & Porton, 1999, pp. 422–423). I am not drawing a direct correlation between how children are spoken to in school and their choice to become involved

in risk-taking behaviors, but children need to feel good about themselves in order to take good care of themselves. Bandura (1977) was one of the first, but certainly not the last, to discuss the connection between self-efficacy beliefs and students' decisions to persevere or give up in school.

Teachers who experience success with their struggling learners recognize that their relationships with children set the stage for learning to take place. Perhaps some students can learn from teachers who only share their content, but that is not the case with struggling learners. This quote may be apocryphally attributed to Noel Coward, but no matter who said it, I agree: "Good teachers must primarily be enthusiasts like writers, painters and priests; they must have a sense of vocation—a deep-rooted unsentimental desire to do good" ("Reflections on Education," n.d.). Teachers of struggling learners must have a passion to do what is necessary to encourage a thorny rose bush to grow. Ultimately, it is your passion to teach, your determination not to give up, and your belief in yourself and your students that will help you to persevere until every child starts to bloom.

Part Four

Assessment

Chapter 12   How to Create Effective Assessments

Chapter 13   Formative Versus Summative Assessments

Chapter 14   Practices of Reflective Assessors

How to Create Effective Assessments

Most teachers waste their time by asking questions which are intended to discover what a pupil does not know whereas the true art of questioning has for its purpose to discover what the pupil knows · or is capable of knowing.

ALBERT EINSTEIN

When we started our work together, we began by identifying the three intrinsically connected elements of instruction: goal, strategies, and assessment (Figure 12.1).

We have thoroughly discussed and analyzed the importance of establishing our goals and objectives. We know we have to make sure that the day's goal and objectives are aligned with any mandated curriculum guide we may be required to follow. We know that the strategies must clearly provide the necessary scaffolding that will enable

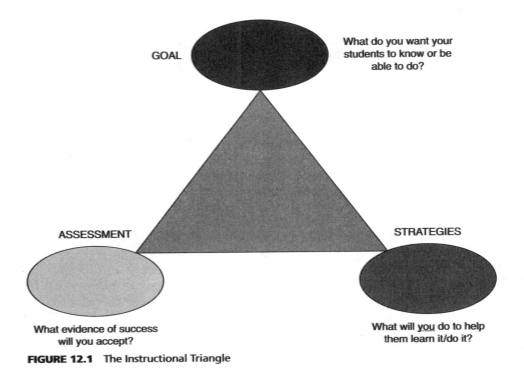

GOAL

What do you want your
students to know or be
able to do?

ASSESSMENT

STRATEGIES

What evidence of success
will you accept?

What will <u>you</u> do to help
them learn it/do it?

FIGURE 12.1 The Instructional Triangle

all of our students to learn or be able to do what we have outlined for the day's goal and objectives. Now we are at the last step of the process: We must learn how to develop the evidence we will accept that each student has mastered the day's goal and objectives.

In this chapter, we will address issues related to teacher-made assessments. We will reserve our discussion of large-scale assessments for the next chapter. For our purposes in this chapter, we will use Stiggins and Chappuis' (2012) definition of teacher-made assessments for learning: "Assessment is, in part, the process of gathering evidence of student learning to inform instructional decisions" (p. 3). Next, we will discuss rubrics. Rubrics clarify the target and help both learners and teachers recognize the levels of mastery that are inherent in any important assignment. Since assessments provide very important data, we will review a few key concepts related to understanding data. Finally, we will discuss formats for alternative types of assessments that can provide information regarding students' mastery of subject matter without relying solely on paper/pencil responses.

TEACHER-MADE ASSESSMENTS

In our daily work, we determine each goal and thus the type of assessment we need to measure our students' mastery of that goal. If we just want a quick snapshot of how well students understand a concept at the most basic introductory level, our assessment will include only a few short declarative-level questions. At first, we are seeking only initial understanding and clarity. However, as our work becomes more involved, our daily assessments should become more sophisticated. We are no longer satisfied with simple responses. We expect our students to be able to think about the content and be able to apply it meaningfully.

As educators/assessors, we have a duty to gather valid and reliable evidence that our students have achieved mastery of our content, to use that data to promote the best in student learning success, and to accurately report on each student's level of achievement (Stiggins & Chappuis, 2012). When struggling learners see the evidence of their hard work in their daily assessment grades, they are provided with concrete proof of the essential link between their effort and their success. I always required my students to keep their own grade sheets and took time daily to have them record all the grades they earned that day.

Our assessments have become an integral part of the instructional process. They mirror our strategies in both content and format. Only as classroom teachers do we know how far our students have progressed; therefore, most of us do not rely merely on textbook assessment materials. Instead, we may use those parts of the text materials that are suited to our needs, but we will rely on our own assessments, which have been driven by previous instructional and assessment results.

Once again, I will tell you a story to help make this clear. When I was getting my ninth graders ready for the Citizenship Tests, there were many materials that had been prepared by the Maryland State Department of Education. Most of the materials were really helpful. However, no one knows what the Empress's students need but the Empress. At the end of every class, I gave a short assessment of that day's material. Based on those results, the following day I reviewed material that most of the students did not learn, and I covered new material. I had to make up all my daily assessments because I was the only person who knew which material I had to teach differently from the previous day and that material also had to be assessed again. The process was iterative, and had I not been so diligent, my very bored and mildly cranky students would never have had the high passing rates we always experienced. I explained to my students what I will explain to you: "This is not *Sesame Street*. The Letter A will not come and squirt orange juice in your eye to make sure you are paying attention! This is work. No one ever said work is fun. It isn't. It's work. I wish I could promise you a life filled with orange juice and giggles, but that would be a lie. I don't lie." My students got tired of that response, but it is all I have.

Sometimes you just have to accept the fact that work is hard. Oh, well—that's why they call it work. Students better tolerate the repetitious nature of some of their work and the nature of assessments if they understand the following: (1) the connections among the assessments, goals, and strategies; (2) the uses of the assessment results; and (3) the integrity of the process.

The Connections Among Goals, Strategies, and Assessments

If your students are old enough to understand the instructional triangle, share it with them. Let them know what you are doing and why. There is no mystery about what you do—nor should there be. When students see the relationships among the daily goal, the strategies they are participating in, and the assessment they are taking, they will accept the assessment as a fair measurement of the teaching and learning process.

The Uses of the Assessment Results

I always explained to my students what I did with the results of my assessments. After I graded all their papers, I reviewed them to see if there were any anomalies. First, I wanted to see if any students struggled on any particular assessment item. Sometimes my wording gets strange, and students may struggle on a particular question not because they didn't master the content, but because they just couldn't figure out what I was asking for. If enough students struggle on one question, but they show mastery on related questions, I delete that question from the total possible, and I rewrite the question immediately. If my question is clear and too many students got it wrong, it still isn't a learner problem; it is again a teacher problem. And again, I delete the question from the total points possible. If none of my students learned a part of the content that was assessed, I assume it is because I didn't teach it. The item in question becomes part of my instructional plan for the following day. However, if there is a subgroup in the class that seems to struggle with a segment of the content, but the majority of the students seem to grasp the material, I have to provide different activities for those students who need corrective practice.

I have used the assessment data to inform my instructional decisions and identify students whose assessment results indicate they need corrective work. Now I am ready to plan for the next day's goal, strategies, and assessments. My students will know how and why their assessment results have been used.

Name____________________

Date________Period________

Julius Caesar **Say, Means, Matters**
Exit Ticket

In a quote by ____________________________, I discovered a theme of ________________.

The quote can be found in Act ______________ on page ______________.

FIGURE 12.2 Successful Exit Ticket

AN EXAMPLE OF A SUCCESSFUL ASSESSMENT This assessment was created by a student teacher working with a mixed-ability group of tenth-grade students attending a suburban high school. The students were completing exercises in "Say, Means, Matters," which enable them to identify who said a quote (i.e., say), put the quote in their own words (i.e., means), and explain the quote's literary purpose (i.e., matters). The *goal* for the day's lesson was "Students will select meaningful quotes from Acts I–IV of *Julius Caesar* and justify their significance by explaining effectively their meaning, purpose, and relationship to theme." The *strategies* used during the lesson included work on their reference sheet titled "Say, Means, Matters." The students were instructed to rephrase the quotes in their own language in the "Means" column. In addition, they were told to explain the literary purpose of the quote (e.g., foreshadowing, contrast to another character) in the "Matters" column. The class worked on each quote's relationship to the major themes of the play so that the students could see how the recurring themes were interwoven at key points in each act of the play. The students were given the exit ticket in Figure 12.2 to complete as the day's *assessment*.

The student teacher collected the exit tickets and analyzed them according to each student's ability to recognize the importance of the quote in relation to the theme. If the quote did not correspond in meaning to the theme, the student teacher placed the exit ticket in the "confused" pile. If the quote indicated a clear connection between the theme and the quote, the ticket was placed in the "got it" pile. If the connection seemed dubious, the ticket was placed in the "not quite" pile. The following day the student teacher regrouped the students according to those three categories, and provided them with three different activities.

The Integrity of the Process

When we began our earliest discussions of the instructional triangle, we recognized that, if there is a disconnect between what students are taught and what they are assessed on, the trust between students and their teachers can be destroyed. We know a great deal more about struggling learners now, and I am sure you will agree that such an act of betrayal will not be tolerated by this population of students. Any teacher who wants to play "gotcha" will find herself in a no-win game with people who believe they have nothing to lose.

I am not sure anyone can make a reasonable or professionally sound case for teaching one concept or set of information and testing on another. Struggling learners are not impressed by power or by figures of authority. I wish they were! If you want your students to respect you and follow your directions, you have to create a solid foundation of trust. Anything that violates that trust can become an obstacle that may or may not be overcome. Assessments that match the value you have placed on topics during instruction, that match by format how the students were instructed, and that have been transparent to the students during instruction add to the message that you want your students to understand: "Measurements are not to provide numbers but insight" (Ingrid Bucher, "Quotes on Assessments," n.d.).

Chapter 12 • How to Create Effective Assessments **163**

Name _____ Date _____				
EXIT TICKET				
$3 \times 3 =$	$6 \times 3 =$	$7 \times 3 =$	$2 \times 3 =$

FIGURE 12.3 Unsuccessful Exit Ticket

AN EXAMPLE OF A MISMATCH   This time we will be visiting a student teacher who was working with second graders in an urban elementary school. Her *goal*, taken from the state curriculum guide, was "Students will demonstrate knowledge of multiplication using three as a factor by working with manipulatives." Her *strategies* included the use of beans, rubber bands, Smart Boards, and chips for bingo. Even when she used facts, the students were given graphics to represent manipulatives. The *assessment* she gave her students is shown in Figure 12.3.

As you can see for yourself, this assessment does not match the way the students were taught during the lesson. When the student teacher handed out this exit ticket, the children were furious. They expected a hands-on assessment, since that was how they had been practicing their number facts during this math lesson. Their comments to her included: "What's this? We haven't been doing this! Why can't we do our work on the Smart Board like we have been practicing?" The individual assessment results were useless, since most of the children put forth very little effort. However, data analysis is possible here; the data tell us that the students learned not to trust their teacher.

RUBRICS

The first time I heard the term *rubric,* I could not believe it was a real word. I was convinced that it was a term made up by specialists in assessment who were sent from the dark side to harass my students and me. I could not have been more wrong. A rubric is actually a scoring tool for student work. It lists the criteria for the work, it provides a grid for the quality of the work from "excellent" to "poor" on each criterion, and it provides a system for indicating topics in order of importance to the grader.

Stiggins, Arter, Chappuis, and Chappuis (2004) said, "Students can hit any target that they can clearly see and [that] stands still for them" (p. 57). One of the best ways to make the target easily visible and stable is to create a rubric for all your long-term projects before the students begin to work on them.

For example, if your goal during a unit on the early colonies was to teach your students the obstacles that English settlers had to overcome when they landed in America during the 17th century and if your students spent a great deal of their time comparing the settlers' lives in England to their lives in the southern and/or New England colonies, the rubric for their final project could emphasize the following: (1) what the original settlers had to be willing to leave to come here, (2) the types of physical and emotional hardships they had to overcome when they arrived, (3) the difference between their expectations and the reality of life in the New World, and (4) the kind of people who would undertake such a journey and survive their ordeals. However, if your rubric, unlike your instruction, emphasized spelling, handwriting, and proper capitalization; the gifts the Native Americans gave to the settlers; the beauty of New England in the spring; and the bounty of the southern colonies—or other issues that were not part of your daily goals and strategies—your rubric would not have been a clear target that stood still throughout the instructional process for your students. The first and most important feature of any rubric is that it matches the instructional goals and strategies that the students were exposed to during instruction.

Next, a rubric must array what you mean by quality. The person who writes the rubric has the right to determine what quality means in this particular context. You might not agree with another teacher's rubric, but each of us has an obligation to determine our expectations for and describe them to our own students.

Template 12.1

Rubric for an Invention Report				
Criteria	Excellent	Good	Fair	Poor
Purpose	The report explains the key purposes of the invention and points out less obvious ones as well.	The report explains all of the key purposes of the invention.	The report explains some of the purposes of the invention but misses key purposes.	The report does not refer to the purposes of the invention.

I like Andrade's (1997) rubric for an invention report (Template 12.1). In her article, Andrade makes a sound argument that students need a clearly articulated rubric that spells out precisely what categories need to be included (e.g., purpose, organization, details, graphics) in order for students to achieve mastery at the excellent level. By clearly outlining her expectations for her students, she has provided the road map for them to follow to reach success. Stiggins and Chappuis (2012) highlight the same attributes of effective rubrics. In addition, they raise the bar for teachers as they create rubrics. "Not only can well-prepared teachers visualize and explain the meaning of success, but they also can impart that meaning to others so as to help them become outstanding performers. *In short, they don't just criticize—they inspire and guide improvement*" (Stiggins & Chappuis, 2012, p. 146).

For struggling learners, rubrics make clear the connection between effort and success. If any student wants to earn an A or a B, the task is clear. Do what you have to do to earn a B, or think outside the box and be creative and thoughtful if you want an A. There is no excuse for anyone to get a D or an F.

Rubrics help students to become better peer editors. I am a very strong editor of anyone else's work as long as I can understand the content, but I am only a fair self-editor. I love this story, and I think it speaks to my point. In my former life, when I was the Coordinator of Reconstitution-Eligible Schools for the State of Maryland, one of my tasks was to review the list of schools that had been *n*ewly *n*amed as reconstitution-eligible. The list was prepared by our office and then sent to the Board of Education to be revealed to the public. This list affected property values, local school agencies, the security of principals' jobs, and other noteworthy considerations. Therefore, the accuracy of this list kept me awake at night. The day the list was ready to be sent to the board, our secretary and I showed it to one last person to be sure it was correct. With cold eyes, our final editor immediately caught our mistake: "The *M*ewly *M*amed Schools." Imagine my horror when she pointed that out to us. Fortunately, we were able to fix the list before it left our office.

We all need a peer editor to help us see what our eyes automatically fix. Using a rubric helps peer editors see the tiny mistakes we miss, as well as our larger conceptual errors. In addition, the more we are able to detect errors in other people's work, the more sensitive we can become to our own mistakes. At least we can accept critical feedback better. I was made very humble on "mewly mamed" day, and I have never forgotten it.

Creating a Rubric

I suggest that, if you are new to creating a rubric, you follow a few basic routines at first. However, we need to review some key vocabulary before we proceed. A *formative assessment* is designed to help students and teachers learn how well the students are mastering material they are studying. Throughout this book, you have read about formative rubrics that I created for daily assessments when I was measuring my students' incremental progress during our unit of study. In this discussion, we will be examining rubrics for *summative assessments*, which are used to determine students' mastery at the end of a unit of study. The following is especially helpful for creating a rubric:

Step One: What is the purpose of the rubric? How will I use the data to inform my next instructional decisions?

Step Two: What stance do I want my students to take? Are they expected to do any of the following?
  - Explain what they have learned
  - Interpret what they have read
  - Look at this issue from a different perspective than their own
  - Reveal new self-understanding from their own life experiences
  - Project characters into a different setting, time, or place

Step Three: What are my criteria? First, I have to list the issues related to this project. Next, I put the topics in rank order. For those topics that have the least energy, I will assign the fewest points.

Step Four: Can I describe my criteria? When I have trouble describing my criteria, I look up models. When I find some models I like, I liberate them and use their language in my rubrics.

Step Five: Do I like my rubric? I try a new rubric out with a class as a formative assessment the first time I use it. As students resubmit their work, I can see for myself if the rubric gave them enough information so that they could redo their work successfully. I grade with an extra touch of kindness on this assignment because the rubric might have misled the students. I keep refining the rubric as I revise the students' papers until I think it finally captures what I value on the assignment.

Step Six: Do my students like the rubric? The next time I use the rubric, I ask my students to evaluate the rubric. If they tell me it helped them know what to do, it is a success.

Grading with a Rubric

As an English teacher, I didn't give any multiple-choice tests, but some of my unit tests had multiple-choice sections. I remember grading all of those sections at once because they were so much easier to correct than essays. However, a rubric makes grading an essay almost as effortless as a multiple-choice test. You have established the criteria, so you know what you are looking for as you read. If you find that all the criteria are met and there are no other intervening issues that your rubric discusses, you know the grade for the paper. Remember that you cannot take off points on a student's paper for anything that is not described in the rubric. As an English teacher, I cannot tolerate a final paper that is not mechanically and grammatically sound. Therefore, I apply the Maryland Functional Writing Test Standards: If writing errors interfere with meaning, the writer will lose XX points for lack of clarity on this assignment. Of course, the rubric will include a category for written expression. I don't think a spelling error in an otherwise outstanding paper should disqualify any student from earning an A; however, if I am constantly distracted by grammatical and mechanical errors to the point that they disrupt the narrative flow, the final score should show evidence of that problem.

Because rubrics are so important, grading becomes a matter of looking for a match between the paper and the criteria. I wish I had known about rubrics when I taught English six out of seven classes a day.

Rubrics from a Learner's Point of View

I want you to remember the last time you took a class in a subject that was a challenge for you. I want you to think about a teacher who really did not like you. Did these two happen simultaneously? Let's pretend they did. You must be pretty resilient because you are a teacher now, but at the time, you felt more at risk than resilient. If you had been given a rubric for your major projects and assignments, would that have made any difference in your attitude? Let's see.

I am going to give all my math teachers a break and recall a teacher I had in one of my graduate classes. There were only nine students in our class. Our professor never learned our names. We were all veteran teachers, but when teachers are students, we don't always behave well. One day we all switched seats to see if he would notice. He did not. When the course began, he assigned a paper that would count as 50% of our grade. He never gave us any directions beyond telling us to write a paper on the topic of the course title. He refused to answer our questions. We whined and complained bitterly. I was named president of the Whiners' Club, and with good reason. I felt completely helpless and hopeless. I do not tolerate vague very well, and I do not like to be ignored.

If we had been given clear directions and a rubric for the paper, I think all nine of us would have felt that we had a fighting chance to meet the professor's expectations. We would have known what he wanted us to explore beyond the title of our course, and we would have known how we were going to be evaluated. I think the quality of our class discussions would have improved because it became him versus us, and that is not a healthy classroom environment. Can you see that even from an adult learner's point of view, the absence of a target that is clearly visible and that stands still can negatively affect every aspect of the teaching and learning process?

However, a good rubric can serve to reinforce the trust and ties between struggling learners and their teachers. Buber said, "The learning community [is] an ever-regenerated community of people who are willing to be present to and for one another" (as quoted in Kramer, 2003, p. 91). When we as teachers provide clarity, and certainly rubrics help us to do that, we have demonstrated our commitment to be present to and for our students.

DATA ANALYSIS

In this brief section on data analysis, we will explore issues related to teacher-made assessments, not standardized tests or mandated statewide assessments. The number of persons participating in these tests is the number of students in your class, a number that is too small from which to generalize; therefore, we will keep our discussions focused on what you alone can learn from your formative and summative assessment results.

There are a few principles that apply to classroom assessments. One is that all assessments contain statistical errors. One such error refers to reliability. Reliability refers to instruments. Reliability is "the degree to which a test consistently measures whatever it measures" (Gay, 1992, p. 161). If a test is reliable, we would expect to see the same or similar scores when the test is readministered. Another statistical error refers to validity. Your assessment may not always measure what you think you are measuring. A test must be valid in terms of what it is measuring and who is taking it (Gay, 1992, p. 155). Suppose you create an assessment for your gifted and talented (GT) students, but administer it to your inclusion class instead. The test designed for GT students is not a valid assessment of what you taught your general education and special education students to learn and to do. However, it may be valid for your GT students.

Another principle that affects teacher-made assessments deals with the relationship between assessment and instruction. "When assessment is integrated with instruction it informs teachers about what activities and assignments will be most useful, what level of teaching is most appropriate, and how summative assessments provide diagnostic information" (McMillan, 2000, p. 5). Wiggins, who has enormous credibility in this arena, believes that assessments should be authentic and provide feedback and opportunities for students to improve their work, rather than simply auditing learning (Wiggins & McTighe, 1998). Wiggins further suggests that the type of assessment affects student engagement in the learning process and that students prepare for assessments more effectively when they know what they will be assessed on and how that knowledge will be measured.

From Goal to Assessment and Beyond

We will use a unit created for *The Miracle Worker* by William Gibson (1956) for this part of our discussion. The students involved in this unit were 25 at-risk ninth graders attending a high school in transition. The school had once been a suburban school that included a vastly White, middle-class catchment area, but by the time these students began attending this school, the demographics had changed. The class included 17 males and 8 females: 45% are African-American, 55% are Caucasian; 40% of the students entered the school as nonacademically promoted ninth graders; and 48% of the students qualified for free and reduced meals.

During this period, teachers were receiving training on new teaching and learning strategies, including Marzano's (1992) Dimensions of Learning. They were exposed to the idea of building a unit plan by determining the objectives, strategies, and assessments at one time to be sure that there would be real harmony among the three. When this unit was written, the teacher made a list of all the goals for the unit and matched it against all of the possible congruent styles of assessments she knew. She did that to be sure that the students would be assessed in accordance with the unit's goals. Again, striving for accord among goals, strategies, and assessment, she chose strategies from the five dimensions of learning she would be emphasizing during instruction to be sure they were aligned with the goals and assessments she had already selected. The written unit test was developed at the same time the unit goals and strategies were established.

The *goals* for this unit included the following: students' mastery of declarative knowledge, procedural knowledge, knowledge of how to solve problems, and knowledge of how to support claims and opinions. At the end of the unit, students were expected to be able to classify, compare, analyze perspectives, construct support, and problem solve. During all phases of instruction, students were expected to show mastery of critical thinking, creative thinking, and self-regulation.

During the course of the unit, such *strategies* as the following were utilized: declarative knowledge related to the time period of the play; procedural knowledge related to sign language, including using a sign language interpreter at the teacher's side during instruction to help the children understand the nature of sign language; problem-solving experiences involving characters from the play; classifying and comparing characters based on their ability to be flexible learners; looking at the plot from the lens of each character's viewpoint; and creating and supporting a position based on the script.

The day prior to the written unit test, each team was given a performance-based assessment worth 25 points. Drawing from a hat, each team randomly selected a scene from the play. The teams were given 10 minutes to prepare their performance of the scene (10 points). Each member of the team had to perform and explain the importance of her character throughout the play (5 points), analyze a problem from the character's perspective (5 points), and construct support for a problem from the play in character (5 points). The students had been given a rubric for this activity the day before so that they could prepare for this section of the assessment.

Figure 12.4 is an excerpt from the summative assessment for the unit: a written test worth 75 points. Even from this small sample from the written unit test, it is

---

THE MIRACLE WORKER

Name _____

Date _____

Period _____

Part One—Short answers (5 points each)

1. Identify the protagonist, antagonist, and deciding factor in this play.
2. Briefly retell the major events in Helen Keller's life, including what happened to her as an adult.
3. Give one example of each of the following and explain each of your choices:
   a. flashback
   b. foreshadowing
4. What would have happened if Captain Keller had kept his promise to Annie when she brought Helen back from the cottage? How do you know?
5. How do we know that Helen has learned language by the end of the play?

FIGURE 12.4 Unit Test—THE MIRACLE WORKER

possible to see that students were required to do higher-order thinking in order to supply effective answers. The second part of the written exam required students to write two brief essays (10 points each), selected from a list of three possible topics, and to use 10 vocabulary words in original sentences that revealed each student's understanding of their meaning (3 points each).

The raw data indicated that 18 of the 22 test takers present for testing that day demonstrated mastery of the material at 70% or better. Of the four students who failed to show mastery, three earned scores between 50% and 69% mastery. Only one student earned a score lower than 50%. The majority of the students did very well on both the short answers and the vocabulary sections of the test. However, the data indicated that those who did the most poorly struggled on the essays, which required them to analyze Helen's situation from a different perspective. It seemed that the students were not cognitively mature enough to do that well. Based on the data from the unit test, the teacher decided to focus the following unit on writing an effective essay by developing a thesis statement and finding good support. The rest of the data revealed that the other Dimensions of Learning strategies were successful for this group on this unit.

The data from the performance-based assessment supported the findings from the written measurement: The majority of the students (20 of 24) showed mastery on every topic except the analysis of Helen's situation from different perspectives. Only four students showed mastery on that construct. Whether the result of assessments involving speaking or writing, the data were clear: Analyzing perspectives needed to be taught as an explicit skill using a different vehicle at a later time.

ALTERNATIVE TYPES OF ASSESSMENTS

Students should be given multiple opportunities to demonstrate what they have learned and how well they have mastered the content in every major unit of study. If there is a real separation between school and life, it is based on the fact that we experience tests in school and performance-based assessments in real life. There are many people who can score highly on any test of basic knowledge about pedagogy, but who have difficulty relating personally to most children.

If you think back to your most recent observation as a teacher or student teacher, you expected to be assessed using a performance-based observation format. Suppose that during your classroom observation you demonstrated proficiency at getting your students to understand rigorous content and they did well on your assessment. How would you feel if your supervisor then, in order to complete your evaluation, asked you to write a short essay on the merits of tying teacher pay to student performance? Can you see how little the paper/pencil instrument would measure what you really know and can do?

It seems clear, then, if you are interested in getting a thorough picture of the multiple skills you have taught your students, that a written assignment will not provide you with the nuanced and revealing picture you really need. For some students, this format only hides what they actually know. For all major assessments, using a performance-based approach will provide more accurate information. "Performance assessments involve students in activities that require them actually to demonstrate performance of certain skills or to create products that demonstrate mastery of certain standards of quality" (Stiggins & Chappuis, 2012, p. 138). Working in teams, students can participate in the type of assessment that is most revealing of all their talents and understandings.

Concerns Related to Sharing Group Grades

One of the problems inherent in group work is that some students really object to sharing important grades with others, but there are valuable guidelines for grading group work that should help you to evaluate each student's contributions. Each member needs to know that everyone is required to carry her share of the load and that no one can sit back and let others do all the work while she does nothing. Suggestions include giving quizzes on content during the group work process, having each student write what she has accomplished (with evidence) to be turned in at the end of each class, and/or allowing senior tutors to evaluate each student's progress using a rubric that you introduced to the class before the project began. It is vital for group cooperation to ensure that individual student performance is assessed and that each member of the group knows how and what every member is doing (Johnson, Johnson, & Smith, 1991).

The final product is often more dynamic and revealing than anything any single student could have produced. Since each student has had a pivotal role in its success, attendance can be improved during the process, and the intrinsic link between effort and success can become increasingly more evident. An outstanding project cannot be accounted for by luck or ease of the task; it can only be the result of hard work and perseverance.

To manage outliers, I always give students who refuse to work with any team to which they have been assigned at least two or three chances (depending on whether it's September or May) to join a group and participate. If a student decides to fail, I will not allow that decision to affect the group. I give the student a project she can do alone. If the student chooses to do the work, we use the same rubric to assess the quality of the final project. If the student chooses not to hand in anything, there is nothing to assess. However, the individual's choice has no impact on any other student.

Decision-Making Matrix

I frequently use the decision-making matrix from the Dimensions of Learning (Marzano, 1992, p. 19). It is a viable summative assessment because it requires students to make decisions using the information they have learned and apply their new learning meaningfully. If the knowledge has truly been integrated into the students' thinking, their solutions to the problems should reveal how well they can apply the new principles they have learned. For struggling learners who prefer a practical approach to learning (Sagor, 1993), this is the most sensible way to evaluate how well they have learned to make decisions within the context of the work they have been doing.

First, I suggest that you teach the students how to use such a matrix in a focus lesson so they know how to apply all the components correctly. When you are sure that the students understand the basic principles, try a sample summative assignment. Suppose that your class has been studying the United States' involvement in World War II. You have emphasized the tension between the isolationists and the interventionists, the demands of the military to get prepared for the war, those in both the United States and Europe who did not want to become involved to help their neighbors, and the victims of the Nazi regime. To make your point clear, as part of your assessment, you give them this story of *Alligator River* (Simon, Howe, & Kirschenbaum, 1995) to read. The students have to use the story as an allegory for your unit of study. When they have finished reading the story, the students will answer the questions and use the matrix in Table 12.1 to decide which character shows the most integrity, which shows the least, and why. They are expected to use what they have learned during the unit to interpret the characters' behaviors in this story. I have tailored the original story of *Alligator River* to meet our needs:

One day, there was a beautiful young girl named Abigail who lived on Orp and wanted to see her handsome boyfriend Alex who lived across the river. She asked everyone to help her get across the river, but no one would help. She could not swim, and the river was filled with people-eating alligators. The only way she could get across the river was if she promised a river boat captain, Ivan, that when she got to the other side of the river, she would give him all her money. He needed the money to build more boats. She knew that Alex really needed her money too, but Abigail was sure that he wanted to see her more than he wanted her money. Finally, Abigail felt she had run out of choices so she crossed the river on Ivan's boat. When she arrived on Alex's side of the river, she gave Ivan all her money. When Alex learned that she had no money, he was very upset with her. He needed the money to save his family from Slug. Abigail became enraged. "Look at all I did for you," she said, and would not listen to his explanation. She met Slug and told Slug her story. Slug had been traveling all over the island beating up and torturing everyone he saw, but especially those people who were like Alex; however, Abigail did not seem to know that. He promised Abigail he would not hurt Alex, just rough him up a little for upsetting her. However, Slug was thrilled at the chance to torture and kill Alex. He immediately found Alex and carried out his plan. When the people on the island, led by their mayor, Cal, heard Alex's screams, they did nothing.

Let me walk you through the process. Do you think Abigail had clear, fair, and reasonable demands of all the other major characters? If so, you would give her a 3 (the criterion weight is 3) and multiply it by 3 (the total possible score under her name) for a weighted score of 9 ($3 \times 3 = 9$). However, I don't think she was very fair to Alex because she refused to listen to his explanation, so I would expect her to receive a reduced score. I would give her a 3 (the criterion weight is 3), but multiply it by 2 (since she didn't earn her total possible score of 3) for a weighted score of 6 ($3 \times 2 = 6$). The students are expected to write their numeric scores for each character on criterion A in the blocks to the right of that criterion and then on the paper write brief explanations for the scores. You will notice that Abigail and Slug have higher possible scores than the other characters. If my students could not name what groups those characters represent, I would know they had not understood the dynamics between powerful forces in the United States and Europe before and during the early years of World War II.

After the students have scored all the characters on the three criteria, they add the numbers in the cells under each name and write the total in the bottom row. Each cell can be identified by the letter that identifies the criterion and the initials for each character. The character with the highest score is the one with the most integrity. Fortunately, none of my students ever chose Slug, who obviously represents the Nazis. The students' explanations for the scores they gave each character on each criterion provide evidence of their understanding of the conflicted roles and postures taken before and during the early years of the war.

TABLE 12.1 Who Shows Integrity?

I. What group from World War II does each character represent?
1. Abigail
2. People on Orp
3. Ivan
4. Slug
5. Cal
6. Alex

II. Fill out the Decision Matrix.
- Write your score in each block.
- On a separate piece of paper, explain each score.
- Based on your final scores, rate each character's demonstration of integrity from most to least.

Decision Matrix

Alternatives	Abigail (AB)	People on Orp (P)	Ivan (I)	Slug (S)	Cal (C)	Alex (AL)
Criterion weight	1. (3)	2. (2)	3. (2)	4. (3)	5. (2)	6. (2)
A) Has clear, fair, and reasonable demands and expectations (3)						
B) Acts for the well-being of others (3)						
C) Keeps his/her word (2)						
Total						

Source: Matrix from Marzano, 1992, p. 110; original content from Simon et al. (1995).

Summary

Assessments provide teachers and students with meaningful information. They are no longer creatures from the dark side that have been devised to trick you or find out what you might not have noticed. A good assessment is a mirror of both teacher and student performance during any unit of study. A reflective, data-sensitive teacher recognizes that items on an assessment that no students could answer represent topics that were either not taught or not taught well. Those items lack reliability and/or validity and should be deleted from the total possible score.

Teacher-made assessments should match the teaching goals and strategies presented on a daily basis. Although teachers can only control the tests they create and administer, their classroom assessments can be a valuable mirror that shows the strengths and weaknesses from both sides of the teacher-learner relationship.

As educators and educational researchers have finally begun to talk to each other using language we can both understand, some models have been developed that allow students to understand how they will be assessed and what criteria will be used during the process. Students have benefited the most from this dialog, but now a new generation of teachers has begun to embrace educational research as an important teaching and learning tool.

Rubrics and performance-based assessments have clarified what we want students to do to provide evidence of mastery, how we want the work to be done to show various levels of mastery, and what we mean by each level of proficiency. Students, even struggling learners, own the decisions they make regarding the grades they earn. It is difficult to claim that a teacher "gave me a C" on a major assignment when the student had the rubric prior to completing the project and did exactly what was described as satisfactory work. Teachers who use rubrics effectively can easily respond to a child who didn't do the work but doesn't want the grade of "C" by saying: "When you look at your work and the matrix, it's clear that you gave yourself a 'C.'" Had the student wanted a better grade, the path to an A or a B was clearly delineated.

Perhaps the best attribute of effective assessments is that they provide both teachers and students new ways of exhibiting students' originality and creativity. During a mock trial the All Stars held as we studied for the Citizenship Test, students used their prior knowledge of district court procedures, the decision-making matrix, and the rules of evidence to determine whether or not the "accused" was innocent or guilty. Surprisingly, during this mock trial, despite their proclivity for finding every defendant guilty, the jury acquitted the defendant in this case. Their performance demonstrated that the students had learned the declarative knowledge that was required for the test and could access the higher-level-thinking skills we had been developing in this and other units. The students and I talked about that trial long after the test was taken and passed.

Barnaby C. Keeney, who was president of American University, said, "At college age, you can tell who is best at taking *tests* and going to school, but you can't tell who the best people are. That worries the hell out of me" ("Brainy Quotes," n.d.). We may never create an assessment for those things that really matter: kindness, empathy, wisdom, and tolerance for others. However, in the meantime, at least we can create assessments that measure how well our students have learned what we said we were going to teach them.

Formative Versus Summative Assessments

Not everything that can be counted counts and not everything that counts can be counted.

ALBERT EINSTEIN

When we discuss the world of high-stakes assessments, we might be looking at life through the sight of a shotgun or the eyepiece of a microscope; it all depends on what you believe about how the assessments will be used. Is it their aim to maim? Or is it their intent to improve? Graham Allison (1969) said, "Where you stand depends on where you sit" (p. 711). The interpretation of the goal and effects of statewide assessments is normally a function of where one sits. Policy makers believe that the only way to hold schools accountable for teacher–student performance is to have assessment results that can, in their minds, demonstrate schools' proficiency. Many teachers want to be able to have sufficient time to allow students to study their content in depth and not be controlled by a curriculum guide that forces them to cover the content quickly in order to be ready for statewide tests. The public hears the rhetoric on both sides, but there is still little clarity available on the effects of high-stakes testing, especially on struggling learners.

We will use Maryland as our case for this discussion for two primary reasons: (1) Except for Kentucky, Maryland was normally at the forefront in the national reform movement, and (2) I know what happened in Maryland because I was an active participant in the early days of designing interventions for struggling learners. Policy decisions in Maryland regarding school reform are outgrowths of restructuring that can be traced back to the 1980s, when Governor William Donald Schaefer commissioned an investigation into the state of Maryland's public schools. The subsequent report of the Governor's Commission on School Reform, submitted to Governor Schaefer in August 1989, was in part a response to the national policy debates on the quality of U.S. schools. In the cover letter to the governor dated 1991, Walter Sondheim, Jr., wrote, "The winds of criticism of public school education...are blowing...vigorously in America." Because of what has become popularly known as the "Sondheim Report," the State of Maryland initiated significant reform initiatives, including testing programs in grades three through eight. In 2003, Maryland extended its accountability measures into grades 9–12. Although Maryland has always been a leader in statewide reform, almost every state now utilizes high-stakes assessments. Currently, teacher pay and student performance on the assessments are being linked in order to receive the highly competitive "Race to the Top" money from the federal government. Could the stakes get any higher?

We will discuss a variety of assessments in this chapter. We will begin with formative assessments, which are used to inform students and teachers during instruction, but are not used for grading purposes. Next, we will move to summative assessments. Students cannot revise products or answers after summative assessments have been completed. These assessments are used to create grades and, in the case of state-mandated tests, to measure student performance, providing data that can have far-reaching consequences. Next, we will discuss high-stakes assessments, what their effects on struggling learners are, and what teachers can do to help these students prepare for high-stakes tests. The data are not as clear as one might think on this topic. Remember that, if there were no standards of accountability, schools that failed to meet any reasonable standards could continue to do so *with impunity*.

FORMATIVE ASSESSMENT

In our last chapter, we discussed teacher-made assessments that are designed to measure students' ability to reach daily goals and objectives. We made sure that our strategies helped our students reach their goals and that the parts of the instructional triangle were truly aligned. However, in this chapter, we are using more universal vocabulary, which can get very confusing.

Vocabulary

Let's be sure we all use the same terms the same way. A *formative* assessment is a lot like tasting the gravy before you serve it. You constantly taste it and then fix it to make it better before you serve it to your guests. In the same way, students can revise their work as a result of feedback on their formative assessment. That is the main purpose of using formative assessments. However, they can also be used to assess work habits, learning styles, and so on. Essentially, formative assessments are teaching and learning tools for both teachers and students.

Benchmark tests are predictive in nature and are closely linked to statewide assessments. They are not formative assessments because formative assessments are intrinsically linked to instruction. Benchmarks tell teachers how their students are likely to perform on upcoming statewide tests. They are given at discrete intervals so teachers know how and where to refine their students' skills.

A *summative* assessment is a final evaluation tool. A unit test, a final exam, and the results or outcome of a program as evaluated by any measurement qualify as summative assessments. When you serve your gravy to your guests, whether it is delicious or not, it has been submitted for summative assessment.

When and How Do We Use Formative Assessments?

We use formative assessments while the students are working, when they ask questions, and as they perform tasks. When you are evaluating your students to create your teams, you are using one type of formative assessment: "What type of worker is this student?"

Formative assessments are designed to provide critical information to both teachers and students. The best example I can give you is the rough draft of an essay. Students write their rough drafts at home or in class. When their peer editors review their papers, the rough draft is a formative assessment that is measured by a peer against the class standards. The peer editor tells the student writer what to do to improve or upgrade the paper in order to demonstrate mastery on the final draft.

If the student writer wants to share his work with another peer editor or a parent in order to receive additional feedback, that is fine. Therefore, the student writer has multiple opportunities to use formative assessments to improve the work before it comes to the teacher in its final draft form. However, once it is submitted to the teacher as a final draft, it is submitted for a summative assessment. The goal of the formative assessments has been to improve the writing; the goal of the summative assessment is to measure the finished writing against the standards that have been set. Marshall (2007) helps us to frame the difference between formative assessments and summative assessments. Formative assessments help teachers and students move forward, while "the essence of summative assessments" is that they look backward (p. 1).

One virtue of formative assessments is that the results are provided immediately. There is no long delay between handing in the paper and receiving the results. Peer editors need to review other students' work promptly in order to allow the writers time to make all the necessary revisions. Formative assessments reinforce the importance of timely feedback to everyone.

An Example of a Formative Assessment

You have just taught your class a lesson on categorizing. Your *goal* is "As a result of participating in this lesson, students will be able to place objects in the correct category based on the construct given by the teacher." Your *strategies* have included categorizing by shape, size, type of animal, and function. For today's *formative assessment*, you ask each child to put the items in Figure 13.1 under the categories pet and tool. To be sure that reading is not an issue, each word is accompanied by a picture, and the two categories are well defined before the children begin their work.

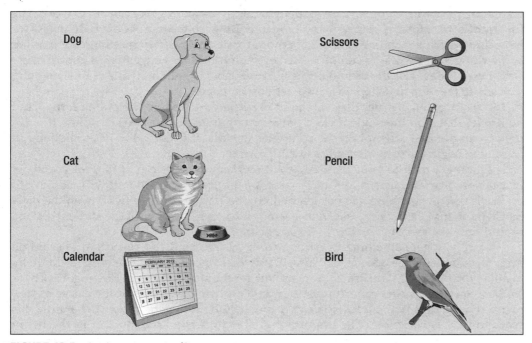

FIGURE 13.1 Am I a pet or a tool?

1. I am capable of performing this task.
2. If I try, I will get all the help I need.
3. Ultimately, I am responsible for completing my work.
4. I can always ask for help along the way.
5. When I hand in my final product, I will have reached my goal!

FIGURE 13.2 Yes, I can!

As a result of this assessment, you determine that nine children do not know how to categorize. The very next day you must create alternative, corrective work for those children. Six children seem to have an age-appropriate level of understanding of the concept, and you can create practice exercises for them. However, five of your students show clear mastery. These students should be given enrichment work on this topic while the other students are doing their work. You may have to rearrange your teams in order to respond to the formative assessment data, but the data drive instruction. You can resume your normal instructional teams for the next piece of instruction so the children can return to their more-familiar working partners.

Reluctant Workers

Formative assessments are especially appealing to struggling learners because the results are not threatening. Once a student hands in something, we can get to work. The first hurdle, of course, is getting something in writing from some of our students. As we have said before, struggling learners are more comfortable using computers for reading and writing. I had access to computers in my room, and I see computers in almost every class I visit today. Use the technology that is available to help motivate your struggling learners to take the first step: to put something on paper.

If a struggling learner does not hand in homework, reduce the points earned, but do not let that stop the student from participating in the entire project. Allow the student to do the first attempt on the computer in class. It is crucial to get something in writing to begin the formative assessment process.

Finding a path to your most reluctant workers must be a part of your planning, instruction, management, and, finally, assessment process. A student with nothing to do has learned something: He has learned how to fail. It's time to teach even the most recalcitrant student how to pass. Ask a senior tutor or a member of the student's team, or find time yourself, to work with this student.

Once you get something in writing from this student, you can begin to build on even the simplest idea. Coach, encourage, use the computer, and use other technology to allow the student to illustrate his ideas, but get the student's ideas flowing. Feedback from encouraging peers can promote reluctant students' attempts at formative assessments. Phone calls home from you can help the student to get support to continue his work until it is complete. The important goal is to remind the student of the list in Figure 13.2. You can put this list on a sign in your room and/or make copies for individuals to put in their notebooks.

SUMMATIVE ASSESSMENTS

Summative assessments are given at the end of a period of instruction. They are designed to measure whether long-term learning goals have been met. They are not intended to give immediate feedback to learners; they can shape curricular and scope and sequence decisions at the local educational agency, and they are used to determine annual yearly progress. Therefore, these are powerful instruments that can have long-term and far-reaching effects.

There are a variety of formats: Selected response items include multiple choice, true–false, and matching. Short-answer responses include fill-in-the-blank and one- or two-sentence responses. Assessments calling for extended written responses and performance assessments are also given (Coffey, 2010). However, statewide assessments seem to use more of the selected and short-answer response formats because assessments with extended written responses and performance assessments require trained graders, making it more difficult to get results returned to schools in a timely manner.

An Example of a Summative Assessment

Teachers give summative assessments at the end of a unit when they wish to "look backwards" (Marshall, 2007, p. 1) to measure whether their student have met the unit's long-range goals, which come from the statewide curriculum guide. Suppose a seventh-grade class has just completed a unit on the Civil War. The *goals* for the unit included the following: The students will be able to demonstrate mastery of the declarative knowledge regarding the war—that is, dates, names of important generals, basic facts of key battles, and issues surrounding support from Great Britain and France. The students will be able to demonstrate the ability to analyze perspectives from the northern states, southern states, slaveholders, slaves, and abolitionists. The students will be able to construct support for their opinions using information from a variety of sources. The *strategies* included reading the text, visiting the library, reading information online, writing about the war, and role-playing scenes from different perspectives. The class participated in many classroom discussions, was visited by military historians from a nearby Army base, and had various hands-on learning experiences. The *summative assessment* included the following:

PART ONE: SHORT ANSWERS

1. *Who were the two greatest generals on each side of the war? Defend your choices.*
2. *Which nations supported the North? The South? Why? What were the results of their support?*
3. *What did our guest believe was the turning point of the war? What does our text indicate? Why is there still so much controversy surrounding this issue?*
4. *If you were a Northern soldier from Maryland during the war, what would you say to your brother who was fighting for the South?*
5. *A runaway slave is at your door. You and your family are abolitionists. What will you do? Explain.*

PART TWO: ESSAYS

The results from this test were not used to drive instruction the following day; the data were used to inform future planning decisions and to create final grades for the students. Students could not correct their work and resubmit it; they had completed their unit of study and had demonstrated whether or not they had achieved mastery of the knowledge and skills goals established for that unit.

Three essay questions were provided, and the students could select two out of the three choices provided.

HIGH-STAKES TESTS AND STRUGGLING LEARNERS

The purpose of this discussion is not to examine the merits of high-stakes testing; over the years, the accountability movement has only grown stronger and more powerful. The purpose of our discussion is to (1) provide a brief history of the testing movement in order to put it into a context that allows you to understand the intended consequences of the policies involved; (2) discuss some of the findings from research studies related to high-stakes testing, especially in terms of struggling learners; and (3) unpack the findings from the research and place them in the context of what we know to be true about struggling learners so that these students profit from the experience of studying for high-stakes tests, rather than suffering unintended negative consequences.

Historical Context of the Accountability Movement

NATIONALLY   During the 1980s, many states required what Maryland called the Functional Tests for high school graduation and reported that students' passing rates were consistently improving; however, students showed little or no improvement on a highly regarded, nationally administered examination, the *National Assessment of Educational Progress* (NAEP). The discrepancy between students' scores on the basic competency exams and on the NAEP accounted in part for the national movement to raise the standards for graduation examinations (Heubert, 2010). To protect future generations of struggling learners from courses designated as "basic" with no evidence of rigor or agreed-upon content standards, the accountability movement worked hard to make every school provide *all* its students with a standards-based, appropriately rigorous curriculum.

IN MARYLAND   From almost the beginning of the statewide reform movement in Maryland, the consensus among the key stakeholders and the members of the Maryland State Board of Education was framed around the belief that accountability as managed through statewide assessments was the only reliable hope for change. The board started by testing elementary and middle school students; however, the results did not drill down to individual elementary and middle school students for almost a decade. During the 1990s, the board shifted into gear and started looking at measuring individual student performance at the high school level.

The board's high-stakes testing policy reflects its assumption that the high school assessment program can reform educational policies and practices. The current High School Assessments are designed to measure both school and student progress toward meeting Maryland's High School Core Learning Goals in the following subjects: English, government, algebra/data analysis, and biology. The graduating class of 2009 was the first to be required to pass all the assessments in order to graduate (School Improvement in Maryland@msde.state.md.us, 2010).

The Maryland State Department of Education (MSDE) understood almost from the beginning of this initiative that some students could be disadvantaged by the Maryland State Board of Education's Resolution #1998–1, which made passing the High School Assessments a graduation requirement. "In the fall of 1999, the State Board adopted a forty-nine million-dollar Academic Intervention Plan. The purpose of the plan was to close the gap between high performing high school students and their less successful peers" (*Every Child Achieving*, 1999, p. 8).

I served on the PreK–12 Academic Intervention Steering Committee and participated in many discussions regarding the importance of protecting struggling learners from the unintended consequences of high-stakes testing. I worked with knowledgeable, well-intentioned educators from across the state and across the nation who were looking at viable means of holding schools, teachers, and students accountable for meeting reasonable standards. The inevitable tensions that we are facing now were well known to us then. We expected problems with depth versus breadth of content coverage; we expected to hear teach-to-the-test arguments; we were not oblivious to the problems the tests would cause. However, I believed then, as I do now, that we do need an assessment system, and I will tell you why.

As always, I want to begin by telling you a true story. This event, which was covered by the national press, occurred when I had been the Coordinator of Reconstitution-Eligible Schools for about a month. One of the high schools that was under state monitoring was described to me as being very problematic for several reasons: (1) The building was old and in need of substantial repair, (2) the neighborhood was unsafe, (3) some of the problems from the neighborhood spilled over to the school grounds, and (4) there had been serious problems in the past with the school's schedule. As a former high school person, I became most alarmed when I heard item 4. A high school that does not have a good schedule is a train wreck waiting to happen. However, my 20+ years of high school experience had not prepared me for what I was about to see.

The state monitor and I went to visit this high school during the first week of school. As we traveled through the building during class time, we saw students circling the building on every floor. Classrooms were virtually empty. Almost no one was teaching because the students were walking the halls. When I asked for an explanation, I was told that students' schedules were so useless, the students did not go to class. For example, the students were assigned to classes they had already taken and passed or to classes they were not eligible to take. There were a few teachers in the hallways and some administrators, too, but they seemed more concerned with making sure the boys were not wearing hats than with the fact that the students were not in class.

About a week after my initial visit, the principal of the school suspended 1,500 students at one time. The students refused to return to their classes after the principal had told them to do so, and she suspended all of them. Although this was the most explosive and notorious of all of the reconstitution-eligible high schools' problems, it was not unique. If we did not have an accountability system in place, the kind of leadership in the building that would have allowed these problems to occur could still be there today, and there would be no consequences for students, teachers, or administrators. Of course, there was sufficient blame to go around, but it should not have stopped at the building level. Administrators at the local education agency were well aware of the toxic situation at this school and had not taken the necessary steps needed to put students in classes and provide the leadership that such a school clearly required.

Unintended Negative Consequences of the Policy

It does appear that high-stakes tests can have devastating effects on struggling learners. If there is a positive correlation between high-stakes testing and increased dropout rates—and this is still not clear from the data—this is a critical issue because high school dropouts face many serious problems and are at a distinct disadvantage. "The annual income for a high school dropout in 2005 was $17,299 compared to $26,933 for a high school graduate" (Alliance for Excellent Education, 2007, p. 1). If we further disaggregate by gender, the numbers help to clarify the feminization of poverty. Females who drop out of high school only earn 60% of what their male counterparts are paid (Dallman-Jones, 2006).

"Dropouts are much more likely than their peers who graduate to be unemployed, living in poverty, receiving public assistance, in prison, on death row, unhealthy, divorced, and ultimately single parents with children who drop out from high school themselves" (Bridgeland, DiIulio, & Burke Morison, 2006, p. 2). Dropouts are not the only ones who pay the price for their poor decisions; research conducted at Princeton University demonstrated that each dropout over his lifetime costs the nation approximately $260,000 (Alliance for Excellent Education, 2007).

According to Croninger and Lee (2001), social problems that have been associated with dropping out of school, such as delinquency and poverty, can threaten adolescent dropouts' well-being and life expectancy. Social ills such as homelessness, substance abuse, and violence can compromise the safety of adolescent dropouts and those who encounter them. It is vitally important for our students, as well as our society, that we learn how to prepare our struggling learners for high-stakes tests so they can stay in school and graduate.

As we have been saying throughout this text, the impact of the relationship between teachers and struggling learners can never be overemphasized. Croninger and Lee (2001) investigated whether students' access to social capital, which they define as "valuable forms of interpersonal assistance" (p. 549), can reduce the chances that students will choose to drop out of school. They found that, "although teacher-based forms of social capital are generally beneficial for *all* students, those who benefit *most* are students at risk of dropping out of school. This is especially true for socially at-risk students who enter high school with low educational expectations and a history of school-related problems" (p. 569).

According to Bridgeland et al. (2006), of those dropouts they interviewed "four out of five wanted better teachers and three-fourths wanted smaller classes with more individualized instruction. More than half (55 percent) felt that more needed to be done to help students who had problems learning" (p. iii). These responses echo the voices of many struggling learnes who have never received the type and intensity of intervention they require to succeed in school. The impact of educational and social deficits on struggling learners, when combined with the demands of high-stakes tests, is sure to make well-intentioned teachers' efforts more important than ever before.

What Research Tells Us

"Advocates of high-stakes testing argue that providing incentives for students to take learning more seriously will result in greater student motivation and effort. Opponents argue that these policies set low-achieving students up to fail, citing evidence that extrinsic and negative incentives...will only undermine students' efforts" (Roderick & Engel, 2001, p. 219). We can apply what we know to these arguments to see if what we have learned about struggling learners can help us to determine if high-stakes tests work for or against them.

First, advocates for and opponents of high-stakes tests make the faulty assumption that incentives or disincentives will make students take learning more seriously. I hope you see the flaw in that argument for struggling learners. Motivational theory is unambiguous in that no incentive is useful unless it is both valued and the goal is considered attainable. Struggling learners' efforts are intrinsically tied to their self-efficacy beliefs. Because you have been paying attention, you know that struggling learners normally have a strong adverse reaction to any high-stakes tests. We know that they have a compromised sense of self-efficacy and that, unless a teacher or a lot of teachers have convinced them that they are capable of passing the tests, they may not even try.

Struggling learners begin any new undertaking with negative self-talk: "This is too hard. I can't do it. I don't care. This is stupid. I don't understand this; I never will." Ultimately, the negative self-talk can become reframed as hostility or utter indifference.

If we want struggling learners to take learning more seriously, we have to begin with a caring teacher who establishes a climate where everyone is respected. Incentives and disincentives mean nothing to struggling learners if the teacher does not establish a safe and caring environment. The teacher must also make it absolutely clear to every student that the goals are attainable. We know that, if the teacher provides the scaffolding, practice, and climate, most struggling learners will attempt the tasks required to pass any tests. However, these students have a grim notion of the future; telling a ninth or tenth grader that, unless he passes one of the HSA exams, he may not graduate is a meaningless threat if he does not have any plans to graduate. Struggling students will try to pass high-stakes tests only if they believe the teacher believes they can *and* if the necessary scaffolding has been provided.

In an evaluation of the effects of high-stakes testing on struggling learners, Roderick and Engel (2001) noted that, even with teachers who provided high levels of support, the students with the lowest skills would not attempt the work because they felt that the goals were unattainable, they had no control over what happens to them, and/or their skills were too low to be able to accomplish the tasks. Therefore, it appears to be the combination of a caring teacher and the appropriate scaffolding that determines whether or not the most reluctant of all struggling learners will even attempt to do any work. In their examination of the results of their study, Roderick and Engel (2001) pointed out that "the majority of students with low work effort during the school year seemed to have needs that were not addressed during the school year...those students ... need more intensive intervention and support" (p. 221).

This is one of the unintended benefits of high-stakes testing. We have uncovered the group we have been talking about, a group that has gone unrecognized by the broader public until now. These are the students who lower schools' scores, who fail the HSAs, who do not pass classes because they refuse to do the work, and who do not graduate. These students appear to be nameless, faceless, and useless until you teach them.

I can see some of their faces in my mind's eye even today. Let me tell you about two of them. One of my favorites was a very tall youngster who, when he was in the eighth grade, used to pull four chairs together so he could sleep all day. When he was an All Star, he was a wonderful student. He read quickly and well. He was a fabulous mimic. He could always make us laugh. I hope he is OK; I often think about him.

I will always love my little "Lovely Lady." One time I took the All Stars on a trip to NASA. I told the children that my sister, who was working there at the time, might stop by to see us. When Lovely Lady saw my sister, Susie, who looks a lot like me, she ran up and gave my sister a big hug and said, "Aunt Susie, I am so glad to see you!" Lovely Lady will always be precious to me. These are not people we can afford to throw away; these are wonderful people who deserve all the help we can give them.

Matching Theory to Practice

In order to help struggling learners attempt high-stakes tests in your content area, let's review what we know to be true about their issues. Even though the current High School Assessments will be replaced by the new assessments to be aligned with the Common Core of State Standards, this list holds true across time, test, and place.

1. They do not see the connection between effort and success.

You cannot wait to demonstrate the connection between effort and success until the results of the HSAs are returned. Your struggling learners need to see immediate connections between their effort and their success on a regular basis. Every time you practice any facet of the HSA, keep a Chart of Success visible in your room. As the number of students who achieve success on your drills or exercises increases, create a graph that displays their growth. Struggling students need to see concrete evidence of improvement and to be convinced that there really is an authentic link between their effort and their success.

2. They are distrustful of adults.

We have had many discussions throughout this book on the importance of creating a trusting relationship between struggling learners and their teachers. Truly, the data are very compelling on this issue. However, to support your endeavors specifically targeted to HSA exams, (a) make sure your assessments mirror in format and content the goals and strategies they are designed to measure and (b) assign journal writing on this topic. Would you expect any student to perform a solo at a recital on a piece he never practiced? Of course not. That is why your practice for the "big day" must mirror how your students will be expected to perform when the test booklets are distributed and they must do their best by themselves.

Using a journal allows your students to talk about how they feel about the test; however, you must respond in writing to their journal entries. Let them know that you understand their anxiety and that you have faith in them. Fill your room and your heart with encouragement for their effort and respect for their success.

3. They must have sufficient scaffolding before they will attempt new tasks.

In order to get your struggling learners ready for the HSA in your content area, go to the website for your state education agency, and get as many examples of published test items as you can. Beginning with the first week of school, use these test items as part of your warm-up on a regular basis. You want your students to become very familiar and comfortable with the test format as soon as possible.

Each state offers support for teachers and administrators. For example, the School Improvement in Maryland website is excellent. For the English HSA, the site provides sample test items and answers, as well as the goal, expectation, and indicator aligned with each test item. These items can be used as samples for your warm-up, formative assessments, and motivation. (You can also consider the question "How can you use this data to guide instruction?" at http://hsaexam.org.) You need to mirror as much of the test format as possible so that when the students take the summative assessment from the state, it will not be a new experience for them.

Next, when you review the answers to the sample questions with the class during your drills, be sure that every student understands how the answer was reached. Make sure that each student can explain the easy questions, as well as the most challenging ones, to your satisfaction.

The MSDE website, School Improvement in Maryland, also provides rubrics to help students and teachers score brief constructed responses. Post these rubrics and use them every time you assign a brief constructed response. Allow peer editors to use the rubrics to assess formative assessments on brief constructed responses. The more frequently your students use the rubrics, the better they will become at knowing when they have written a response at the 3 level. Since 3 is the highest level, they will experience success before the test is administered, and that can give them the confidence they will need to attempt to do the work on the test.

4. They need effective praise during instruction in order to maintain effort.

According to Brophy (1981), effective praise is delivered contingently. Students do not even hear global comments, which they consider meaningless. Students process only praise that is meant for them and is based on a particular act that the student performed well. The praise describes the qualities of the accomplishment. The student recognizes that the teacher was paying attention to the student and his work. The reward that accompanies the praise is based on both the performance or outcome and the effort that was needed to accomplish the task.

5. They need to be active learners.

As we know, struggling learners become bored easily with routine tasks, and that is one reason why we advocate discovery learning. However, in some cases repetitious drills are inevitable. Giving each team a chance to create questions for the other teams to answer keeps students actively engaged. Once your students are familiar with the format of assessment questions, allow them to create questions, provide the answers, and have a challenge match between the teams. This is an excellent periodic review for the skills that you have been working on in your unit of study that correlate with the warm-up questions from the HSA sample items that you have been using. Long before you begin formal preparations for the HSA, your students will know the following: (a) The goal has real value in that it is intrinsic to what they are currently learning in class, (b) they have the skills needed to reach the goal, and (c) you will provide all the scaffolding they will need. Surround your students with words of encouragement (Figure 13.3) and samples of their success, and you will see progress on both their effort and their outcomes.

"Destiny is not a matter of chance; it is a matter of choice."
William Jennings Bryan

FIGURE 13.3   What will YOU choose?

Summary

In this chapter, we have refined our understanding of assessments by clarifying their two categories: formative and summative. A formative assessment is used during the instructional process to inform both students and teachers of what incremental gains the students are making and how the teaching and learning process should be changed daily so that the students can achieve greater success. Students are given multiple opportunities to correct their work. There are no grades attached to this work, only indications of the degree of progress made.

Summative assessments, however, are designed to provide evidence of mastery at the end of a unit of study, after a year of studying a given content area, or at any other designated time. The stakes are high, and students are not given any opportunities to correct their work once it has been submitted. The data are analyzed, but are not necessarily used for instructional decisions to be made in the near future.

Both forms of assessment require teachers to be aware of reliability, validity, and careful test construction. Of course, all teacher-made assessments must be intrinsically aligned with the state curriculum goals and teacher-selected strategies for the day and/or the unit of study.

I think I am most offended by the theory that high-stakes tests hurt struggling learners because it assumes that struggling learners are not capable of handling rigorous content and performing well on assessments that measure their ability to understand difficult content. I know that is just not true. However, I also know, and so do you, that struggling learners who are expected to learn using traditional stand-and-deliver methodology will be as unsuccessful now as they always have been.

FIGURE 13.4 My future will be fabulous!

Teaching students who have a low sense of self-worth using repetition, sage on the stage, and other historically failed techniques, in combination with punitive threats, will not motivate this population of students. Therefore, the flaw in the theory is not that it assumes the tests create the increased dropout rate; it is the dependence on outmoded teaching strategies and warnings of meaningless punishment that do not result in change that we must address. The tests were designed to hold students, teachers, and administrators accountable for their decisions. If we do not want a two-tiered society where only the privileged can compete and the rest serve their needs, we must prepare everyone to participate and compete in the 21st century.

When you work with older students, it is important to recognize that they have their own hopes and dreams. I suggest you post Figure 13.4 in your room and let the students fill it with a list of all their goals. Use their visions of success to help them reach for *their* stars.

Practices of Reflective Assessors

Who dares to teach must never cease to learn.

JOHN COTTON DANA

W e are at an interesting and inevitable point in our journey: the end. We will review the major points we have made throughout this part on assessments and provide some suggestions for best practices for effective reflection on assessments. However, since this is the last chapter in our book, we will also look back together at the entire journey. What have we learned that will help us to find more success with our struggling learners? How do we know that we are using our new knowledge effectively?

In the Introduction to this book, I made some promises to you. I need to reflect on whether or not I kept those promises. Rousseau said, "He who is the most slow in making a promise is the most faithful in the performance of it" ("Think Exist," n.d.). I made my promises to you slowly and judiciously; as I review them with you, I hope you will agree that I have tried to be faithful to my word.

ASSESSMENT

Effective Daily Assessments

When we began discussing assessments, we looked at ways of assessing how well our students mastered our daily goals. We created our own assessments and tried to be sure that they matched in format, emphasis, and content what we had done during our instructional delivery. Our students were never surprised by our assessments; in fact, most of our struggling learners could have predicted what would be on their assessments because they trusted us. As effective assessors, we learned to delete items that are unclear due to poor phrasing on our part, items that only a few students got correct because we did not teach the content well, and/or items that captured confusion on the part of a majority of students. Our daily assessments cannot be generalized because they are designed for a small sample of students. However, they are very important in helping us to plan the next day's instruction and letting us know how well our students are processing our content in small, discrete steps.

How Do We Reflect on Our Success on Daily Assessments?

You will need a partner in order to answer my questions following the two scenarios in this section. If you really can't find a partner, write your answers alone and then read over your own responses at a later date to see if you agree with your original ideas. Let's get started.

- Teacher A
  Teacher A teaches math. The goal for today's lesson was mastery of multiplication facts for 2×1 through 2×10. The children were given a variety of strategies to memorize, understand, and use manipulatives to master the number facts. At the end of this practice, the students were given an exercise sheet (10 items) from their arithmetic text. The results were as follows:

  5 students = 100% mastery
  7 students = 70% mastery
  10 students = 60% mastery
  3 students = 20% mastery

  Teacher A concluded that, since 88% of her class achieved a passing score (60%), she did not have to reteach the content to all her students and she could move on to the next set of lessons, which she did. However, the following day she provided scaffolding for the three students who performed poorly on the assessment.

- Teacher B
  Teacher B teaches social studies. The class has been studying the causes of the American Revolution. The goal of today's lesson was for the children to understand the issues involved in the Boston Tea Party. The teacher wanted the children to learn that throwing the tea into the harbor was an act of rebellion against the tax on tea, which the colonists resented; however, the British felt entitled to tax the people they were protecting. The students dressed up, and each got to participate in the re-enactment of the Tea Party. At the end of the re-enactment, every student had the opportunity to see the event from both the colonists' and the British points of view. Teacher B created his own assessment (10 items) to measure the students' understanding of both sides of the issue. The results were as follows:

  6 students = 100% mastery
  4 students = 80% mastery
  7 students = 70% mastery
  3 students = 50% mastery
  3 students = 30% mastery

Teacher B was thrilled with his results and chose not to do any reteaching. The students moved on to the next step toward the Revolutionary War, and the six students who failed to show mastery received no further clarification or help regarding this topic.

With your partner, answer the following:

1. How well did each teacher use assessments and their results?
2. How do you know?
3. What will happen to those students who failed to reach adequate mastery in each class?
4. What would you suggest to each teacher regarding those students?

Of course, if you are giving assessments that cover longer periods of work or are more complicated than just a 10-item assessment, we know that the use of rubrics helps teachers define the qualities and quantity of work required to meet their standards and helps both teachers and students see that target clearly. As a reflective educator, you must constantly re-evaluate the effectiveness of your rubrics to be sure they capture the content and the quality you want to measure. Let's review the steps to creating a rubric and then decide how you can reflect on the quality of your rubrics:

1. What is the purpose of the rubric?
2. What do I want my students to do?
    a. Explain
    b. Interpret
    c. Look at the issue from a different perspective than their own
    d. Reveal new self-understanding
    e. Project characters into a different setting, time, or place
3. What are my criteria?
4. Can I describe my criteria clearly and explicitly?
5. Do I like my rubric?
6. Do my students like the rubric?

You can create a table such as Table 14.1 to help you re-evaluate the effectiveness of any of your current rubrics.

Finally, use multiple types of indicators so that students who do not perform well on paper/pencil assessments can still demonstrate how well they have learned the key concepts taught in class. A reflective assessor wants to know who has learned what, how well they have learned it, and how much additional support is needed for every student to achieve mastery.

Formative and Summative Assessments

Next, we must look at the essential differences between formative and summative assessments. Are you grading your daily quizzes? Are you grading your students on their practice exercises and using their grades to determine report card grades? Do you know the difference between formative and summative assessments? A little exercise might help to clarify this point.

TABLE 14.1	Rubric for rubrics					
Current rubric	Purpose is clear	Students know what to do	Criteria are easy to find	Criteria are explicit	I like my rubric	Students like my rubric
Score 5 = Great 4 = Good 3 = Fair 2 = Poor						
Changes Needed (for score of 3 or lower) Be specific						

Answer the following questions with either "I did the right thing" or "I made a mistake," and show your answers to a partner or another educator you trust:

1. I gave a drill on a subject we had not studied yet. I wanted to see how much prior knowledge my students had on this topic. I graded this drill.
2. I gave a test at the end of an introductory lesson on T. S. Eliot. I counted this grade on the students' report cards.
3. I gave a practice exercise on why westward expansion embraced the belief in "Manifest Destiny." Since we had just started discussing this concept, I returned the papers with no grades, just comments.
4. I asked students to write in their journals about the rigorous content we had covered in class today. I did not grade their journal entries; I just made comments to the students who handed in their journals to me.
5. I created a rubric for an end-of-the-class assessment and used the grade the students earned as part of their final grade for the unit.

It is very important that you know how and when to use formative and summative assessments. Be sure you know the right answers to each of the items above, so you will remember not to assign grades to formative assessments.

Now, give advice to Mrs. Novice. She is getting ready for a parent–teacher conference with Mr. and Mrs. Turtle because their son Tommy has received a failing grade from Mrs. Novice. She is worried about the conference because Mr. Turtle sounded so irate on the phone. The following is a list of Tommy's grades in Mrs. Novice's class.

Class drill	6/10
Class drill	4/10
Class drill	7/10
Class drill	3/10
Class drill	4/10
Unit test	40/50
Class drill	5/10
Journal	8/10
Project	10/15
	72/135 = 53%

Does Mrs. Novice have cause to be concerned? Write her a note helping her to prepare for the conference.

Although Mrs. Novice's arithmetic is accurate, do you see any flaws in her judgment that would cause Tommy's parents to be concerned? Less than 50% of her grades come from summative assessments. Mrs. Novice has confused the use of formative assessments, which are designed to help Tommy learn, and summative assessments, which are graded assignments that should be counted toward his report card grade. When Mrs. Novice removed the formative assessments from her grades, Tommy demonstrated that he could perform satisfactorily on the summative assessments. Remember that your grading policy should reflect how assessments are supposed to be used. Formative assessments can earn a check, check +, or check –. I prefer the use of comments when the students' work warrants the time and effort on my part. However, since formative assessments are a teaching, not a grading tool, I do not suggest that they should ever be given a serious point or grade value; that defeats their purpose. Only assignments that measure learning over time, that cannot be redone, and that have substantial point and/or grade values should contribute significantly to students' report card grades. I use the daily work as evidence of students' work habits, but not as data to support final grades.

High-Stakes Testing and Struggling Learners

As you know, I am an advocate of high-stakes testing for all general education students. The results of these tests have highlighted the need for differentiated programs for the largely invisible population we have been discussing. Struggling learners need caring teachers who provide them with the support they require to make the connection between effort and success. Struggling learners succeed when they have teachers who help them to believe that with the appropriate scaffolding they can overcome any obstacle standing in their way and can achieve success, which has so often seemed beyond their reach.

Teachers who know how to establish a safe and caring climate help struggling learners to understand that they are all deserving of care and respect. As you review the assessments you are using to prepare your struggling learners for the statewide tests they must pass, ask yourself these questions:

1. Do my warm-ups match the format of the statewide tests?
2. Do my practice exercises match the format, content, and style of the statewide tests?
3. Are my students aware of the state's rubric?
4. Do they know how to use the rubric to evaluate their own papers?
5. Do my students know how to make up questions that mirror the state's questions?
6. Do my students understand what the state test is measuring?
7. Do my students understand the connection between the curriculum and the assessment?
8. Does my instruction make the connections between the curriculum and the assessment explicit?
9. Have I created an encouraging and supportive climate for my students?
10. Can every student in my class explain how she arrived at the correct answers on the state's sample items?

This could be a very useful list for you and other teachers on your grade level or in your department. You could even show some leadership by asking for time at a grade level or department meeting to discuss this list. Teachers who have created useful exercises for their students could be asked to share what they have created, and everyone, especially the students, would profit from this experience. You can share this list with your chair first to be sure everyone is comfortable with this approach. Your chair may prefer to share the list with the other teachers. Remember that the real goal is to get help to the students; be gracious and just make sure the list is shared. Even if the list undergoes some adjustments to fit your school, grade, or content, the approach is sound, and its use should result in measurable benefits for the students.

WHAT HAVE WE LEARNED ABOUT STRUGGLING LEARNERS?

We began our journey together by determining that we would address ourselves primarily to the needs of struggling learners. I promised you that above all I would devote my energy and attention to exploring and explaining who they are and how they function. In Chapter 2, I said, "For the purposes of this text, any student who is in one or more of the following categories will be considered a struggling learner who is at risk for school failure: 1. Children who live in unstable families and communities, 2. Children who are unsuccessful in meeting school-based standards, 3. Children who have an external locus of control, and 4. Children who have a limited and/or grim notion of the future." If you are to find success with your struggling learners, we have to be sure that these definitions capture the students you work with every day.

Obviously, the first category concerns the circumstances of the children's lives. If I have not made the point clear to you yet, let me do so now: Race is not as highly correlated with being at risk as poverty is. In general, poor people in the United States live what Thoreau described as "lives of quiet desperation" ("Think Exist," n.d.). We are unforgiving of *all* our poor. Nevertheless, the state of financial well-being does not keep any child from becoming at risk. There are too many children who come from privileged families of all races and ethnicities who are left waiting for hours at after-school events because their parents are too busy with their business and/or social lives to remember to pick up their children. Children who are waiting for hours have a lot of time to feel unlovable and unloved. Bear in mind that three out of the four categories deal with behaviors that result from negative self-efficacy beliefs, not life circumstances.

Many struggling learners are not the least bit cognitively impaired, and yet they have failed to reach school-based standards for their age. One of the major factors contributing to their failure to thrive in school is their entrenched connection to hopelessness. Dodinsky ("Search Quotes," n.d.) once advised his readers, "Look at hopelessness in the face and say: 'We are simply not meant to be together.'" Struggling learners believe that they are meant to be together.

Another reason for their poor performance in school is that they do not believe there is any connection between their effort and their success—so why try? Let's connect this category to the one before. If you cannot affect change in your home, if you do not see your parents try to succeed in their lives, and if no one makes it clear to you that trying is the only path to succeeding, how could you know that success comes as a result of effort? Worse still, if your parents work very hard, but because of their lack of education and skills they never have enough money, how could hard work equal success to you?

The intrinsic connection between effort and success is not an intuitive or innate piece of knowledge; it must be learned. If it has not been learned by the time children start school, those children are already entering school at a unique disadvantage. By the time children begin kindergarten, they are what Dr. Nancy Grasmick, Maryland's former State Superintendent of Schools, referred to as the "geriatric set" because she knew from research that a great deal of brain development occurs prior to the age of 5. Her comment has been validated by recent brain research. "Harry Chugani has been able to obtain PET scans from a representative sample of individuals of all ages" (Wolfe, 2010, p. 78). From his studies, neuroscientists have determined that the amazing amount of growth between birth and age 4 is not replicated again until adolescence (Wolfe, 2010).

By the time youngsters get to high school, many of them have become absolutely convinced that there is no connection between effort and success because, according to many school board policies, after they have been retained once in elementary school and once in middle school, they have to be promoted even if they do nothing at all. When those young people walk into their first ninth-grade class, they are fully persuaded they don't have to do any work and they will still be passed on to the next grade. As we have said before, students who are at risk do not have learning disabilities; they suffer from compromised self-efficacy beliefs, fail to recognize the connection between effort and success, and feel powerless and hopeless.

Let's be sure you know how to recognize an at-risk child. I will describe three students, and you determine which are at risk.

> *Donte*—Donte is a 12-year-old African-American male. He lives with his mother and two sisters. He is very interested in music. When his mother is at work, he stays home to take care of his younger sister. When he grows up, he wants to become a music teacher.

Is he at risk? Explain.

> *Diamond*—Diamond is a 13-year-old Caucasian female who is placed in special education. She lives with her grandmother. She has not heard from her mother in several years. She attends school regularly and has a good rapport with her teachers. When she grows up, she wants to be a hairdresser.

Is she at risk? Explain.

> *Dawn*—Dawn is a 9-year-old African-American female. She lives at home with her parents and her older brother. She does not attend school regularly. When she is there, she is usually asleep. The social worker is having difficulty finding out why she misses so much school. When Dawn talks, she rarely talks or thinks about her future.

Is she at risk? Explain.

These were pretty easy, weren't they? Did the students' socioeconomic status have any bearing on your decisions? Did the children's races have any influence on your decisions? Of course not. What were you looking for? Indicators of problems that showed you the child was experiencing significant stressors that prevented the child from participating in school well, and, of course, the absence of any signs of hope for a better future was a key signal that one child who came from an intact family was at risk for failure.

Many years ago I presented a program to the Harford County School Board regarding help for at-risk students. Following my presentation, there was some discussion about struggling learners. I noted that at that time we were only at the "point one out" phase; we needed to move beyond recognition to being able to intervene. This is the same pattern that has been true for any group of students who has needed clinical as well as educational expertise. Now that we know who we are talking about, what do we do next? You and I have moved well beyond recognizing struggling learners; we know some successful strategies for helping them flourish in school.

Successful Strategies

Let's put together what we know to be true about how struggling learners function in school and compare that knowledge to my suggestions for successful teaching strategies to see if the two are truly aligned (Table 14.2).

TABLE 14.2 Helpful Strategies

Struggling Learners (Sagor, 1993)	Porton's Pointers	Match (Yes or No)
1. Low in self-confidence	These students require caring teachers who will help improve self-efficacy. Begin with activities they can easily master before tackling more difficult tasks.	
2. Avoiders	These students require consequences for missing school that are worse than if they had attended. Makeup tests, for example should be harder. In addition, these students must be made to understand that their presence *matters*.	
3. Distrustful of adults	*Everything* must be transparent and honest.	
4. Limited and grim notion of the future	Provide explicit explanations constantly of how changes in behavior can result in better outcomes.	
5. Behind in academic skills	Discovery learning and cooperative groups can be used to fill in gaps and encourage students to get help from others.	
6. Impatient with routine and are often considered disruptive	Discovery learning and cooperative groups are good for keeping these students out of trouble.	
7. No political sense	These students need explicit explanations of • Chain of command • Power structure	
8. Practical learners	Honest explanations for *why* they are learning the content and how it relates to the real world are provided before every lesson.	
9. See no relationship between effort and success	Every day, in every lesson, at every opportunity, these students must be helped to understand that, unless they try, they cannot succeed. If they choose to change their destiny, they can do it. Examples of real-life people like the students who have succeeded despite life's circumstances and examples of people who have excelled in each content area despite earlier failures can help make the point. This must be a constant theme and must be reinforced at every opportunity.	
10. Externalizers	Students must be helped to understand this: "If it is to be, it is up to *me*." Use concrete data at all times to reinforce this concept.	

For the most part, I have described a group of students much like any other, but struggling learners need to be given multiple opportunities to make the connection between effort and success. They require every chance to move from an external to a more internal locus of control; therefore, their teachers have to tell them explicitly how and why to do that. Using cooperative learning groups and discovery learning techniques, teachers keep their struggling learners actively engaged in meaningful projects and activities for which the students share some of the responsibility.

Your Turn

This time I want you to work by yourself. If you feel there is a match between each of Sagor's (1993) characteristics of discouraged learners and my pointers, write what strategies you are using in your class to make the match work for you and your students. If you feel that any of my pointers do not completely capture what needs to be done, rewrite them for yourself, and then write the specific strategies and activities you are using with your students to help them move from being at risk to resilient.

I urge you to remember that being the sage on the stage is not successful with this population. It may have worked for you when you were a student, but these students do not come to school with the same goals and aspirations you had, and they may not even consider graduating from high school to be a desirable ambition. You need to think about school and life from their perspective and make connections with them in order for them to form any worthwhile bond with you. You will be able to move them from where they are to where you hope they will be only if they truly believe you care about them. Einstein said, "Love is a better teacher than duty" ("Think Exist," n.d.)

How Do We Know We Are Being Effective?

We know that in order to be effective the points of our instructional triangle must be aligned (Figure 14.1). If our lesson plans are not well written, nothing else will work.

Effective Planning

Take your best lesson plan and create a triangle. What is your goal? At the bottom right, list your strategies, and at the bottom left, look at the assessment to see what it measures. If the goal and the strategies and the assessments are all on the same topic, you have passed the first test of effective teaching. Good work! A lot of teachers do not

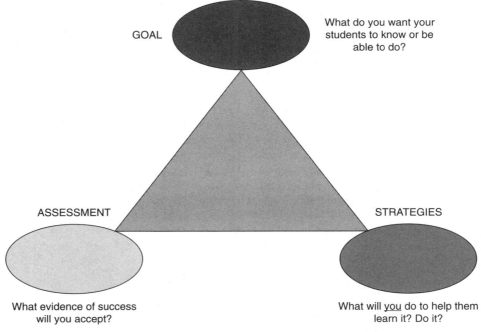

FIGURE 14.1 The Instructional Triangle

know how important that is and do not even look over their plans to see if their plans meet these criteria.

Effective Management

Classroom management is an art unto itself. It requires sensitivity with a firm hand, a soft touch and a hard line. The goal is to teach children self-control, although at times, the person who requires the most self-control is the teacher. Classroom management is best achieved by carefully planning lessons that keep children actively engaged in their work and by keeping a good sense of humor ready at all times.

Rules, Routines, and Boundaries

When we began our discussion on management, we examined three basic concepts: rules, routines, and boundaries. Let's make sure you remember what they mean and how to use them.

Your Turn

In each of the following scenarios, does the teacher need to use a rule, a routine, or a boundary? Explain to each teacher what is wrong with her or his response to the children's behavior.

- Ms. Giant has a class that is always late for recess. They have difficulty getting in line, getting down the hallways quietly, and entering any room appropriately. She is threatening to take away their recess.
- Mr. Safe has a bully in his class. He threatens everyone. Yesterday he called a quiet, studious boy "gay." Mr. Safe is concerned the label will stick; he is going to make the bully write a letter apologizing to the quiet boy. Mr. Safe has promised the bully he will not read the letter before giving it to the other student.
- Ms. Well has a rule in her class that every student must stand when she enters the room. Two little girls are tired and don't want to stand when she comes in. Ms. Well makes the whole class practice standing for an hour.

Room Arrangement

Although room arrangement may not seem as important as rules, routines, and boundaries, if you cannot reach a child who is in trouble or causing trouble, serious problems can occur quickly. Use your imagination or borrow some from a friend and create a room where children are able to move, work, and learn—but most of all, where you can get to every student in your room quickly. When you return to your classroom tomorrow, look at it from this perspective. Would I think you have done the best job you can with the space you have been allotted? Good! Let's move on.

Angry Children

We are all painfully aware that many children in today's society are enraged at the adults in their lives and that a lot of them have good cause to be. The following is what I was told by a student; practice your response to this child because you may hear a story a lot like this:

MRS. P.   Lisa, I love you. You always get your work done and then help others. Sometimes you even come over and help me.

LISA   Mrs. P., don't you ever tell me you love me again. I can't believe you said that to me.

MRS. P.   Lisa, I am so sorry. I never meant to hurt your feelings. I will never say it again. It's just that I really care for you. What happened?

LISA   One time I borrowed something from my mother without asking. My mother put a hot iron on my hand. She kept it there and said she was doing it because she loved me.

MRS. P.   *Your Turn . . .*

Effective Praise

This is an ongoing issue for so many teachers—and one I do not really understand. I hear teachers say, "Good job," and watch children blow it off as if it were raindrops. It takes only slightly longer to say, "I like the way you took your time to think about your answer." Then the child thinks, "Wow, she noticed that I was thinking. I like that!" The difference reminds me of the sounds of white noise versus what you hear from intelligent conversations. You can teach with praise or lose teachable moments. If you really want to be successful with struggling learners, look up the section on effective praise. Decide which of Brophy's (1981) suggestions would work best for your class, and write them down. The next time you see a student perform very well, use one of Brophy's ideas to praise her, and see for yourself the difference that specific, contingent praise makes. I know you will start to see a difference in the following: (1) the student's attitude, (2) the student's attitude toward you, and (3) the student's willingness to try. Give me one good reason not to use this technique. Right—I knew you would see it my way.

Effective Instruction

Every page in this book is about instruction because planning and management are essential ingredients of effective instruction. Although a great deal of the discourse covers my instructional history, this is only one model of one teacher's experience. My hope is that you will extrapolate from my experiences and use them to help you make your own teaching more successful. I do not want to oversimplify a fairly complex process, but the essentials of good teaching are summarized in Table 14.3.

TABLE 14.3 Elements of Effective Instruction

1. Cooperative learning groups help students to learn in a safe and social learning environment.
2. Students need to construct meaning for themselves.
   - They must be motivated.
   - They must be able to access prior knowledge.
   - They must be able to put the new meaning into a context.
   - They must be able to use language to process what they have learned.
   - They must have opportunities to explain the relationships between the new ideas they have just acquired and other experiences, other readings, and other related issues they have studied.
3. Students must have the opportunity to be taught using materials that are appropriate to their cognitive strengths.
4. Students must believe they can learn, and all the scaffolding they need to learn must be provided.

In order to be sure you have reached the indicators in Table 14.3, stand quietly in the back of the room on a day while your children are involved in independent practice and on another day while they are completing their assessments. Ask yourself the following questions:

1. Are the children on task?
2. Do they know what to do?
3. Is the classroom noise the sound of children who are working or the sound of children who are stressed?
4. Do the children get help from other children on their team?
5. Do the children take ownership for their work?
6. Are the children actively and meaningfully engaged?
7. Are there any children who have their heads resting on their desks? Why?
8. Are there any children who seem to be wandering around the room for no reason? Why?

9. Does every child have work that is appropriate for her cognitive ability?
10. Do children with special needs have all the accommodations that their Individual Educational Programs require?
11. Are enrichment activities provided for students who ought to have them?
12. Are you satisfied with the children's behavior in your class? Why?

If you are satisfied with your answers to those questions, you should feel very good about yourself as a teacher. You have done an excellent job at getting your students ready for any task that they may have to accomplish.

Summary

The woods are lovely, dark and deep, But I have promises to keep....

Robert Frost

In the Introduction to this book, I made several promises to you. I promised that you would meet some wonderful people, and I hope you have enjoyed all of the delightful students and teachers I have introduced to you. I told you that you would hear some very unpleasant stories, and unfortunately, I had to describe some events that still make me very sad. Through all this, I hope you have learned some new ways of teaching that you can add to your repertoire.

A Different Kind of Classroom: Teaching with Dimensions of Learning by Marzano (1992), *At-Risk Students: Reaching and Teaching Them* by Sagor (1993), and *Brain Matters: Translating Research into Classroom Practice* by Wolfe (2010) are part of my library, and I highly recommend them to you. I also really enjoyed reading *Shadow Children: Understanding Education's #1 Problem* by Dallman-Jones (2006). It answers some questions that I do not address in this book and will help to round out your understanding of this very intriguing population. Read everything you can that makes sense to you and create as clear and balanced a picture for yourself of what puts struggling learners at greater risk and what helps them to succeed. I promised to help you find effective ways to reach and teach your students. Use your own good judgment and base your ideas on sound theory, and you will be fine.

Finally, make sure you have an appropriate and professional relationship with every student you teach. Children need to know you value them before they will value what you teach. A smile can do a lot for a child who has not seen one for days. For years, my students used to come to my room to see me on Monday mornings for their "Hi, honey" security check-in. It didn't cost a thing, but it meant the world to us.

Be well—be good to yourself and the children you teach.

APPENDIX 1

Figures, Tables, and Templates

CHAPTER 1

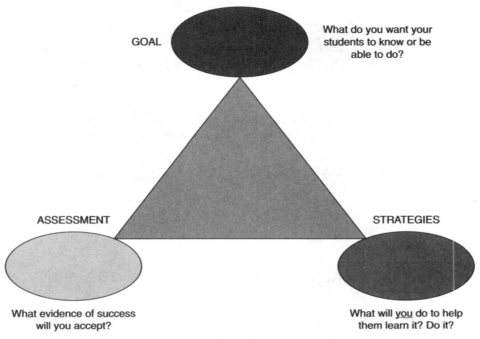

GOAL — What do you want your students to know or be able to do?

ASSESSMENT — What evidence of success will you accept?

STRATEGIES — What will you do to help them learn it? Do it?

FIGURE 1.1   The Instructional Triangle

Today's Goals: *What will we be learning today?*
Today's Strategies: *What activities will we use to help us reach our goals?*
1
2
3
Today's Assessment: *How will I know if each of you reached our goals?*
Paper-pencil?   Demonstration?   One-on-one response with me?   Other?

How many points for participation?   How many points for cooperation?

FIGURE 1.2   Message Board

TABLE 1.2   Observation Topic: Motivation

Student's Name	Time	Activities	Student's Involvement			Observations
			A	S	W	
1		Warm-Up				
		Motivation				
		Guided Practice				
		Indep. Practice				
		Assessment				
		Closure				
2		Warm-Up				
		Motivation				
		Guided Practice				
		Indep. Practice				
		Assessment				
		Closure				
3		Warm-Up				
		Motivation				
		Guided Practice				
		Indep. Practice				
		Assessment				
		Closure				

A stands for Actively involved; **S** stands for Somewhat involved; **W** stands for Withdrawn from the activity.

Template 1.1

Lesson Plan Template—Generic		

Lesson Title:

Lesson Unit:

GOAL	State Curriculum (SC) Statewide or local systemwide goal	Common Core State Standards (CCSS). Goal based on grade level and CCSS standard
Lesson Objective	As a result of today's lesson, students will be able to	
Materials Needed	Make the list. Check to see that all items are present. During the lesson, if you find you need something not on the list, write the item in the margin.	
Warm-Up Time:	Use this to *activate prior knowledge*.	
Motivation Time:	What will you do to engage students in today's topic? *Why* are they learning the new information?	
Guided Practice Time:	Introduce the topic. *Model* how to construct meaning/organize information/store new learning *or* how to perform the task/create the product/share the performance.	
Independent Practice Time:	Working with their teams, *students practice* the new learning. During this phase, errors are eliminated, strengths are praised, and students learn from each other. Using differentiated group assignments will help students with the wide variety of skills, interests, and abilities they need to succeed. Discovery learning is the essence of this phase.	
Assessment Time:	*Each student must supply evidence of the extent to which he mastered content or skill development as described in today's goal.* Use data from this assessment for tomorrow's instruction.	
Closure Time:	Ask students a question about key attitudes and learning in today's lesson: What did you learn today? What was the best part of today's lesson? What did you learn from each other today? How are you going to use today's lesson?	
Homework	Make homework relevant and practice oriented. Do not assign drill and kill exercises!	

Template 1.2

Lesson Plan Template—Differentiation		

Lesson Title:

Lesson Unit:

GOAL	SC Statewide or local systemwide goal	CCSS Goal based on grade level and CCSS standard
Lesson Objective	As a result of today's lesson, students will be able to	
Materials Needed	Make the list. Check to see that all items are present. During the lesson, if you find you need something not on the list, write the item in the margin.	
Warm-Up Time:	Use this to activate prior knowledge. Each of the three groups should have a warm-up that addresses the assessment from the previous day.	

Motivation Time:	(Whole group) What will you do to engage students in today's topic? Why are they learning the new information?
Guided Practice Time:	While groups 2 and 3 are working on their warm-up, call group 1 for guided practice. From now on, the process is the same, but the expectations reflect the nature of each of the groups. Introduce the topic. Model the task/product/performance.
Independent Practice Time:	Working with their groups, students practice the new learning. During this phase, errors are eliminated, strengths are praised, and students learn from each other. When group 1 is sent back to do independent practice, group 2 is brought up for guided practice. When group 2 is sent back, group 3 comes up. In the meantime, if group 1 is finished, targeted students can help group 2 students with their independent practice. When group 3 returns for independent practice, groups 1 and 2 can come up and demonstrate their products or skills together.
Assessment Time:	Each student must supply evidence of the extent to which he mastered content or skill development as described in today's goal. *This does not have to be a paper/pencil assessment; demonstration of processes should be performed, not assessed, using a paper/pencil format.* Use data from this assessment for tomorrow's instruction.
Closure Time:	(Whole group) Ask students a question about key attitudes and learning in today's lesson: What did you learn today? What was the best part of today's lesson? What did you learn from each other today? How are you going to use today's lesson?
Homework	Homework Make homework relevant and practice oriented. Each group should get its own homework assignment. Avoid drill and kill exercises, especially for the below-grade-level group!

Template 1.3

Lesson Plan Template—Generic

Lesson Title:

Lesson Unit:

GOAL	(SC) CCSS
Lesson Objective	As a result of today's lesson, students will be able to
Materials Needed	
Warm-Up Time:	
Motivation Time:	
Guided Practice Time:	
Independent Practice Time:	
Assessment Time:	
Closure Time:	
Homework	

CHAPTER 3

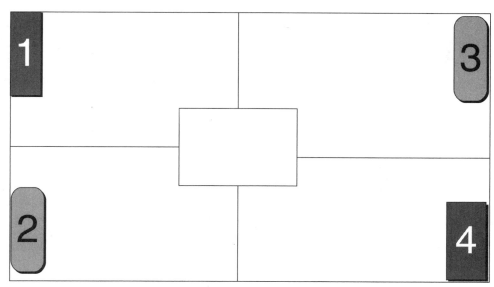

FIGURE 3.1 Drill Placemat

TABLE 3.1	Member Contributions			
Using a rating scale of 1 = No help to 4 = Best help, rate each team member on the following questions.	Did the team member give good answers to team thought questions?	Did the team member find answers in the text to support team answers?	Did the team member complete his/her share of the work?	Did the team member help clarify points so that all of the team understood what was being discussed during one-minute pause-and-discuss reflections?
Member 1				
Member 2				
Member 3				
Member 4				

CHAPTER 4

Template 4.1

Guidelines for Reflection on Planning

As we move through the reflection process during the planning phase, please keep the following suggestions in mind:

1. Keep a journal or notebook.
2. After you write your plan, reflect on whether or not your plan demonstrates the guiding principles of the instructional triangle.
3. Check your plan to be sure that you have provided access to success for *all* your students.
4. Review your plan again to be sure that you have provided yourself with some alternatives in case you need them.
5. Use your journal when you have completed your unit plan, when you have created a new activity or exercise, or when you are making a difficult decision.

Template 4.2

Planning Template—Reflection

Lesson Title—Introduction to Structured Writing Assignment SWA
Lesson Unit—SWA

Reflections	Lesson Component
This comes to us from the guide.	GOAL (SC) Statewide or local systemwide goal or goals taken from appropriate CCSS standards. Lesson Objective As a result of today's lesson, students will be able to find the FAT–P.
According to the guide, we hand out a lot of materials. Do we want to do this? I think that will put them off. After we show them what a prompt looks like, I think we should make copies of only the top paragraphs. We will need visual aids for our visual learners. They like color coding a lot. We can make our FAT–P color coded to help our visual learners.	Materials Needed Make the list. Check to see that all items are present. During the lesson, if you find you need something not on the list, write the item in the margin.
Time: 10 minutes We can use the drill to find out how much they know about the HSA and the writing process (i.e., prewriting, writing a rough draft, peer editing, and writing a final draft).	Warm-Up Use this to activate prior knowledge.
Time: 10 minutes I think we need to think of ways we can help our class believe that we can get every student to pass. What about bringing back students from prior years to talk to them about their experiences?	Motivation What will you do to engage students in today's topic? How will you help students understand the importance of today's lesson?
Time: 15 minutes Model how to find the FAT–P. We have to decide if we want to teach all of it together or one piece at a time.	Guided Practice Introduce the topic. Model how to construct meaning/organize information/store new learning *or* how to perform the task/create the product/share the performance.

Reflections	Lesson Component
Time: 15 minutes We have to create activities that will make finding the FAT–P interesting. Perhaps we can create some competition between the teams for finding the FAT–P.	Independent Practice Working with their teams, students practice the new learning. During this phase, errors are eliminated, strengths are praised, and students learn from each other. Using differentiated group assignments will help students with the wide variety of skills, interests, and abilities they need to succeed. Discovery learning is the essence of this phase.
Time: 10 minutes We have to create an assessment that will allow us to see how well each student was able to reach today's goal without frustrating the students so that they become discouraged immediately.	Assessment Each student must supply evidence of the extent to which she mastered content or skill development as described in today's goal. Use data from this assessment for tomorrow's instruction.
Time: 5 minutes We need to think about a quick closure for today that will help students leave class feeling positive about themselves.	Closure Ask students a question about key attitudes and learning in today's lesson: What did you learn today? What was the best part of today's lesson? What did you learn from each other today? How are you going to use today's lesson?
If they are ready, they will do Homework A: Write an opening paragraph of a prompt that includes a FAT–P. If not, they will do Homework B: Define each of the letters in the FAT–P.	Homework Make homework relevant and practice oriented. Avoid drill and kill exercises!

Template 4.3

Template for Reflection on Planning

1. Review your lesson plan and write down the following:
   a. Goal:
   b. Strategies:
   c. Assessments:
2. How do you know that your strategies will help the students reach the goal?
3. How do you know that the assessments measure the goal?
4. What will you do with the results of the assessments?
5. Where do you expect the students to face challenges during the lesson?
6. What provisions have you put into place to help your students overcome the challenges?
7. What enrichment activities do you have planned for students who already have mastered your goal?
8. What strategies do you have in place for students with psychosocial issues? What would trigger their use?
9. What evidence will you accept that this lesson was a success?
10. What have you learned from reflecting *in* action and *on* action?

CHAPTER 5

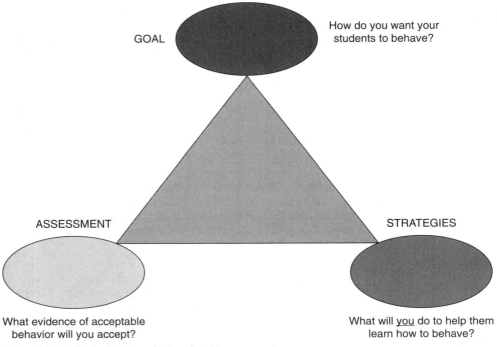

GOAL

How do you want your students to behave?

ASSESSMENT

STRATEGIES

What evidence of acceptable behavior will you accept?

What will <u>you</u> do to help them learn how to behave?

FIGURE 5.1   The Instructional Triangle—Management

CHAPTER 6

FIGURE 6.1 "Cheerleading" Sign

TABLE 6.1	Effective Praise

1. is delivered contingently
2. specifies the particulars of the accomplishment
3. shows spontaneity, variety, and other signs of credibility that suggest clear attention to the student's accomplishment
4. rewards attainment of specified performance criteria (which can include effort, however)
5. provides information to students about their competence or the value of their accomplishments
6. orients students toward better appreciation of their own task-related behavior and thinking about problem solving
7. uses students' own prior accomplishments as the context for describing present accomplishments
8. is given in recognition of noteworthy effort or success at difficult (for this student) tasks
9. attributes success to effort and ability, implying that similar successes can be expected in the future
10. fosters endogenous attributions (students believe that they expend effort on the task because they enjoy the task and/or want to develop task-relevant skills)
11. focuses students' attention on their own task-relevant behavior
12. fosters appreciation of, and desirable attributions about, task-relevant behavior after the process is completed.   (Brophy, 1981, p. 26)

CHAPTER 7

TABLE 7.1	Guidelines for Ineffective Praise

According to Brophy (1981), ineffective praise

1. is delivered randomly or unsystematically.
2. is restricted to global positive reactions.
3. shows a bland uniformity that suggests a conditional response made with minimal attention.
4. rewards mere participation without consideration of performance, processes, or outcomes.
5. provides no information at all or gives students no information about their status.
6. orients students toward comparing themselves with others and thinking about competing.
7. uses the accomplishments of peers as the context for describing students' present accomplishments.
8. is given without regard to the effort expended or the meaning of the accomplishment.
9. attributes success to ability alone or to external factors such as luck or low task difficulty.
10. fosters exogenous attributions (students believe that they expend effort on the task for external reasons—to please the teacher, win a competition or reward, etc.)
11. focuses students' attention on the teacher as an external authority who is manipulating them.
12. intrudes into the ongoing process, distracting attention from task-relevant behavior. (p. 26)

CHAPTER 8

Template 8.1

Template for Reflection—Management

1. What are the essential differences among rules, routines, and boundaries?
2. Why do you need each?
3. How do you teach rules? Routines? Boundaries?
4. When do you teach rules? Routines? Boundaries?
5. What are some of the fundamental questions you need to ask yourself after you have set up your room?
6. What is the fundamental difference between effective and ineffective praise?
7. Are you using effective praise to help your struggling learners recognize the connection between effort and success? How do you know?
8. Are you using effective praise to make sure that your students understand their progress over time? In light of the difficulty of the task? How do you know?
9. Why is it important to have an appropriate teacher–student relationship with your students?
10. How do you define classroom climate? How does it affect classroom management?
11. How can you tell when the climate has changed in your room? What should you do?
12. What message do you give your students when you dress like a professional? Why is that important?
13. What is the significance of describing the behavior and not the child?
14. Are you listening to yourself carefully to be sure you are describing the behavior and not the child? How do you know?
15. What do you do when you make a mistake in front of the class? Why?
16. When you make decisions, whose interests come first? How do you know?
17. Are you comfortable with the quality of your teaching? Explain.
18. What are you willing to do to improve?
19. What does current brain research tell you about the types of management goals you should be using with your students?
20. Does your reflection journal indicate that you are becoming more aware of the intricacies of teaching and learning?

CHAPTER 10

FIGURE 10.2 Problem-Solving System

TABLE 10.1   Lesson Plan—My Name

Lesson Title: My Name

Lesson Unit:

GOAL	This is a focus lesson that is designed to help students make meaning from a reading selection, write their response, and share their response with others.
Lesson Objective	*As a result of today's lesson, students will be* able to respond to a reading selection in writing in a personal and meaningful manner.
Materials Needed	A copy of "My Name" by Sandra Cisneros Placemat paper and writing utensils for everyone on the team
Warm-Up Time:	1. What are some of your favorite names? 2. How are people in your family named? 3. What name do you wish you had? Why? 4. What name do you really dislike? Why?
Motivation Time:	Read "My Name" to the class. Tell the class that they will be reading the piece to each other in their teams. Explain that we will be learning about ourselves by responding to Cisneros' story of her name and how she feels about her name. We will be writing about our names, how we got them, how we feel about them, and what they mean to us.
Guided Practice Time:	**Part I.** First, using one team as a model, I start reading "My Name"; when I stop, another person starts reading. After that, I explain that the group continues reading that way until the reading has been completed. **Part IV.** Last, I read my response to the class.
Independent Practice Time:	**Part II.** Second, the teams read the entire selection. **Part III.** Third, each student writes his/her own response. When all of the responses have been written, each student reads his/her response to the team. Finally, the team selects the one student who will read his/her response to the class. Each team has one person read to the class.
Assessment Time:	What does your name not say about you? Explain.
Closure Time:	What was the best part of today's lesson? Why?

TABLE 10.2   All Stars Problem-Solving Game

Today we are going to practice how to solve problems together. There are no right or wrong answers. However, there is a rubric that your senior tutors will apply to each team's solutions. Each team will be given its own problem. Using the problem-solving system posted in our classroom (Figure 10.2), your team must examine and evaluate the problem from all sides. Together, you will look for the most promising outcomes for each of the parties described in the incident.

Problem 1

Your best friend's life at home is terrible. He sleeps at your house a lot. His mother no longer lives at home. His father has been using drugs ever since she left. There is never enough food for your friend to eat, but he doesn't like to eat at your house all the time. He has become very sad and moody. He isn't interested in hanging out with your friends anymore. He doesn't sleep well. He has started giving his stuff away. When you try to make plans with him, he doesn't seem involved or interested. If you tell your mom about him, he will feel that you have betrayed his trust in you. You don't think his father cares about him. What should you do?

Problem 2

You live at home with your mother. She does not make enough money to pay the bills. She needs you to get a part-time job to help pay the bills. She is desperate and talks to you all the time about how much she needs money. Your boyfriend has a job. He is always complaining because you are never available to see him when he isn't working. You really miss being with him, but you need to help out at home, and you are looking for a job. What should you do?

Problem 3

You hang out with a tough crowd. You like them, but you know they can be very mean. They are cyber bullying one boy in your class because they are sure he is gay. You don't really care if he is gay or not, but you don't want to say anything because you don't want to be their next victim. You saw the boy in school, and he looks terrible. One of the kids in your class said that she heard that the boy isn't gay, but he's really miserable because of all the cyber bullying he is getting. Your sister told you about a boy in another school who killed himself because he was the target of cyber bullying. You believe her. What should you do?

Problem 4

Your friends have "borrowed" a car that belongs to a neighbor down the street. Your little "brother" just called to say that your friends are outside waiting for you. You know they don't own a car; you look out your window and recognize the car they are driving. Last month you were released from the local juvenile detention facility. Your foster family said that, if you get arrested again, they are sending you back to the Department of Social Services. You don't want to punk out. What should you do?

Rubric:

Score each team on its solutions. All scorers must agree on the team's score and explain the score to the team after announcing it.

   4 = Excellent solution. All parties' needs are met. Response shows original thought and creative solutions to the problem.

   3 = Good solution. Most parties' needs are met. Response shows adequate thinking to resolve the problem.

   2 = Fair solution. Some parties' needs are met. Response shows thought, but parts of the problem are left unresolved.

   1 = Poor solution. No party's needs are really met. Response shows immature thought, and the problem remains largely unsolved.

Assessment:

A friend of yours lives in a foster home he really likes. He has told everyone that he expects this foster family to adopt him. You know the son of the family, and he has confided in you that since his dad lost his job, the family's plans have changed. They will not be adopting your friend. Your friend finally seems happy. You hate to be the one to spoil his happiness. What should you do?

Template 10.1

Lesson Plan Template—Constructivist

Lesson Title:

Lesson Unit:

GOAL	CCSS Goal based on grade level and CCSS standard
	SC State Curriculum *This comes from the state* *curriculum guide.*
Lesson Objective	As a result of today's lesson, *students will be able to* . . . *This comes from* the state curriculum guide or the CCSS and refers to the goal for the day.
Materials Needed	As the teacher, you need to have the materials needed for the day's journey.
Warm-Up Time:	During the warm-up, your job is to access prior knowledge. Constructivists believe that learning is contextual and can be obtained only in relation to prior knowledge.
Motivation Time:	According to those who believe in discovery learning, motivation is essential to learning. If learners do not understand why they are learning, they are unlikely to be active participants in the process.
Guided Practice Time:	When discovery learning methods such as problem solving are employed, you must model the process to be used so that each team can follow the process carefully and correctly. No answers have been pre-established. Only the process and the path are clearly outlined.
Independent Practice Time:	Learning is an active process: Knowledge is gained through a personal and social construction of meaning. During independent practice, students, working in teams, create meaning for themselves using the constructs you shared during guided practice. The findings are their own and should build on their prior knowledge of the topic under study.
Assessment Time:	The assessment should mirror the strategies used during instruction. However, in order to determine each student's mastery of the goal, this work must be done independently.
Closure Time:	Learning involves language. When you ask effective closure questions, you learn a lot about how the students feel about their experiences. This information is very useful in planning similar experiences for future classes.
Homework	Learning takes time. Practice at new learning should be a daily feature of each student's routine. As long as the practice is useful, and not onerous, it provides the repetition needed for effective learning to take place.

CHAPTER 11

TABLE 11.2 Reflective Questions for Class Discussions

1. What kinds of questions did you ask your students? How do you know?
2. Did you call on boys or girls more often? How do you know?
3. Were your questions provocative, or did they usually result in yes or no answers?
4. Did you ask other students to respond to students' replies?
5. Was there any evidence that some children changed their minds as a result of the discussion? How do you know?
6. Were the children actively engaged in the discussion? How do you know?
7. Were the children challenging each other for proof, or did they accept each other's responses?
8. Did anyone bring up a topic that was completely off track? What did you do?
9. Did you see evidence of more mature thinking from your students?
10. When the children left your classroom, were they still talking about the topic?

TABLE 11.3 Reflective Questions for Discovery Learning

1. After I establish my goal for the lesson, what is more important, the answer or what the children learn as they work toward finding the answer?
2. Will cooperative learning teams help my students during this lesson? Why? How?
3. Do my children need to access their prior knowledge in order to be successful?
4. Do my children need to know why they are participating in this lesson in order to be motivated?
5. Do my students work at different rates of speed? Do I have a system for allowing students to finish at different rates?
6. Are my students learning this content by following the protocol inherent in this discipline or by hearing about it? Which is more effective?
7. Why did I choose the strategies I used for this lesson?
8. Were my students involved during the entire lesson? How do I know?
9. What do my assessment results reveal about my students' mastery of today's goals and objectives?
10. Would I use the same strategies again for this lesson? Why?

TABLE 11.4 Reflections for Positive Relationships with Students

1. Do you treat every student in your class with respect, courtesy, and kindness?
2. Do you let your students know about you and your life outside of school?
3. Do you tell your students funny stories about yourself as a child?
4. Do you feel attached (appropriately) to any of your classes?
5. Do any of your students feel appropriately attached to you?

CHAPTER 12

TABLE 12.1	Decision Matrix					
Alternatives	**Abigail (AB)**	**People on Orp (P)**	**Ivan (I)**	**Slug (S)**	**Cal (C)**	**Alex (AL)**
Criterion weight	1. (3)	2. (2)	3. (2)	4. (3)	5. (2)	6. (2)
A) Has clear, fair, and reasonable demands and expectations (3)						
B) Acts for the well-being of others (3)						
C) Keeps his/her word (2)						
Totals						

Source: Matrix from Marzano (1995).1992, p. 110; original content from Simon et al. (1995).

CHAPTER 13

1. I am capable of performing this task.
2. If I try, I will get all the help I need.
3. Ultimately, I am responsible for completing my work.
4. I can always ask for help along the way.
5. When I hand in my final product, I will have reached my goal!

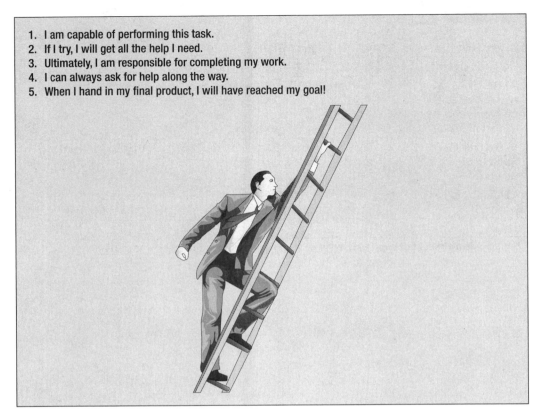

FIGURE 13.2 Encouraging Words

"Destiny is not a matter of chance; it is a matter of choice."

William Jennings Bryan

FIGURE 13.3 Effort Matters

FIGURE 13.4 My Future Will Be Fabulous!

CHAPTER 14

TABLE 14.1	Rubric for Rubrics					
Current rubric	Purpose is clear	Students know what to do	Criteria are easy to find	Criteria are explicit	I like my rubric	Students like my rubric
Score 5 = Great 4 = Good 3 = Fair 2 = Poor						
Changes Needed (for score of 3 or lower) Be specific						

TABLE 14.2 Reflections for HSA Preparation

1. Do my drills match the format of the statewide tests?
2. Do my practice exercises match the format, content, and style of the statewide tests?
3. Are my students aware of the state's rubric?
4. Do they know how to use the rubric to evaluate their own papers?
5. Do my students know how to make up questions that mirror the state's questions?
6. Do my students understand what the state test is measuring?
7. Do my students understand the connection between the curriculum and the assessment?
8. Does my instruction make the connections between the curriculum and the assessment explicit?
9. Have I created an encouraging and supportive climate for my students?
10. Can every student in my class explain how she arrived at the correct answers on the state's sample items?

TABLE 14.3	Is There a Match?	
Struggling Learners (Sagor, 1993)	**Porton's Pointers**	**Match (Yes or No)**
1. Low in self-confidence	These students require caring teachers who will help improve self-efficacy. Begin with activities they can easily master before tackling more difficult tasks.	
2. Avoiders	These students require consequences for missing school that are worse than if they had attended. Makeup tests, for example, should be harder. In addition, these students must be made to understand that their presence *matters*.	
3. Distrustful of adults	*Everything* must be transparent and honest.	
4. Limited and grim notion of the future	Provide explicit explanations constantly of how changes in behavior can result in better outcomes.	
5. Behind in academic skills	Discovery learning and cooperative groups can be used to fill in gaps and encourage students to get help from others.	
6. Impatient with routine and often considered disruptive	Discovery learning and cooperative groups are good for creating meaning and keeping these students out of trouble.	
7. No political sense	These students need explicit explanations of • Chain of command • Power structure	
8. Practical learners	Honest explanations for *why* they are learning the content and how it relates to the real world are provided before every lesson.	
9. See no relationship between effort and success	Every day, in every lesson, at every opportunity, these students must be helped to understand that, unless they try, they cannot succeed. If they choose to change their destiny, they can do it. Examples of real-life people like the students who have succeeded despite life's circumstances and examples of people who have excelled in each content area despite earlier failures can help make the point. This must be a constant theme and must be reinforced at every opportunity.	
10. Externalizers	Students must be helped to understand this: "If it is to be, it is up to *me*." Use concrete data at all times to reinforce this concept.	

TABLE 14.4   Reflections for Implementation of Lesson Plans

1. Are the children on task?
2. Do they know what to do?
3. Is the classroom noise the sound of children who are working or the sound of children who are stressed?
4. Do the children get help from other children on their team?
5. Do the children take ownership for their work?
6. Are the children actively and meaningfully engaged?
7. Are there any children who have their heads resting on their desks? Why?
8. Are there any children who seem to be wandering around the room for no reason? Why?
9. Does every child have work that is appropriate for her cognitive ability?
10. Do children with special needs have all the accommodations that their Individual Educational Programs require?
11. Are enrichment activities provided for students who ought to have them?
12. Are you satisfied with the children's behavior in your class? Why?

APPENDIX 2

Interstate New Teacher Assessment
and Support Consortium Standards

The education departments at many U.S. colleges are guided by a set of national standards for teacher education, the Interstate New Teacher Assessment and Support Consortium (INTASC) Standards. These standards are designed to clarify the principles that should guide each department's practices and policies as it supports the development of future teachers. The INTASC Standards are included here because the more familiar you are with them, the more transparent the expectations for proficiency will be.

STANDARD 1: CONTENT PEDAGOGY

The teacher understands the central concepts, tools of inquiry, and structures of the discipline(s) he or she teaches and can create learning experiences that make these aspects of subject matter meaningful for students. (Theme: grounding in content or subject matter)

KEY INDICATORS—The Candidate:

- demonstrates an understanding of the central concepts of his or her discipline.
- uses explanations and representations that link curriculum to prior learning.
- engages students in interpreting ideas from a variety of perspectives.
- uses methods of inquiry that are central to the discipline.
- uses interdisciplinary approaches to teaching and learning.
- evaluates resources and curriculum materials for appropriateness to the curriculum and instructional delivery.

STANDARD 2: STUDENT DEVELOPMENT

The teacher understands how children learn and develop, and can provide learning opportunities that support their intellectual, social, and personal development. (Theme: grounding in human development theory)

KEY INDICATORS—The Candidate:

- evaluates student performance to design instruction appropriate for social, cognitive, and emotional development.
- evaluates student performance to design instruction appropriate for social, cognitive, and emotional development.
- provides opportunities for students to assume responsibility for and be actively engaged in their learning.
- encourages student reflection on prior knowledge and its connection to new information.
- accesses student thinking as a basis for instructional activities through group/individual interaction and written work (listening, encouraging, discussion, eliciting samples of student thinking orally and in writing).

STANDARD 3: DIVERSE LEARNERS

The teacher understands how students differ in their approaches to learning and creates instructional opportunities that are adapted to diverse learners. (Theme: grounding in differentiation)

KEY INDICATORS—The Candidate:

- designs instruction appropriate for students' stages of development, learning styles, strengths, and needs.
- selects approaches that provide opportunities for different performance modes.
- accesses appropriate services or resources to meet exceptional learning needs when needed.
- adjusts instruction to accommodate the learning differences or needs of students (times and circumstance of work, tasks assigned, communication and response modes).
- uses knowledge of different cultural contexts within the community (socio-economic, ethnic, cultural) and connects with the learner through types of interaction and assignments.
- creates a learning community that respects individual differences.

STANDARD 4: MULTIPLE INSTRUCTIONAL STRATEGIES

The teacher understands and uses a variety of instructional strategies to encourage students' development of critical thinking, problem solving, and performance skills. (Theme: grounding in implementation of instruction)

KEY INDICATORS—The Candidate:

- selects and uses multiple teaching and learning strategies (a variety of presentation/explanation) to encourage students in critical thinking and problem solving.
- encourages students to assume responsibility for identifying and using learning resources.
- assumes different roles in the instructional process (instructor, facilitator, coach, audience) to accommodate content, purpose, and learner needs.

STANDARD 5: MOTIVATION AND MANAGEMENT

The teacher uses an understanding of individual and group motivation and behavior to create a learning environment that encourages positive social interaction, active engagement in learning, and self-motivation. (Theme: grounding in the relationship between classroom management and effective learning)

KEY INDICATORS—The Candidate:

- encourages clear procedures and expectations that ensure students assume responsibility for themselves and others, work collaboratively and independently, and engage in purposeful learning activities.
- engages students by relating lessons to students' personal interests, allowing students to have choices in their learning, and leading students to ask questions and solve problems that are meaningful to them.
- organizes, allocates, and manages time, space, and activities in a way that is conducive to learning.
- organizes, prepares students for, and monitors independent and group work that allows for full and varied participation of all individuals.
- analyzes classroom environment and interactions and makes adjustments to enhance social relationships, students' motivation/engagement and productive work.

STANDARD 6: COMMUNICATION AND TECHNOLOGY

The teacher uses knowledge of effective verbal, nonverbal, and media communication techniques to foster active inquiry, collaboration, and supportive interaction in the classroom. (Theme: grounding in effective communication with students)

KEY INDICATORS—The Candidate:

- models effective communication strategies in conveying ideas and information and when asking questions (e.g., monitoring the effects of messages, restating ideas and drawing connections, using aural, visual, and kinesthetic cues, being sensitive to nonverbal cues both given and received).
- provides support for learner expression in speaking, writing, and other media.
- demonstrates that communication is sensitive to gender and cultural differences (e.g., appropriate use of eye contact, interpretation of body language and verbal statements, acknowledgement of and responsiveness to different modes of communication and participation).
- uses a variety of media communication tools to enrich learning opportunities.

STANDARD 7: PLANNING

The teacher plans instruction based upon knowledge of subject matter, students, the community, and curriculum goals. (Theme: grounding in effective planning)

KEY INDICATORS—The Candidate:

- plans lessons and activities to address variation in learning styles and performance modes, multiple development levels of diverse learners, and problem solving and exploration.
- develops plans that are appropriate for curriculum goals and are based on effective instruction.
- adjusts plans to respond to unanticipated sources of input and/or student needs.
- develops short and long-range plans.

STANDARD 8: ASSESSMENT

The teacher understands and uses formal and informal assessment strategies to evaluate and ensure the continuous intellectual, social, and physical development of the learner. (Theme: grounding in use of assessment to inform instruction)

KEY INDICATORS—The Candidate:

- selects, constructs, and uses assessment strategies appropriate to learning outcomes.
- uses a variety of informal and formal strategies to inform choices about students' progress and to adjust instruction (e.g., standardized test data, peer and students self-assessment, informal assessments such as observation, surveys, interviews, students' work, performance tasks, portfolio, and teacher-made tests).
- uses assessment strategies to involve learners in self-assessment activities to help them become aware of their strengths and needs, and to encourage them to set personal goals for learning.
- evaluates the effects of class activities on individuals and on groups through observation of classroom interaction, questions, and analysis of student work.
- maintains useful records of student work and performance and can communicate student progress knowledgeably and responsibly.
- solicits information about students' experiences, learning behavior, needs and progress from parents, other colleagues, and students.

STANDARD 9: REFLECTIVE PRACTICE: PROFESSIONAL DEVELOPMENT

The teacher is a reflective practitioner who continually evaluates the effects of his/her choices and actions on others (students, parents, and other professionals in the learning community) and who actively seeks out opportunities to grow professionally. (Theme: grounding in reflection and self-evaluation)

KEY INDICATORS—The Candidate:

- uses classroom observation, information about students, and research as sources for evaluating the outcomes of teaching and learning as a basis for experimenting with, reflecting on, and revising practice.
- uses professional literature, colleagues, and other resources to support self-development as a learner and as a teacher.
- consults with professional colleagues within the school and other professional arenas as support for reflection, problem-solving and new ideas, actively sharing experiences and seeking and giving feedback.

STANDARD 10: SCHOOL AND COMMUNITY INVOLVEMENT

The teacher fosters relationships with school colleagues, parents, and agencies in the larger community to support students' learning and well-being. (Theme: grounding in community partnerships)

KEY INDICATORS—The Candidate:

- participates in collegial activities designed to make the entire school a productive learning environment.
- links with counselors, teachers of other classes and activities within the school, professionals in community agencies, and others in the community to support students' learning and well-being.
- seeks to establish cooperative partnerships with parents/guardians to support students' learning.
- advocates for students.

REFERENCES

Allensworth, E., & Easton, J. Q. (2005). *The on-track indicator as a predictor of high school graduation.* Chicago, IL: Consortium on Chicago School Research.

Alliance for Excellent Education. (2007). *The high cost of high school dropouts: What the nation pays for inadequate high schools* (Issue Brief 10). Washington, DC: Author.

Allison, G. T. (1969). Conceptual models and the Cuban missile crisis. *American Political Science Review, 63,* 689–718.

Andrade, H. G. (1997). *Understanding rubrics.* Retrieved from http://learnweb.harvard.edu/alps/thining/docs/rubricar.htm

Armour-Thomas, E. (1992). Intellectual assessment of children from culturally diverse backgrounds. *School Psychology Review, 21*(4), 552–565.

Auger, R. W., Seymour, J. W., & Roberts, W. B. (2004). Responding to terror: The impact of September 11 on K–12 schools and schools' responses. *Professional School Counseling, 7,* 220–230.

Azzi-Lessing, L. (2010). Meeting the mental health needs of poor and vulnerable children in early care and education programs. *Early Childhood Research and Practice, 12*(1). Retrieved from http://ecrp.uiuc.edu/v12n1/azzi.html

Balfanz, R., & Herzog, L. (2005, March). *Keeping middle grades students on track to graduation: Initial analysis and implications.* Presentation given at the second Regional Middle Grades Symposium, Philadelphia, PA.

Bandura, A. (1977). *Social learning theory.* New York, NY: General Learning Press.

Bandura, A. (1989). Human agency in social cognitive theory. *American Psychologist, 44*(9), 1175–1184.

Barkley, E. F., Cross, K. P., & Major, C. H. (2005). *Collaborative learning techniques: A handbook for college faculty.* San Francisco, CA: Jossey-Bass.

Baron-Cohen, S. (2003). *The essential difference: The male and female brain.* New York, NY: Basic Books.

Barton, J., Heilker, P., & Rutkowski, D. (1997). *Fostering effective classroom discussions.* Retrieved from http://www.mhhe.com/socscience/english/tc/discussion.htm

Beegle, D. M. (2003). Overcoming the silence of generational poverty. *Talking Points, 15*(1), 11–20.

Berk, L. A. (2000). *Child development* (5th ed.). Boston, MA: Allyn & Bacon.

Berk, R. A. (2003). *Professors are from Mars, students are from snickers.* Sterling, VA: Stylus Press.

Bernard, M. E. (2006). It's time we teach social-emotional competence as well as we teach academic competence. *Reading and Writing Quarterly, 22*(2), 103–119. doi:10.1080/10573560500242184

Bettenhausen, S. (1998). Make proactive modifications to your classroom. *Intervention in School and Clinic, 33*(3), 182–183.

Bloom, B. S. (1956). *Taxonomy of educational objectives: Handbook 1. The cognitive domain.* New York, NY: David McKay.

Bluestein, J. (2008). *The win–win classroom.* Thousand Oaks, CA: Corwin Publishing.

Bohn, A. (2006, Winter). A framework for understanding Ruby Payne. *Rethinking Schools Online, 21*(2). Retrieved from http://www.rethinkingschools.org/archive/21_02/frame212.shtml

Bondy, E., & Ross, D. D. (2008). The positive classroom. *Educational Leadership, 66*(1), 54–58.

Boxer, P., Edwards-Leeper, L., Goldstein, S. E., Musher-Eizenman, D., & Dubow, E. F. (2003). Exposure to "low-level" aggression in school: Associations with aggressive behavior, future expectations, and perceived safety. *Violence and Victims, 18*(6), 691–705.

Brabec, K., Fisher, K., & Pitler, H. (2004). Building better instruction: How technology supports nine research-proven instructional strategies. *Learning and Leading with Technology, 31*(5), 6–11.

Braithwaite, R. (2001). *Managing aggression.* New York, NY: Routledge.

Bridgeland, J. M., DiIulio, J. J., Jr., & Burke Morison, K. (2006). *The silent epidemic: Perspectives of high school dropouts.* Retrieved from http://www.gatesfoundation.org/nr/downloads/ed/thesilentepidemic3-06final.pdf

Brooks-Gunn, J., & Duncan, G. J. (1997). The effects of poverty on children. *Future of Children, 7,* 55–71.

Brophy, J. (1981). Teacher praise: A functional analysis, *Review of Educational Research, 51*(5). doi:10.3102/00346543051001005

Bruner, J. (1996). *The culture of education.* Cambridge, MA: Harvard University Press.

Calderhead, J. (1989). Reflective teaching and teacher education. *Teaching and Teacher Education, 5*(1), 43–51.

Callicott, K. J., & Park, H. (2003). Effects of self-talk on academic engagement and academic responding. *Behavioral Disorders, 29*(1), 48–64.

Carskadon, M. A. (Ed.). (2002). *Adolescent sleep patterns: Biological, social and psychological influences.* Cambridge, UK: Cambridge University Press.

Center on the Social and Emotional Foundation for Early Learning. (2007). *Helping children understand routines and classroom schedules* (What Works Brief Training Kit #3). Nashville, TN: Author. Retrieved from www.vanderbilt.edu/csefel/

Christian, S. (2009). *Children of incarcerated parents.* Denver, CO: National Conference of State Legislatures.

Cisneros, S. (1984). *The house on Mango Street.* Houston, TX: Arte Publico Press.

Clark, D. (2011). *Bloom's taxonomy of learning domains.* Retrieved from Big Dog & Little Dog's Performance Juxtaposition at http://www.nwlink.com/-donclark/hrd/bloom.html

Coffey, H. (2010). Summative assessment. *Learn NC.* Retrieved from http://www.learnnc.org/lp/pages5233

Cohen, E. G. (1973). Modifying the effects of social structure. *American Behavioral Scientist, 15*(6), 861–879.

Connor, P. (2011). *Your role as classroom discussion facilitator.* Retrieved from http://tilt.colostate.edu/tips/tip.cfm?tipid=110

Costa, A., & Garmston, R. (1994). *Cognitive coaching: A foundation for Renaissance schools.* Norwood, MA: Christopher Gordon.

Cranton, P. A. (1998). *No one way.* Toronto, Canada: Wall and Emerson.

Croninger, R., & Lee, V. E. (2001). Social capital and dropping out of high school: Benefits to at-risk students of teachers' support and guidance. *Teachers College Record, 103*(4), 548–581.

Cummings, C. (2000). *Winning strategies for classroom management.* Alexandria, VA: Association for Supervision and Curriculum Development.

Cushman, K. (2003). *Fires in the bathroom: Advice for teachers from high school students.* New York, NY: New Press.

Daggett, W. R., Cobble, J. E., & Gertel, S. J. (2007). *The environment of the struggling learner.* Rexford, NY: International Center for Leadership in Education.

Dallman-Jones, A. (2006). *Shadow children: Understanding education's # 1 problem.* Lancaster, PA: RLD Publications.

Daniels, D. C. (2002). Becoming a reflective practitioner. *Middle School Journal, 33*(4), 52–56.

Davis, H. A. (2003). Conceptualizing the role and influence of student–teacher relationships on children's social and cognitive development. *Educational Psychologist, 38*(4), 207–234.

Dweck, C., & Leggett, E. (1988). A social-cognitive approach to motivation and personality. *Psychological Review, 95,* 256–273.

Eckholm, E. (2009, July 4). In prisoners' wake, a tide of troubled kids. *The New York Times.* Retrieved from http://www.nytimes.com/2009/07/05/us/05prison.html

Edelson, D. C., Gordin, D. N., & Pea, R. D. (1999). Addressing the challenges of inquiry-based learning through technology and curriculum design. *Journal of the Learning Sciences, 8*(3/4), 391–450.

Eide, B., & Eide, F. (2006). Brains on fire: The multimodality of gifted thinkers. *New Horizons for Learning.* Retrieved from http://home.avvanta.com/building/spneeds/gifted/eide.htm

Einstein, A. (n.d.). Quotations retrieved from http://einstein-quotes.com

Every child achieving: A plan for meeting the needs of the individual learner: Maryland's preK–12 academic intervention initiative. (1999). Adopted October 27, 1999, by the Maryland State Board of Education.

Fauth, R. C., Brady-Smith, C., & Brooks-Gunn, J. (2001). *Poverty and education: An overview, children and adolescents.* Retrieved from http://education.stateuniversity.com/pages2330/Poverty-Education.html

Feiler, A. (2010). *Engaging "hard to reach" parents: Teacher–parent collaboration to promote children's learning.* West Sussex, UK: Wiley-Blackwell.

Ferraro, J. M. (2000). *Reflective practice and professional development.* Retrieved from ERIC Clearinghouse on Teaching and Teacher Education, ERIC Identifier ED449120, at http://searcheric.org/digests/ed449120.html

Finest Quotes. (n.d.). Quotations retrieved from http://finestquotes.com

Flavell, J., Friedrichs, A., & Hoyt, J. (1970). Developmental changes in memorization processes. *Cognitive Psychology, 1*(4), 324–340.

Ford, D. Y. (2005, Winter). Intelligence testing and cultural diversity: Pitfalls and promises, *Newsletter of the National Research Center on the Gifted and Talented.* Retrieved from http://www.gifted.uconn.edu/nrcgt/newsletter/winter05/winter052.html

Fordham, S., & Ogbu, J. U. (1986). *Black students' school success: Coping with the "burden of 'acting White.'"* In R. Muuss & H. Porton (Eds.), (1999). *Adolescent behavior and society: A book of readings* (5th ed., pp. 189–207). New York, NY: McGraw-Hill.

Forum on Child and Family Statistics. (2010). *America's children in brief: Key national indicators of well-being 2010.* Retrieved from http://www.childstats.gov/americaschildren/beh.asp

Freiberg, H. J., & Lamb, S. M. (2009). Dimensions of person-centered classroom management. *Theory into Practice, 48,* 99–105. doi:10.1080/00405840902776228

Garbarino, J. (1983). Children's response to community violence: What do we know? *Infant Mental Health Journal, 14*(2), 113–115. doi:10.1002/1097-0355(199322)14.2<103::AID-IMHJ2280140204>3.0.CO;2-6

Gardner, H. (1983). *Frames of mind: The theory of multiple intelligences.* New York, NY: Basic Books.

Gay, L. R. (1992). *Educational research: Competencies for analysis and application* (4th ed.). New York, NY: Macmillan.

Gibson, W. (1956). *The miracle worker.* New York, NY: Pocket Books.

Gilligan, C. (1977). In a different voice: Women's conceptions of self and morality. *Harvard Educational Review, 47,* 481–517.

Ginott, H. G. (1972). *Teacher and child: A book for parents and teachers.* New York, NY: Macmillan.

Ginsburg, M. (1978). *Mushroom in the rain.* New York, NY: Aladdin Paperbacks.

Glass, G. V. (2002). Time for school: Its duration and allocation. In A. Molnar (Ed.), *School reform proposals.* Greenwich, CT: Information Age Publishing.

Goldberg, M. D. (1994). A developmental investigation of intrinsic motivation: Correlates, causes, and consequences in high ability students. *Dissertation Abstract International,* 55-04B, 1688.

Goldstein, A. P. (1999). *Low-level aggression: First steps on the ladder to violence.* Champaign, IL: Research Press.

Goodell, E. (2007). Poverty specialist: Language does matter. *The Dartmouth.* Retrieved from http://theDartmouth.com/2007/11/12/news/poverty

Goodreads. (n.d.). Quotations retrieved from http://goodreads.com

Gottfried, A. E. (1990). Academic intrinsic motivation in young elementary school children. *Journal of Education Psychology, 82*(3), 525–538.

Graham, S., Kratochwill, T., Lucariello, J., McCombs, B., Rimm-Kaufman, S., & Semrud Clikeman, M. (2010). Applications of psychological science to teaching and learning: Gaps in the literature. *American Psychological Association, 100*(3), 363–406.

Hall, L. A. (2007). Understanding the silence: Struggling readers discuss decisions about reading expository text. *Journal of Educational Research, 100,* 132–141.

Hall, L. A. (2009). Struggling reader, struggling teacher: An examination of student–teacher transactions with reading instruction and text in social studies. *Research in the Teaching of English, 43*(3), 286–309.

Hartjes, E. (2009). *Welcome to teachers at risk.* Retrieved from http://www.teachersatrisk.com/2009/04/26/my-web-20-took-kit

Hartley, L. P. (1953). *The go-between.* The New York Review of Books.

Hartman, H. J. (2010). *A guide to reflective practice.* New York, NY: McGraw Hill.

Hatton, N., & Smith, D. (1995). Reflection in teacher education: Towards definition and implementation. *Teaching and Teacher Education, 11,* 33–49.

Hein, G. E. (1991, October). *Constructivist learning theory.* Paper presented at the International Committee of Museum Educators Conference Jerusalem, Israel. Retrieved from http://www.exploratorium.edu/ifi/resources/constructivistlearning.html

Helms, J. (1992). Why is there no study equivalence in standardized cognitive-ability testing? *American Psychologist, 47,* 1083–1101.

Henderson, N., & Milstein, B. B. (1999). *Survivor's pride: Building resilience in youth.* Solvang, CA: Resiliency in Action Training & Publications.

Henry, M. A., & Sutton, J. (1999, October). *Action research: Personal, professional, and powerful.* Paper presented at the meeting of Mid-continent Research for Education and Learning, Denver, CO.

Heubert, J. D. (2010). *High stakes testing: Opportunities and risks for students of color, English-language learners, and students with disabilities.* Wakefield, MA: National Center on Accessible Instructional Materials. Retrieved from http://aim.cast.org/learn/historyarchive/bacgroundpapers/ncac_hi

Highberg, N. P. (2010). Leading effective classroom discussions on controversial issues. *Chronicle of Higher Education.* Retrieved from http://chronicle.com/blogPost/Leading-Effective-Classroom/238

Hillocks, G. (1995). *Teaching writing as reflective practice.* New York, NY: Teachers College Press.

Hoffman Kaser, C. (n.d.). *Arranging the physical environment of the classroom to support teaching/learning* (Series on Highly Effective Practices—Classroom Environment). Retrieved from http://education.odu.edu/esse/docs/classroomenvironments.pdf

Hoffman Kaser, C. (n.d.). *Teaching students to self-monitor their academic and behavioral performance* (Series on Highly Effective Practices—Self Monitoring). Retrieved from http://education.odu.edu/esse/docs/selfmonitoring.pdf

Holland, D. C., & Eisenhart, M. A. (1988). Moments of discontent: University women and the gender status quo. *Anthropology and Education Quarterly, 19*(2), 115–138.

Huitt, W. (2004). Observational (social) learning: An overview. *Educational Psychology Interactive.* Valdosta, GA: Valdosta State University. Retrieved from http://www.edpsycinteractive.org/topics/scocog/soclrn.html

Jacob, B. A. (2001). Getting tough? The impact of high school graduation exams. *Educational Evaluation and Policy Analysis, 23*(2), 99–121.

Janssen, F., de Hullu, E., & Tigelaar, D. (2008). Positive experiences as input for reflection by student teachers. *Teachers and Teaching: Theory and Practice, 14*(2), 115–127. doi:10.1080/13540600801965903

Jensen, E. (2008). *Brain based learning.* Thousand Oaks, CA: Corwin Press.

Johnson, D. W., Johnson, R. T., & Smith, K. A. (1991). *Cooperative learning: Increasing college faculty instructional productivity* (ASHE-FRIC Higher Education Report No. 4). Washington, DC: School of Education and Human Development, George Washington University.

Kennelly, L., & Monrad, M. (2007). *Approaches to dropout prevention: Heeding early warning signs with appropriate interventions.* Washington, DC: National High School Center, American Institutes for Research.

Kerr, M. A., & Schneider, B. H. (2008). Anger expression in children and adolescents: A review of the empirical literature. *Clinical Psychology Review, 28*(4), 559–577.

King Rice, J. (2003). *Teacher quality: Understanding the effectiveness of teacher attributes.* Washington, DC: Economic Policy Institute.

Kozol, J. (1991) *Savage inequalities: Children in America's schools.* New York, NY: Crown Publishers.

Kramer, K. P. (with Gawlick, M.). (2004). *Martin Buber's I and thou: Practicing living dialogue.* Mahwah, NJ: Paulist Press.

Kreber, C. (2006). Developing the scholarship of teaching through transformative learning. *Journal of Scholarship of Teaching and Learning, 6*(1), 88–109.

Kritzer, J. (2000). *Promoting resilience: Helping young children and parents affected by substance abuse, domestic violence, and depression in the context of welfare reform.* New York, NY: National Center for Children in Poverty, Columbia University.

Kritzer, J., & Lefkowitz, J. (2006). *Helping the most vulnerable infants, toddlers, and their families* (Pathways to Early School Success Issue Brief No. 1). New York, NY: National Center for Children in Poverty, Columbia University.

Kritzer, J., Theberge, S., & Johnson, K. (2008). *Reducing maternal depression and its impact on young children: Toward a responsive early childhood policy framework* (Project Thrive Issue Brief). New York, NY: National Center for Children in Poverty, Columbia University.

Lee, H. (1960). *To kill a mockingbird.* New York, NY: Lippincott.

Linsin, M. (2011). *Losing control of your class? Here's how to get it back.* Retrieved from http://www.smartclassroommanagement.com/2011/01/22/losing-control-of-your-classroom/

Little, P. F. B. (2005). Peer coaching as a support to collaborative teaching. *Mentoring and Tutoring, 13*(1), 83–94. doi:10.1080/13611260500040351

Loeber, R., Burke, J. D., Lahey, B. B., Winters, A., & Zera, M. (2000). Oppositional defiant and conduct disorder: A review of the past 10 years, Part 1. *Child and Adolescent Psychiatry, 39*(12), 1468–1484.

Long, N. J., Morse, W. C., & Newman, R. G. (Eds.). (1996). *Conflict in the classroom: The education of at-risk and troubled students* (5th ed.). Austin, TX: Pro-Ed.

Lowenstein, L. F. (1983). Developing self-control and self-esteem in disturbed children. *School Psychology International, 4*(4), 229–235.

Lynch, S., Hurford, D. P., & Cole, A. (2002). Parental enabling attitudes and locus of control of at-risk and honors students. *Adolescence, 37.* Retrieved from http://www.questia.com/googleScholar.qst?docId=5000640263

Mager, R. F. (1972). *Goal analysis.* Retrieved from http://eric.ed.gov

Marshall, B. (2007). Assessment in English. In *Handbook of primary English.* Retrieved from www.nate.org.uk

Marzano, R. J. (1992). *A different kind of classroom: Teaching with dimensions of learning.* Alexandria, VA: Association for Supervision and Curriculum Development.

Marzano, R. J. (with Marzano, J. S., & Pickering, D.). (2003). *Classroom management that works: Research-based strategies for every teacher.* Alexandria, VA: Association for Supervision and Curriculum Development.

Mayer, G. R., & Ybarra, W. J. (2004). *Teaching alternative behaviors schoolwide: A resource guide to prevent discipline problems.* Los Angeles, CA: Los Angeles County Office of Education.

McEvoy, A. (2005). *Teachers who bully students: Patterns and policy implications.* Paper presented at the Hamilton Fish Institute's Persistently Safe Schools Conference, Philadelphia, PA. Retrieved from http://civilitypartners.com/yahoo_site_admin/assets/docs/teachers_who_bully_students.239164537.pdf

McKinney, S. E., Flenner, C., Frazier, W., & Abrams, L. (2006). *Responding to the needs of at-risk students in poverty* (Working Paper No. 17). Aiken, SC: University of South Carolina.

McMillan, J. H. (2000). Fundamental assessment principles for teachers and school administrators. *Practical Assessment, Research and Evaluation, 7*(8). Retrieved from http://pareonline.net/getvn.asp?v=7&n=8

McWhirter, J. J., McWhirter, B. T., McWhirter, A. M., & McWhirter, E. H. (1998). *At-risk youth: A comprehensive response for counselors, teachers, psychologists, and human service professionals.* Belmont: CA: Brooks/Cole-Thompson Learning.

Mena Marcos, J. J., Sanchez Miguel, E., & Tillema, H. (2009). Teacher reflection on action: What is said (in research) and what is done (in teaching). *Reflective Practice, 10*(2), 191–204. doi:10.1080/14623940902786206

Messali, J. (2010). *The effect of motivation on academic achievement.* Retrieved from http://www.ehow.com/facts_5804273_effect-motivation-academic-achievement.html

Midgley, C., & Edelin, K. C. (1998). Middle school reform and early adolescent well-being: The good news and the bad. *Educational Psychologist, 33*(4), 195–206.

Moje, E. B., & Dillion, D. R. (2006). Adolescent identities as demanded by science classroom discourse communities. In D. E. Alvermann, K. A. Hinchman, D. W. Moore, S. F. Phelps, & D. R. Waff (Eds.), *Reconceptualizing the literacies in adolescents' lives* (2nd ed., pp. 85–106). Mahwah, NJ: Lawrence Erlbaum.

Moritz-Rudasill, K., Reio, T. G., Jr., Stipanovic, N., & Taylor, J. (2010). A longitudinal study of student–teacher relationship quality, difficult temperament, and risky behavior from childhood to early adolescence. *Journal of School Psychology, 48*(5), 389–412.

Morse, M. S., Allsopp, D., & McHatton, P. (2009). Cultivating caring relationships between teachers and secondary students with emotional and behavioral disorders: Implications for research and practice, *Research and Special Education, 30*(2), 108–125.

Murray, C., & Pianta, R. C. (2007). The importance of teacher–student relationships for adolescents with high incidence disabilities. *Theory into Practice, 46,* 105–112.

Muuss, R. E. (1996). *Theories of adolescence* (6th ed.). New York, NY: McGraw Hill.

Muuss, R. E., & Porton, H. D. (Eds.). (1999). *Adolescent behavior and society: A book of readings* (5th ed.). New York, NY: McGraw Hill.

National Science Foundation, Division of Science Resources Statistics. (2011). *Women, minorities, and persons with disabilities in science and engineering: 2011* (Special Report NSF11-309). Arlington, VA: Author. Retrieved from http://www.nsf.gov/statistics/wmpd/

Neild, R. C., & Balfanz, R. (2006). *Unfulfilled promise: The dimensions and characteristics of Philadelphia's dropout crisis, 2000–2005.* Baltimore. MD: Center for Social Organization of Schools, Johns Hopkins University.

Nelson, J., Smith, D., & Dodd, J. (1991). A review of self-management outcome research conducted with students who exhibit behavioral disorders. *Behavioral Disorders, 16,* 169–179.

No Child Left Behind. (n.d.). *Is YOUR child being left behind?* Retrieved from http://www.nochildleftbehind.com/

Norden, J. (2007). *Understanding the brain: Course guidebook.* Chantilly, VA: The Great Courses, The Teaching Company.

Northwest Educational Technology Consortium. (2011). *Early connections: Technology in early childhood education.* Retrieved from http://www.netc.org/earlyconnections/primary/classroom.html

O'Connor, M. C. (2011). Teachers hold the real keys to whiteboard effectiveness. *Education Week.*, 30(35) 15–16.

Ormrod, J. E. (1999). *Human learning* (3rd ed.). Upper Saddle River, NJ: Merrill/Pearson Education.

Oxford Dictionaries Online. (n.d.). Retrieved from http://oxforddictionaries.com/

Ozan, O., & Kesim, M. (2011, March). Providing scaffolding by using mobile applications in connectivist learning environment. In *Book of abstracts of the conference: Mobile learning: Crossing boundaries in convergent environments* (Bremen, Germany). Retrieved from http://creactivecomments.org/licenses/by-nc-nd/3.01/

Palmer, D. (2005). A motivational view of constructivist-informed teaching. *International Journal of Science Education,* 27(15/16), 1853–1881.

Patterson, S. M., & Albers, A. B. (2001). Effects of poverty and maternal depression on early childhood development. *Child Development,* 72(6), 1794–1813.

Payne, R. (1996). Understanding and working with students and adults from poverty. *Instructional Leader* (Texas Elementary Principals and Supervisors Association), 9(4), 1–4.

Pianta, R. C., Hamre, B., & Stuhlman, M. (2003). *Handbook of psychology.* Wiley Online. doi:10.1002/0471264385.wei0710

Pianta, R. C., Stuhlman, M., & Hamre, B. (2002). How schools can do better: Fostering stronger connections between teachers and students. *New Directions for Mental Health Services,* 2002(93), 91–107.

Quillen, I. (2011). Summer educators "mix up" learning with technology. *Education Week.* Retrieved from http://ew/articles/2011/06/15/35summertech.h30.html

Quote Garden. (n.d.). Quotations retrieved from http://quotegarden.com

Quotes on Assessment. (n.d.). Quotations retrieved from http://QuotesofAssessment.com

Quotes on Teaching. (n.d.). Quotation Retrieved from http://www.freewebs.com/hwyl/Quotes/learning.html

Ramsden, P. (1972). *Learning to teach in higher education.* London: Routledge.

Rich, J. M. (1992). *Innovations in education* (6th ed.). Needham Heights, MA: Allyn & Bacon.

Rich, M. (2008, July 27). Literacy debate: RU really reading? *The New York Times.* Retrieved from http://www.nytimes.com/2008/07/27/books/27reading.html?page. . .

Roderick, M., & Engel, M. (2001). The grasshopper and the ant: Motivational responses of low-achieving students to high-stakes testing. *Educational Evaluation and Policy Analysis,* 23(3), 197–227.

Roosevelt, T. (1910). Excerpt retrieved from http://www.theodore-roosevelt.com/trsorbonnespeech.html

Rossi, R., & Montgomery, A. (Eds.). (1994, January). *Education reforms and students at risk: A review of the current state of the art.* Retrieved from http://www2ed.gov/pubs/EDReformStudies/EdReforms/title.html

Sagor, R. (1993). *At-risk students: Reaching and teaching them.* Swampscott, MA: Watersun Publishing.

Scheeringa, M. S., & Zeanah, C. H. (2001). A relational perspective on PTSD in early childhood. *Journal of Traumatic Stress,* 14(4), 799–815.

Schön, D. (1983). *The reflective practitioner.* San Francisco, CA: Jossey-Bass.

Schön, D. (1987). *Educating the reflective practitioner.* San Francisco, CA: Jossey-Bass.

School Improvement in Maryland. (2012). http://mdk12.org/assessments/high_school/index.html

School Improvement in Maryland. (2011). *What is HSA?* Retrieved from http://mdk12.org/assessments/high_school/index.html

Schunk, D. H., & Zimmerman, B. J. (2006). Competence and control beliefs: Distinguishing the means and ends. In P. A. Alexander & P. H. Wenne (Eds.), *Handbook of educational psychology* (2nd ed., pp. 349–367). Mahwah, NJ: Lawrence Erlbaum.

Search Quotes. (n.d.). Quotations retrieved from http://wwwsearchquotes.com

Shindler, J. (2010). *Transformative classroom management.* San Francisco, CA: Jossey-Bass.

Silva, E. (2009). Teachers at work: Improving teacher quality through school design. *Education Sector Reports. Retrieved from* http://www.afterschoolresources.org/kernel/images/Teachers_at_Work.pdf

Simon, S. B., Howe, L. W., & Kirschenbaum, H. (1995). *Values clarification.* New York, NY: Warner Books.

Slavin, R. E., & Braddock, J. H. (1993). Ability grouping: On the wrong track. *College Board Review,* 68(2), 11–17.

Smith, A., & Bondy, E. (2007). *"No! I won't": Understanding and responding to student defiance. Education and Treatment of Children,* 31, 351–280. http://findarticles.com/p/articles/mi_qa3614/is_200704/ai_n1943 . . .

Smith, J., Brooks-Gunn, J., Kowhen, D., & McCarton, C. (2001). Transitions on and off welfare: Implications for parenting and children's cognitive development. *Child Development,* 72, 1512–1533.

Smith, M. K. (2009). The social/situational orientation to learning. *The encyclopedia of informal education.* Retrieved from www.infed.org/biblio/learning-social.htm

Sprenger, M. (1999). *Learning and memory: The brain in action.* Alexandria, VA: Association for Supervision and Curriculum Development.

Sprick, R. S., Borgmeier, C., & Nolet, V. (2002). Prevention and management of behavior problems in secondary schools. In M. A. Shinn, H. W. Walker, & G. Stoner (Eds.), *Interventions for academic and behavior problems II: Preventive and remedial approaches* (pp. 373–401). Bethesda, MD: National Association of School Psychologists.

Stapleton, A. (2009). *Effects of divorce on age and gender on childhood aggression* (Unpublished thesis). Huntington, WV: Marshall University.

Stiggins, R. J., Arter, J. A., & Chappuis, S. (2004). Classroom assessment for student learning: Doing it right, using it well. Alexandria, VA: Association for Supervision and Curriculum Development.

Stiggins, R. J., & Chappuis, J. (2012). *An introduction to student-involved assessment for learning* (6th ed.). Upper Saddle River, NJ: Pearson.

Stigler, J., & Hiebert, J. (1997). Understanding and improving classroom mathematics instruction: An overview of the TIMSS video study, *Phi Delta Kappan 79(1),* 59–115. Retrieved from http://www.acu.edu.au/documents/TIMSS_pdf

Stigler, J. W., & Hiebert, J. (1999). *The teaching cap: Best ideas from the world's teachers for improving education in the classroom.* New York, NY: Free Press.

Svinicki, M., & McKeachie, W. J. (2011). *Teaching tips* (13th ed.). Belmont, CA: Wadsworth.

Taber, K. S. (2009). Constructivism and the crisis in U.S. science education: An essay review. *Education Review, 12*(12). Retrieved from http://edrev.asu.edu/essays/v12n12index.html

Tatum, A. W. (2006). Adolescents' multiple identities and teacher professional development. In D. E. Alvermann, K. A. Hinchman, D. W. Moore, S. F. Phelps, & D. R. Waff (Eds.), *Reconceptualizing the literacies in adolescents' lives* (2nd ed., pp. 65–79). Mahwah, NJ: Lawrence Erlbaum.

Teacher Appreciation Quotes. (n.d.). Quotations retrieved from http://www.teacher-appreciation.info/Quotations_on_teaching/

Thibos, M., Lavin-Loucks, D., & Marin, M. (2007). *The feminization of poverty.* Dallas, TX: J. McDonald Williams Institute.

Think Exist. (n.d.). Quotations retrieved from http://www.thinkexist.com

Thompson, G. K., & Jenkins, J. B. (1993). *Verbal judo: The gentle art of persuasion.* New York, NY: William Morrow.

Turner, H. A., Finkelhor, D., & Ormrod, R. (2006). The effect of lifetime victimization on the mental health of children and adolescents. *Social Science and Medicine, 62*(1), 13–27.

UNICEF. (2007). *Child poverty in perspective: An overview of child well-being in rich countries: A comprehensive account of the lives and well-being of children and adolescents in the economically advanced nations* (Innocenti Report Card 7). Florence, Italy: UNICEF Innocenti Research Centre.

U.S. Census Bureau. (2000). U.S. data sets retrieved from http://factfinder2.census.gov/faces/nav/jsf/pages/index.xhtml

U.S. Department of Education, Office of Educational Research and Improvement. (1992). *Cooperative Learning* (Education Research Consumer Guide No. 1). Retrieved from http://www.eric.ed.gov/PDFS/ED346999.pdf

Vockell, E. L. (n.d.). *Educational psychology: A practical approach* [Online version]. Retrieved from http://education.calumet.purdue.edu/vockell/EdpsyBook/

Walker, H. M., Colvin, G., & Ramsey, E. (1995). *Antisocial behavior in school: Strategies and best practices.* Pacific Grove, CA: Brooks/Cole.

Wiggins, G., & McTighe, J. (1998). *Understanding by design.* Upper Saddle River, NJ: Merrill/Pearson Education.

Willis, J. (2007, Summer). The neuroscience of joyful education. *Educational Leadership, 64.* Retrieved from http://www.ascd.org/publications/educational-leadership/

Wolfe, P. (2010). *Brain matters: Translating research into classroom practice* (2nd ed.). Alexandria, VA: Association for Supervision and Curriculum Development.

Wright, J. (2011). *School-wide strategies for managing defiance/noncompliance.* Retrieved from http://www.interventioncentral.org/index.php/challenging-studen…

Zeichner, K. M., Tabachnik, B. R., & Denmore, K. (1987). Individual, institutional, and cultural influences on the development of teachers' craft knowledge. In J. Calderhead (Ed.), *Exploring teacher thinking.* London, UK: Cassell.

NAME INDEX

A

Albers, A. B., 23, 24
Allensworth, E., 25
Alliance for Excellent Education, 179
Allison, G. T., 173
Allsopp, D., 153
Andrade, H. G., 164
Armour-Thomas, E., 32
Arter, J. A., 163
Auger, R. W., 85
Azzi-Lessing, L., 23

B

Balfanz, R., 25, 26
Bandura, A., 33, 37, 41, 116, 117, 146–147, 156
Barkley, E. F., 38, 41
Baron-Cohen, S., 43
Barton, J., 122
Beegle, D. M., 29, 31, 32
Berk, L. A., 83
Berk, R. A., 67
Bernard, M. E., 64, 71
Bettenhausen, S., 91
Bloom, B. S., 5
Bluestein, J., 64, 65
Bohn, A., 48
Borgmeier, C., 63, 79, 80, 82
Boxer, P., 66
Brabec, K., 28, 30, 78, 79, 80
Braddock, J. H., 36
Brady-Smith, C., 23
Braithwaite, R., 72
Bridgeland, J. M., 179, 180
Brooks-Gunn, J., 23, 24
Brophy, J., 77, 78, 79, 80, 98, 100, 105, 182, 205, 206
Bruner, J., 131, 133, 134
Burke, J. D., 72
Burke Morison, K., 179

C

Calderhead, J., 102
Capote, Truman, 64
Carskadon, M. A., 82
Center on the Social and Emotional Foundation for Early Learning, 63
Chappuis, J., 160, 164, 168
Chappuis, S., 163
Christian, S., 31
Cisneros, S., 135, 136, 153, 209
Clark, D., 5
Cobble, J. E., 25
Coffey, H., 177

Cohen (col 2)

Cohen, E. G., 26, 34, 40, 95
Cole, A., 29
Collier, Robert, 27
Colvin, G., 83
Connor, P., 122
Costa, A., 49
Cranton, P. A., 102
Croninger, R., 179
Cross, K. P., 38
Cummings, C., 91
Cushman, K., 67

D

Daggett, W. R., 25
Dallman-Jones, A., 22, 31, 179, 195
Daniels, D. C., 48
The Dartmouth, 32
Davis, H. A., 68
Dean, Elizabeth, Dr., 40
de Hullu, E., 102
Denmore, K., 102
DiIulio, J. J., Jr., 179
Dillion, D. R., 154
Dodd, J., 64
Dubow, E. F., 66
Duncan, G. J., 24
Dweck, Carol, 33

E

Easton, J. Q., 25
Eckholm, E., 30, 31
Edelin, K. C., 68
Edelson, D. C., 140, 141, 142
Educating the Reflective Practitioner, 48
Edwards-Leeper, L., 66
Eide, B., 132
Eide, F., 132
Einstein, A., 35, 130, 142, 148, 159, 173, 192
Eisenhart, M. A., 25
Engel, M., 180
Every child achieving, 178

F

Fauth, R. C., 23, 24, 26
Feiler, A., 86
Finch, Atticus, 114
Finest Quotes, 121
Finkelhor, D., 76
Fisher, K., 28, 78
Flavell, J., 80
Ford, D. Y., 32
Fordham, S., 26

Ford, Henry, 25, 32, 146
Forum on Child and Family Statistics, 23
Freiberg, H. J., 103
Friedrichs, A., 80

G
Garbarino, J., 85
Gardner, H., 6
Garmston, R., 49
Gay, L. R., 166
Gertel, S. J., 25
Gibson, William, 166
Gilligan, C., 44, 99
Ginott, H. G., 77, 78, 79, 83, 85, 87, 102, 105,
    110, 113
Ginsburg, Mirra, 124, 125
Glass, G. V., 36, 37
The Go-Between, 93
Goldberg, M. D., 10
Goldstein, A. P., 66, 94, 95
Goldstein, S. E., 66
Goodell, E., 32
Gordin, D. N., 140
Grasmick, Nancy, Dr., 96, 190

H
Hall, L. A., 154
Hamre, B., 67, 68
Hartjes, E., 144
Hartley, L. P., 93
Hartman, H. J., 48, 49
Hatton, N., 102
Heilker, P., 122
Hein, G. E., 131, 133
Helms, J., 32
Henderson, N., 64, 71
Henry, M. A., 49
Herzog, L., 26
Heubert, J. D., 178
Hiebert, J., 84
Highberg, N. P., 122
Hillocks, G., 48, 49
Hoffman Kaser, C., 90
Holland, D. C., 25
Howe, L. W., 169, 170, 213
Hoyt, J., 80
Huitt, W., 116, 117
Hurford, D. P., 29

I
In a Different Voice: Women's Conceptions of Self and
    Morality (article), 99

J
Jacob, B. A., 4
Janssen, F., 102

Jenkins, J. B., 83
Jensen, E., 80, 81, 133
Johnson, D. W., 169
Johnson, R. T., 169
Joppatowne High School, 108

K
Kennedy, Bobby, 24
Kennelly, L., 26
Kerr, M. A., 76
Kesim, M., 117
King, B. B., 154
King Rice, J., 85, 106
Kirschenbaum, H., 169, 170, 213
Kozol, J., 23
Kramer, K. P., 166
Kreber, C., 102
Kritzer, J., 22, 24

L
Lahey, B. B., 72
Lamb, S. M., 103
Lavin-Loucks, D., 32
Lee, H., 11, 114
Lee, V. E., 179
Lefkowitz, J., 22, 24
Leggett, E., 33
Linsin, M., 104
Little, P. F. B., 31
Loeber, R., 72
Long, N. J., 63, 64
Lowenstein, L. F., 78
Low-Level Aggression, 66
Lynch, S., 29

M
Major, C. H., 38
Marin, M., 32
Marshall, B., 75, 77
Maryland State Board of Education, 178
Maryland State Department of Education (MSDE),
    19, 161, 178
Marzano, J. S., 85
Marzano, R. J., 5, 11, 85, 119, 121, 129, 147, 148, 167, 169, 170,
    195, 213
Mayer, G. R., 83
McEvoy, A., 94, 95
McHatton, P., 153
McKeachie, W. J., 49
McMillan, J. H., 166
McTighe, J., 166
Mena Marcos, J. J., 102
Messali, J., 10
Midgley, C., 68
Milstein, B. B., 64, 71
The Miracle Worker, 42, 166, 167

Moje, E. B., 154
Monrad, M., 26
Moritz-Rudasill, K., 104
Morse, M. S., 153
Morse, W. C., 63, 64
Murray, C., 153
Musher-Eizenman, D., 66
Mushroom in the Rain, 124, 150
Muuss, R. E., 23, 156

N

National Science Foundation, Division of Science Resources
    Statistics, 33
Neild, R. C., 25, 26
Nelson, J., 64
Newman, R. G., 63, 64
New York Times, 31, 143–144
Nolet, V., 63, 79, 80, 82
Norden, J., 43

O

O'Connor, M. C., 140
The Odyssey, 108
Of Mice and Men, 44
Ogbu, J. U., 26
Ormrod, J. E., 41
Ormrod, R., 76
The Oxford Dictionary of English, 63–64
Ozan, O., 117

P

Palmer, D., 133
Patterson, S. M., 23, 24
Payne, R., 31, 33
Pea, R. D., 140
Pfarr, Jodi, 32
Pianta, R. C., 67, 68, 153
Pickering, D., 85
Pitler, H., 28, 78
Porton, H. D., 14, 21, 23, 33, 42, 66, 84, 91, 92, 115, 116, 117, 118,
    139, 156, 191, 217

Q

Quillen, I., 140
Quote Garden, 34, 96, 154
Quotes on Assessment., 162

R

Ramsden, P., 102
Ramsey, E., 83
Reio, T. G., Jr., 104
Rich, M., 144
Roberts, W. B., 85
Roderick, M., 180
Roosevelt, T., 100
Rutkowski, D., 122

S

Sagor, R., 6, 20, 24, 26, 107, 169, 191, 192,
    195, 217
Sanchez Miguel, E., 102
Schaefer, William Donald, 174
Scheeringa, M. S., 22
Schneider, B. H., 76
Schön, D., 48, 57, 102
Schon, Donald, 48
School Improvement in Maryland,
    178, 181, 182
Schunk, D. H., 28, 30
Search Quotes, 190
Seymour, J. W., 85
Shindler, J., 94
Silva, E., 106
Simon, S. B., 169, 170, 213
Slavin, R. E., 36
Smith, D., 64, 102
Smith, K. A., 169
Smith, M. K., 132, 133
Sondheim, Walter , Jr., 174
Sprick, R. S., 63, 79, 80, 82
Stiggins, R. J., 160, 163, 164, 168
Stigler, J. W., 84
Stipanovic, N., 104
Stuhlman, M., 67, 68
Sutton, J., 49
Svinicki, M., 49

T

Tabachnik, B. R., 102
Taber, K. S., 140
Tatum, A. W., 154
Taylor, J., 104
Teacher Appreciation Quotes, 78
The House on Mango Street, 135
Thibos, M., 32
Think Exist, 25, 27, 99, 130, 134, 143, 144, 146, 148, 154,
    185, 189, 192
Thompson, G. K., 83
Tigelaar, D., 102
Tillema, H., 102
To Kill a Mockingbird (TKAM), 114, 115, 117–118
Turner, H. A., 76

U

Understanding the Brain, 80
UNICEF, 23
U.S. Census Bureau, 23
U.S. Department of Education, Office of Educational Research
    and Improvement, 38

V

Vockell, E. L., 28, 29

W

Walker, H. M., 83
Wiggins, G., 166
Williams, Doris, 108
Willis, J., 105
Winters, A., 72
Wolfe, P., 80, 81, 124, 190, 195
Wright, J., 70, 72

Y

Ybarra, W. J., 83

Z

Zeanah, C. H., 22
Zeichner, K. M., 102
Zera, M., 72
Zimmerman, B. J., 28, 30

SUBJECT INDEX

A

ability, grouping by, 40–41
absenteeism, 25–26
academic ability
  and motivation, relationship, 10
accessibility, discovery learning and, 141, 142–143
accountability movement (historical context), 178–179
adequate yearly progress (AYP), 36
adult learning, 48
All Stars program, 19, 62
anger, in children, 76
  management, 76–77
  reflective practices, 193
assessment(s), 6–7. *See also*
      instructions
  alternative types of, 168–170
  benchmark tests, 174
  decision-making matrix, 169–170
  definition of, 160
  example, 162, 163
  formative (*see* formative assessments)
  instructional triangle, 159–160
  INTASC Standards, 221
  performance, 168
  rubrics (*see* rubrics)
  sharing group grades, concerns related to,
     168–169
  strategies, goals, and, connections among, 161
  summative (*see* summative assessments)
  teacher-made (*see* teacher-made assessments)
at-risk students. *See* struggling learners
attendance, 25–26
  improving, 27–28
attributions, 28

B

background knowledge, discovery learning and,
    141, 143–144
benchmark tests, 174
biases
  classrooms and, 25
  gender, long-term effects of, 32–33, 34
boundaries
  benefits of, 66
  clear, establishing, 65–66
  defined, 63–64
  reflective practices, 103–104, 193
brain research, 80–82
  elementary school, 80–81
  high school, 81–82
  middle school, 81
  and reflective practices, 105
bullying, 93. *See also* shaming
  teacher, effects of, 94

C

children. *See also* student(s)
  anger in (*see* anger, in children)
  attendance and, 25–26, 27–28
  authority, expectations of, 26–27
  classrooms, safety in, 24–25
  communication, lack of, 24
  external locus of control approach in, 28–30
  gender bias, long-term effects of, 32–33, 34
  generational incarceration in, 30–31, 33
  generational poverty in, 31–32, 33
  limited/grim notion of future, 30–34
  in poverty, 23–24
  retention in grade, 26
  school-based standards, unsuccessful in meeting, 25–28
classroom
  anger, in children, 76–77
  applications, 29–30
  arrangement (*see* classroom arrangement)
  biases and, 25
  cleanliness in, 90–91
  laughter in, 67
  management (*see* classroom management)
  predictability and emotional stability in, 25
  reality in, 76–77
  safety in, struggling learners, 24–25
  technology in, 85
classroom arrangement
  creating, 68–69
  inviting classrooms, 69
  proximity in, 68
  safety and security and, 68–69
  student, easy access to, 68
  technology, easy access to, 69
classroom discussions, effective, 121–124
  assessing, 122
  lesson plan on, 122–124 (*see also* lesson plan(s))
  preparation and effort, 121–122
  reflective teachers and, 148–150
classroom management. *See also* reflective managers,
    practices of
  brain research in (*see* brain research)
  complaining to parents, 85–86
  dressing, importance of, 78
  effective praise (*see* praise, effective)
  guidelines, 75–86
  Harriet's Helpful Hints, 82–86
  noise management, 78, 83
  paying attention to little details, 86
  reflective practices, 104
  skills, 64
  trust building and, 77–78
cleanliness, in classrooms, 90–91
climatology, discovery learning and, 141–144

cognitive simulation, 117
Common Core State Standards, 8, 13, 16, 51–52, 135, 136, 149, 155
communication, 84–85
   lack, struggling learners and, 24
   and technology, INTASC Standards, 221
communities
   unstable, children from (*see* unstable families)
constructing meaning, defined, 5
constructivism, 132–133
   instructional triangle and, 133–134
   learning and, 132–133
content pedagogy, INTASC Standards, 219
contributions, member, 44–45
cooperative learning, 41, 44
   defined, 38
cooperative learning groups, 116–117, 147
courage, definition of, 96
curriculum guide, 49, 50

D

daily assessments, 186–187. *See also* assessment(s)
   effective, 186
daily lessons, specific objectives for, 4–5
data analysis, teacher-made assessments, 166–168
   goals, 166–168
   principles, 166
   reliability, 166
   validity, 166
decision-making matrix, 169–170
declarative knowledge, 5
defiance, handling, 71–72
Dimensions of Learning (DOLs), 114, 119–120, 147, 167, 168, 169
   Dimension Five, 119, 120, 121, 124
   Dimension Four, 119, 120, 121
   Dimension One, 119–120, 121, 124, 147
   Dimension Three, 119, 120, 121, 124, 134
   Dimension Two, 119, 120, 121
discovery learning, 131–144
   application, 134–139
   climatology and, 141–144
   constructivism, 132–133 (*see also* constructivism)
   effective lesson, creating and implementing, 154–155
   lesson plan template and, 134, 135
      (*see also* lesson plan(s))
   problem-solving system, 136–139
   reflective teachers and, 151–152
   science and, 139–144
   technology and, 139–144
disgracing, 93–94
diverse learners, INTASC Standards, 220
divorce, struggling learners and, 22
DOLs. *See* dimensions of learning (DOLs)
dopamine, levels
   in adolescence, 81
dressing, importance of
   in classroom management, 78

dropouts
   increased rates, high-stakes tests and, 179
drug rehabilitation center
   problem-solving system and, 139

E

effective daily assessments, 186. *See also* assessment(s)
efforts
   grouping by, 41
   and success, connections, 28–29
egregious errors
   vs. fixable errors, 106
elementary school, brain research and, 80–81
enrichment group, 12
expectations, for children, 26–27
"externalizers," 29
external locus of control approach, in children
   attributions, 28
   classroom applications, 29–30
   effort and success, connections, 28–29
   ownership of failures or successes, 29

F

failure, ownership of, 29
families
   unstable, children from (*see* unstable families)
family stress model, 24
FAT-P. *See* form, audience, topic, and purpose (FAT–P)
5 E plan, 7
fixable and forgivable mistakes, 90–93
   bullying, 93
   vs. egregious errors, 106
   lesson plans, wrong, 91, 92
   mean girls and, 93
   routine, need of, 91–93
   sarcasm, 93
   vs. unforgivable, 97–98
   untidy classroom, 90–91
Ford, Henry, 146
formative assessments, 164. *See also* assessment(s)
   example, 175–176
   goal of, 175
   method and time of using, 175
   reluctant workers, 176
   vocabulary, 174
   vs. summative assessments, 173–182, 187–188
form, audience, topic, and purpose (FAT–P), 50–51
frontal cortex, of brain, 81
functional citizenship test, 6

G

gender
   bias, long-term effects of, 32–33, 34
   contributions, valuing, 44–45
   grouping by, 43–45
   ineffective praise and, 99
   single-gender teams, 44
generational incarceration, 30–31, 33

generational poverty, 31–32, 33
gifted and talented (GT) students
    assessment for, 166
goal(s)
    to assessment and beyond, 166–168
    strategies, and assessments, connections among, 161
goals, in planning process, 4–5
    daily lessons, specific objectives for, 4–5
    declarative knowledge in, 5
    procedural knowledge, 5
"good teachers get good students" system, 107
grade, retention, 26
grading
    group work, concerns related to sharing, 168–169
    with rubrics, 165
grouping, strategies, 35–45
    by ability, 40–41
    cooperative learning (*see* cooperative learning)
    creation of, 38–41
    current schoolwide practices in, 37
    by effort, 41
    by gender, 43–45
    history of, 36–37
    by interests, 42
    students, 36–37
    by talents, 41–42
    by values, 42–43
group work
    grading, concerns related to sharing, 168–169
GT students. *See* gifted and talented (GT) students

H

Harriet's Helpful Hints, 82–86, 105–106
High School Assessment (HSA), 50, 178
high school, brain research and, 81–82
high school science, discovery learning and, 140–141
high-stakes tests, struggling learners and, 178–182
    accountability movement (historical context), 178–179
    increased dropout rates, 179
    matching theory to practice, 181–182
    practices of reflective assessors, 188–189
    research, results of, 180–181
    unintended negative consequences of policy, 179–180
Hobson v. Hanson, 36
HSA. *See* High School Assessment (HSA)

I

iconic activities, learning and, 133
incarceration, generational, 30–31, 33
Individualized Education Program (IEP), 22, 97
Individuals with Disabilities Education Improvement Act (IDEA), 22, 42

instructional triangle, 4–7, 49, 159–160
    assessment (*see* assessment(s))
    constructivist learning theory and, 133–134
    goals in (*see* goal(s))
    novice, lesson plan of, 118
    reviewing, 133–134
    strategies in (*see* strategies)
instruction, differentiated, 12–16
    guidelines for, 12
    lesson plan, 13
    in practice, 12–16
    routines in, 12
    worksheets, 15
instructions. *See also* assessment(s)
    classroom discussions, effective, 121–124
    differentiated (*see* instruction, differentiated)
    discovery learning, 131–144 (*see also* discovery learning)
    examining, instructional triangle for, 4–7
    guidelines, 113–130
    instructional triangle, 159–160
    for lesson plan (*see* lesson plan(s))
    novice's plan, 118–121 (*see also* novice, lesson plan of)
    planning for (*see* planning, for instruction)
    reflective practices, 194–195
    veteran's plan, 114–118 (*see also* veterans, lesson plan of)
INTASC. *See* Interstate New Teacher Assessment and Support Consortium (INTASC) Standards
integrity, of assessment process, 162–163
interests, grouping by, 42
"internalizers," 29
Internet, 49
Interstate New Teacher Assessment and Support Consortium (INTASC) Standards, 219–222
    assessment, 221
    communication and technology, 221
    content pedagogy, 219
    diverse learners, 220
    motivation and management, 220
    multiple instructional strategies, 220
    planning, 221
    reflective practice: professional development, 222
    school and community involvement, 222
    student development, 219
intrinsic motivation, 10

J

journal entry, for struggling learners, 20–22

K

knowledge
    declarative, 5
    procedural, 5

L

language usage, in generational poverty, 31–32
"learned helplessness," 28

learning
   adult, 48
   constructivism and, 132–133
   cooperative, 38, 41, 44
   iconic activities and, 133
   motivation, 133
   self, 48
   symbolic activities and, 133
   time required, 133
lesson plan(s), 7–12, 114–118
   alignment of, 152–154
   on classroom discussions, 122–124 (*see also* classroom
        discussions, effective)
   for differentiated instruction, 13
   5 E plan, 7
   formatting, 7–8
   math, 14
   motivation and academic ability, relationship, 10
   of novice, 118–121 (*see also* novice, lesson plan of)
   primary-level reading, 124–129
   strategies, 11
   student teacher's story, 8–10
   success, 11–12
   template, 8, 134, 135 (*see also* discovery learning)
   of veteran, 114–118 (*see also* veterans, lesson plan of)
   wrong, forgivable mistakes, 91, 92
lessons
   daily, specific objectives for, 4–5
   declarative, 5
   plans (*see* lesson plan(s))
   procedural, 5
Life Skills classes, 20, 33

M
management
   classroom (*see* classroom management)
   discovery learning and, 141, 144
   mistakes in (*see* mistakes, in management)
   reflective practices, 193
   skills (*see* management skills)
   student–teacher relationships and (*see* student-teacher
        relationships)
management skills, 61–72. *See also* reflective managers,
        practices of
   boundaries in (*see* boundaries)
   classroom (*see* classroom management)
   classroom arrangement (*see* classroom arrangement)
   positive energy (*see* positive energy, of teachers)
   routines in (*see* routines)
   rules in, 62–63
Maryland
   accountability movement (historical context), 178–179
Maryland Functional Writing Test Standards, 165
Maryland's Tomorrow program, 19
message board, 7
middle school, brain research and, 81
mistakes, in management, 89–99
   fixable *vs.* unforgivable, 97–98

   forgivable (*see* fixable and forgivable mistakes)
   teaching, as career, 98
   unforgivable (*see* unforgivable mistakes)
motivation, 5–6
   and academic ability, relationship, 10
   discovery learning and, 141, 142
   intrinsic, 10
   learning and, 133
   and management, INTASC Standards, 220
multiple instructional strategies
   INTASC Standards, 220

N
NAEP. *See National Assessment of Educational Progress* (NAEP)
National Assessment of Educational Progress (NAEP), 178
National Science Education Standards, 140
NCLB. *See* No Child Left Behind (NCLB)
neuroimaging, 105. *See also* brain research
No Child Left Behind (NCLB), 36, 37, 45
noise management, in classroom, 78, 83
novice, lesson plan of, 118–121. *See also* lesson plan(s)
   in action, 120–121
   evaluating, 119–120
   instructional triangle, 118
   review, 121

O
objectives, for daily lessons, 4–5
observational learning, 116–117
ownership, of failures and successes, 29

P
"parentified," 76
performance assessments, 168. *See also* assessment(s)
planning
   grouping strategies, effective (*see* grouping, strategies)
   for instruction (*see* planning, for instruction)
   INTASC Standards, 221
   reflections about, 56–57
   reflective practices, 192–193
   struggling learners, identifying (*see* struggling learners,
        identifying)
planning, for instruction, 3–17
   defined, 3
   differentiated instruction (*see* instruction, differentiated)
   instructional triangle (*see* instructional triangle)
   lesson plans (*see* lesson plan(s))
   reflection during (*see* reflective planners)
positive energy, of teachers
   clearing desk, 71
   defiance, handling, 71–72
   quick intervention, 70–71
   response of student, 69–72
poverty
   generational, 31–32, 33
   struggling learners and, 23–24
PowerPoint presentation, 85
practice, differentiation in, 12–16

praise, effective, 77, 82–83, 105
   Brophy's guidelines for, 105
   guidelines for, 78–80
   reflective practices, 194
praise, ineffective, 107
   damages, 98–99
   gender issues, 99
   general education students, 99
   guidelines for, 98–99, 107
   for struggling learners, 99
predictability, 25
primary-level, reading lesson plan, 124–129
   reflective teachers and, 150–151
problem-solving system, 136–139
   drug rehabilitation center and, 139
procedural knowledge, 5
proximity, in classroom arrangement, 68
punishment, 93–94

R

racism, status expectations and, 26
rapport, positive, 67. *See also* student-teacher relationships
reconstitution-eligible schools, 96
reflection(s)
   about planning, 56–57
   guidelines for, 49–50
   importance of, 102
   modalities, 48
   planning template, 51–52
   written, 48–49
reflective assessors, practices of, 185–195
   angry children, 193
   daily assessments, success on, 186–187
   effective daily assessments, 186
   effective praise, 194
   formative and summative assessments, 187–188
   high-stakes testing and struggling learners, 188–189
   management, effective, 193
   overview, 185
   planning, effective, 192–193
   room arrangement, 193
   rules, routines, and boundaries, 193
   successful strategies, 191–192
reflective managers, practices of, 101–109
   brain research, 105
   Brophy on, 105
   effective praise, Brophy's guidelines for, 105
   fixable *vs.* egregious errors, 106
   Ginott on, 105
   Harriet's Helpful Hints, 105–106
   ineffective praise, guidelines for, 107
   mistakes, improving, 107
   overview, 101–102
   scenarios, 107–109
   teachers' performance, effects on struggling learners, 106–107
   in vocation and a profession, 104–105

reflective planners, practices of, 47–57
   need for, 48–49
   practicing together, 50–53
   scenarios, response to, 53–56
   strategies for, 49–50
reflective practices. *See also* specific entries
   positive student–teacher relationships, 104
   professional development, INTASC Standards, 222
   room arrangement, 104
   rules, routines, and boundaries, 103–104
reflective teachers
   alignment and alliances, 152–154
   classroom discussions and, 148–150
   discovery learning and, 151–152
   effective lesson, creating and implementing, 154–155
   passion, 146
   practices of, 145–155
   primary reading lesson and, 150–151
   questions, 154
   self-efficacy beliefs, 146
Rehabilitation Act, 22
responsibility, and unforgivable mistakes, 95–96
retention in grade, 26
room arrangement
   reflective practices, 104, 193
routines
   defined, 63
   in differentiation, 12
   establishing, 64–65
   need of, forgivable mistakes, 91–93
   reflective practices, 103–104, 193
rubrics, 50, 51, 160. *See also* assessment(s)
   for an invention report, 164
   creation of (steps), 164–165
   grading with, 165
   helps peer editors, 164
   from a learner's point of view, 165–166
   overview, 163–164
   problem-solving game, 137
   terminological description, 163
rules
   defined, 62–63
   reflective practices, 103–104, 193

S

sarcasm, 93
school and community involvement
   INTASC Standards, 222
science, discovery learning and, 139–144
   high school science, 140–141
   National Science Education Standards, 140
scientific visualization, 141
self-efficacy, 117, 146
   To Kill a Mockingbird and, 117–118
self-learning, 48
sense of humor, 67, 84. *See also* student-teacher relationships
sexual dimorphism, 43
shaming, 93–94

sleep, requirement, 82
social learning theory, of Bandura, 41
Sondheim Report, 174
stability
    emotional, in classrooms, 25
status characteristics and expectation states, theory of, 26
strategies, 5–6. *See also* instructions
    activities, 6
    goals, and assessments, connections among, 161
    grouping (*see* grouping, strategies)
    lesson plan and, 11
    motivation, 5–6, 10
    successful, 191–192
structured writing assignment (SWA), 51–52
struggling learners, 12. *See also* children
    and assessment, 6–7
    high-stakes tests and (*see* high-stakes tests, struggling
        learners and)
    identifying (*see* struggling learners, identifying)
    ineffective praise for, 99
    predictability and emotional stability and, 25
    reflective planners, practices of (*see* reflective planners,
        practices of)
struggling learners, identifying, 19–34
    external locus of control approach in, 28–30
    future, limited/grim notion of, 30–34
    journal entry for, 20–22
    school-based standards, unsuccessful in meeting, 25–28
    from unstable families and communities (*see* unstable
        families)
student development
    INTASC Standards, 219
student(s). *See also* children
    grouping, 36–37
    ignoring, unforgivable mistakes, 96–97
    teachers and, relationships (*see* student-teacher relationships)
    well-being, positive energy and, 69–72
student-teacher relationships
    alignment and alliances, 152–154
    appropriate, benefits and burdens, 67–68
    management and, 66–68
    positive, and reflective practices, 104
    positive rapport, 67
    sense of humor in, 67, 84
substance abuse, 23
success
    effort and, connections, 28–29
    lesson plan and, 11–12
    ownership of, 29
summative assessments, 164–165. *See also* assessment(s)
    example, 177
    goal of, 175
    overview, 177
    vs. formative assessments, 173–182, 187–188
SWA. *See* structured writing assignment (SWA)
symbolic activities, learning and, 133

T
talents, grouping by, 41–42
targeting, and unforgivable mistakes, 94–95
teacher-made assessments. *See also* assessment(s)
    assessment results, uses of, 161–162
    data analysis, 166–168
    definition of, 160
    example, 162, 163
    goals, strategies, and assessments, connections among, 161
    overview, 160–161
    principles, 166
    process integrity, 162–163
    reliability, 166
    rubrics (*see* rubrics)
    validity, 166
teacher quality, importance of, 106–107
teacher(s)
    bullying, effects of, 94
    cognitive simulation, role in, 117
    goal, 98
    ignoring students, 96–97
    performance, effects on struggling learners, 106–107
    positive energy of (*see* positive energy, of teachers)
    reflective (*see* reflective teachers)
    reflective, need for, 48–49
    students and, relationships (*see* student-teacher
        relationships)
teaching
    as career, 98
    reflective, need for, 48–49
Teaching Tips, 49
team leaders, 39
team recorders, 39
team spokespersons, 39
team supplies persons, 39
technology
    in classroom, 85
    discovery learning and, 139–144
time constraints, discovery learning and,
        141, 144
time worksheets, 15
tracking, history of, 36–37

U
unforgivable mistakes, 93–97
    disgracing, 93–94
    fixable *vs.,* 97–98
    ignoring students, 96–97
    irresponsibility, for safety children, 95–96
    targeting a child, 94–95
unstable families, 22–25
    divorce, 22
    impacts, on children, 23
    planning for children in, 25
    poverty, 23–24
    substance abuse, 23

V

values, grouping by, 42–43
veterans, lesson plan of, 114–118. *See also* lesson plan(s)
  analyzing perspectives, 114–115
  cooperative learning groups, 116–117
  evaluation by students, 118
  interview questions, 116
  observational learning, 116–117
  standard of, 116
violence, 31, 66, 76
vocabulary
  formative assessments, 174

W

workers, reluctant
  formative assessments, 176
worksheets
  time, 15
written reflections, 48–49

Y

YouTube video, 85